COMP MADE S

160 PAGES — PAPERBACK

Access 97 for Windows
Moira Stephen
0 7506 3800 1   1997

Access for Windows 95 (Version 7)
Moira Stephen
0 7506 2818 9   1996

Access for Windows 3.1 (Version 2)
Moira Stephen
0 7506 2309 8   1995

NEW
Compuserve
Keith Brindley
0 7506 3512 6   1998

Designing Internet Home Pages
Lilian Hobbs
0 7506 2941 X   1996

Excel 97 for Windows
Stephen Morris
0 7506 3802 8   1997

Excel for Windows 95 (Version 7)
Stephen Morris
0 7506 2816 2   1996

Excel for Windows 3.1 (Version 5)
Stephen Morris
0 7506 2070 6   1994

NEW
Explorer (Version 4.0)
Sam Kennington
0 7506 3796 X   1998

NEW
FrontPage 97
Nat McBride
0 7506 3941 5   1998

Hard Drives
Ian Sinclair
0 7506 2313 6   1995

Internet Explorer (Version 3.0)
Sam Kennington
0 7506 3513 4   1997

Internet Resources
P. K. McBride
0 7506 2836 7   1996

NEW
The Internet (Colour Edition)
P. K. McBride   0 7506 3944 X   1998

The Internet for Windows 95 (Second Edition)
P. K. McBride
0 7506 3846 X   1997

Internet for Windows 3.1
P. K. McBride
0 7506 2311 X   1995

Lotus 1-2-3 for Windows 3.1 (Version 5)
Stephen Morris
0 7506 2307 1   1995

MS DOS (Up To Version 6.22)
Ian Sinclair
0 7506 2069 2   1994

Microsoft Networking
P. K. McBride
0 7506 2837 5   1996

Multimedia for Windows 95
Simon Collin
0 7506 3397 2   1997

Multimedia for Windows 3.1
Simon Collin
0 7506 2314 4   1995

Netscape (Version 3.0)
Sam Kennington
0 7506 3514 2   1997

NEW
Netscape Communicator (Version 4.0)
Sam Kennington
0 7506 4040 5   1998

Office 97 for Windows
P. K. McBride
0 7506 3798 6   1997

Office 95
P. K. McBride
0 7506 2625 9   1995

NEW
Pagemaker
Steve Heath
0 7506 4050 2   1998

Powerpoint 97 for Windows
Moira Stephen
0 7506 3799 4   1997

Powerpoint for Windows 95 (Version 7)
Moira Stephen
0 7506 2817 0   1996

NEW
Publisher 97
Moira Stephen
0 7506 3943 1   1998

NEW
Searching The Internet
P. K. McBride
0 7506 3794 3   1998

NEW
Windows 98
P. K. McBride
0 7506 4039 1   1998

Windows 95
P. K. McBride
0 7506 2306 3   1995

Windows 3.1
P. K. McBride
0 7506 2072 2   1994

Windows NT (Version 4.0)
Lilian Hobbs
0 7506 3511 8   1997

Word 97 for Windows
Keith Brindley
0 7506 3801 X   1997

Word for Windows 95 (Version 7)
Keith Brindley
0 7506 2815 4   1996

Word for Windows 3.1 (Version 6)
Keith Brindley
0 7506 2071 4   1994

Word Pro for Windows 3.1 (Version 4.0)
Moira Stephen
0 7506 2626 7   1995

Works for Windows 95 (Version 4.0)
P. K. McBride
0 7506 3396 4   1996

Works for Windows 3.1 (Version 3)
P. K. McBride
0 7506 2065 X   1994

NEW MADE SIMPLE SERIES

PROGRAMMING MADE SIMPLE

200 PAGES • PAPERBACK

By a combination of tutorial approach, with tasks to do and easy steps, the MADE SIMPLE series of Computer Books from Butterworth-Heinemann stands above all others.

- Easy to Follow
- Jargon Free
- Task Based
- Practical Exercises

Thousands of people have already discovered that the MADE SIMPLE series gives them what they want fast! Many delighted readers have written, telephoned and e-mailed us about the Made Simple Computing Series.
Comments have included:
- 'Clear, concise and well laid out.'
- 'Ideal for the first time user.'
- 'Clear, accurate, well presented, jargon free, well targeted.'
- 'Easy to follow to perform a task.'
- 'Illustrations are excellent.'
- 'I haven't found any other books worth recommending until these.'

This best selling series is in your local bookshop now, or in case of difficulty, contact:

Heinemann Publishers, Oxford
PO Box 381
Oxford OX2 8EJ.

Tel: 01865 314300

Fax: 01865 314091

E.Mail: bhuk.orders@repp.co.uk
Credit card sales: 01865 314627

Visit us on the worldwide web: http://www.bh.com

C Programming
Conor Sexton
0 7506 3244 5   1997

C++ Programming
Conor Sexton
0 7506 3243 7   1997

NEW
COBOL
(for the year 2000)
Conor Sexton
0 7506 3834 6   1998

Delphi
Stephen Morris
0 7506 3246 1   1997

Java
P. K. McBride
0 7506 3241 0   1997

Java Script
P. K. McBride
0 7506 3797 8   1997

Pascal
P. K. McBride
0 7506 3242 9   1997

NEW
Unix
P. K. McBride
0 7506 3571 1   1998

Visual Basic
Stephen Morris
0 7506 3245 3   1997

NEW
Visual C++
Stephen Morris
0 7506 3570 3   1998

NEW
Windows 95 Programming
Stephen Morris
0 7506 3572 X   1998

Word 97 for Windows Made Simple

Keith Brindley

Made Simple
BOOKS

Made Simple
An imprint of Butterworth-Heinemann
Linacre House, Jordan Hill, Oxford OX2 8DP
225 Wildwood Avenue, Woburn, MA 01801-2041
A division of Reed Educational and Professional Publishing Ltd

A member of the Reed Elsevier plc group

OXFORD   AUCKLAND   BOSTON
JOHANNESBURG   MELBOURNE   NEW DELHI

First published 1997
Reprinted 1998, 1999

© Keith Brindley, 1997

All rights reserved. No part of this publication
may be reproduced in any material form (including
photocopying or storing in any medium by electronic
means and whether or not transiently or incidentally
to some other use of this publication) without the
written permission of the copyright holder except in
accordance with the provisions of the Copyright,
Design and Patents Act 1988 or under the terms of a
licence issued by the Copyright Licensing Agency Ltd,
90 Tottenham Court Road, London, England W1P 9HE.
Applications for the copyright holder's written
permission to reproduce any part of this publication
should be addressed to the publishers

NORFOLK LIBRARY AND INFORMATION SERVICE	
SUPP	FARR
INV. NO.	C556590
ORD DATE	17/02/00

005.3 WOR

TRADEMARKS/REGISTERED TRADEMARKS
Computer hardware and software brand names mentioned in
this book are protected by their respective trademarks and
are acknowledged

British Library Cataloguing in Publication Data
A catalogue record for this book is available from the British
Library

ISBN 0 7506 3801 X

Typeset and produced by Co-publications, Loughborough
Set in Archetype, Bash Casual, Cotswold Book and Gravity fonts from Advanced Graphics Limited
All screenshots taken with Screen Thief for Windows from Nildram Software (info@nildram.co.uk)
Icons designed by Sarah Ward © 1994
Printed and bound in Great Britain by Scotprint Ltd, Musselburgh, Scotland.

Contents

Preface vii

1 The basics

Starting up 2
Word menus 4
Help me, I'm drowning! 6
Toolbars 10
Buttons 13
Normal view 14
Online layout view 15
Page layout view 16
Outline view 17
Full screen view 18
Zooming 19
Saving a document 20
Opening documents 21
Creating new documents 22
Goodbye – or just au revoir? 24
Summary for Section 1 26

2 Text essentials

Entering text 28
Editing text 30
Selecting text 32
Ooops – a mistake! 36
Cut, copy and paste 38
Drag-and-drop editing 40
Entering symbols 42
Summary for Section 2 44

3 Formatting text

About formatting 46
Character formats 48
Painting a format 53
Paragraph formats 54
Tabs 60
Simple tables 62
More about tabs 64
Borders and shading 66
Summary for Section 3 72

Contents (contd)

4 Sections and pages
- About sections 74
- Setting up a document 76
- Margins 77
- Headers and footers 80
- Line numbers 84
- Columns 86
- Summary for Section 4 90

5 Text control
- Finding text 92
- Replacing 94
- Spelling 96
- AutoCorrect 100
- AutoText 102
- Outlining 104
- Tables 108
- Table conversions 111
- Table formatting 112
- Counting your words 113
- Graphics 114
- Summary for Section 5 118

6 Automatic formatting
- Styles 120
- Character and paragraph styles 123
- Creating styles 124
- More about styles 130
- About templates 134
- Creating a template 136
- Summary for Section 6 138

7 Technical thingamajigs
- Print preview 140
- Printing 142
- Print options 143
- Starting Word at turn-on 144
- Shortcut keys 146
- Toolbars 148
- Summary for Section 7 150

- Index 152

Preface

The computer is about as simple as a spacecraft, and who ever let an untrained spaceman loose? You pick up a manual that weighs more than your birth-weight, open it and find it's written in computerspeak. You see messages on the screen resembling some strange spy code and the thing even makes noises. No wonder you feel it's your lucky day if everything goes right. What do you do if everything goes wrong? Give up.

Training helps. Being able to type helps. Experience helps. This book helps, by providing training and assisting with experience. It can't help you if you always manage to hit the wrong keys, but it *can* tell you which are the right ones and what to do when you hit the wrong ones. After some time, even the dreaded manual will start to make sense, just because you at last know what the writers are wittering on about.

Computing is not black magic. You don't need luck or charms, just a bit of understanding. The problem is that the programs used nowadays *look* simple — but simply aren't. Most are crammed with features you don't need — but how do you know what you don't need? This book shows you what is essential and guides you through it. You will know how to make an action work and why. Less essential bits can wait — and once you start to use a program with confidence you can tackle those bits for yourself.

The writers of this series have all been through it. We know time is valuable, and you don't want to waste it. You don't buy books on computer topics to read jokes or be told you are a dummy. You want to find what you need — and be shown how to do it. Here, at last, you can.

1 The basics

Starting up 2

Word menus 4

Help me, I'm drowning! 6

Toolbars 10

Buttons 13

Normal view 14

Online layout view 15

Page layout view 16

Outline view 17

Full screen view 18

Zooming 19

Saving a document 20

Opening documents 21

Creating new documents 22

Goodbye – or just au revoir? 24

Summary for Section 1 26

Starting up

Basic steps:

First operation you ever do when using Word is to start it up. Use the **Start** button, and access its sub-menu.

Point to the **Programs** menu entry (you don't need to click)

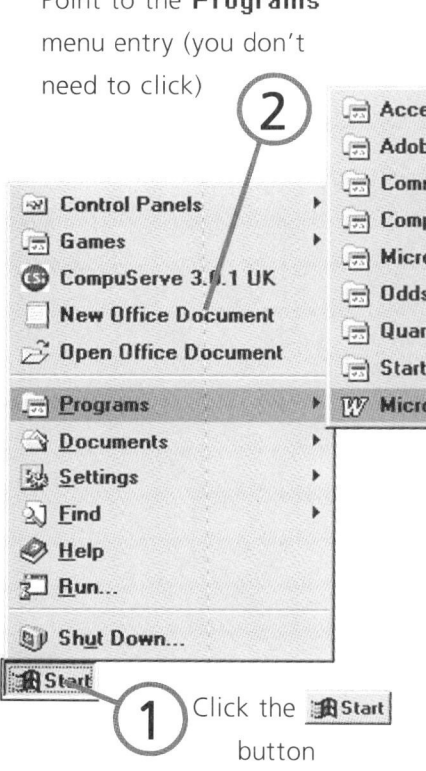

Point to and click **Microsoft Word**

Click the **Start** button

1. Click the **Start** button
2. Point to the **Programs** menu entry — a sub-menu entry pops out.
3. Point to then click the **Microsoft Word** sub-menu entry (if you have Microsoft Office installed on your computer, you'll first have to point to the **MSOffice** sub-menu entry — which will create a further pop-out menu to locate the **Microsoft Word** sub-menu entry)

After starting, you will be presented with the main Word window (shown right — for a completely new and unaltered program). If your copy of Word has been adapted by any other user since installation your screen may display something a little different.

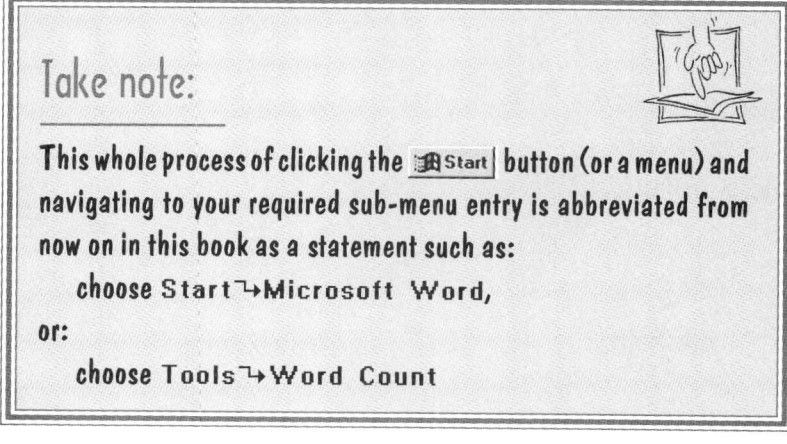

Take note:

This whole process of clicking the **Start** button (or a menu) and navigating to your required sub-menu entry is abbreviated from now on in this book as a statement such as:
   choose Start↪Microsoft Word,
or:
   choose Tools↪Word Count

Tip:

If you use your computer only for word processing, you can setup to run Word each time you turn on your machine — see page 144 for details

Main features of a Word document window are shown below, but don't panic — they'll be looked at shortly. Soon you'll think Word is one of the easiest computer programs to get the hang of — and you'll be right.

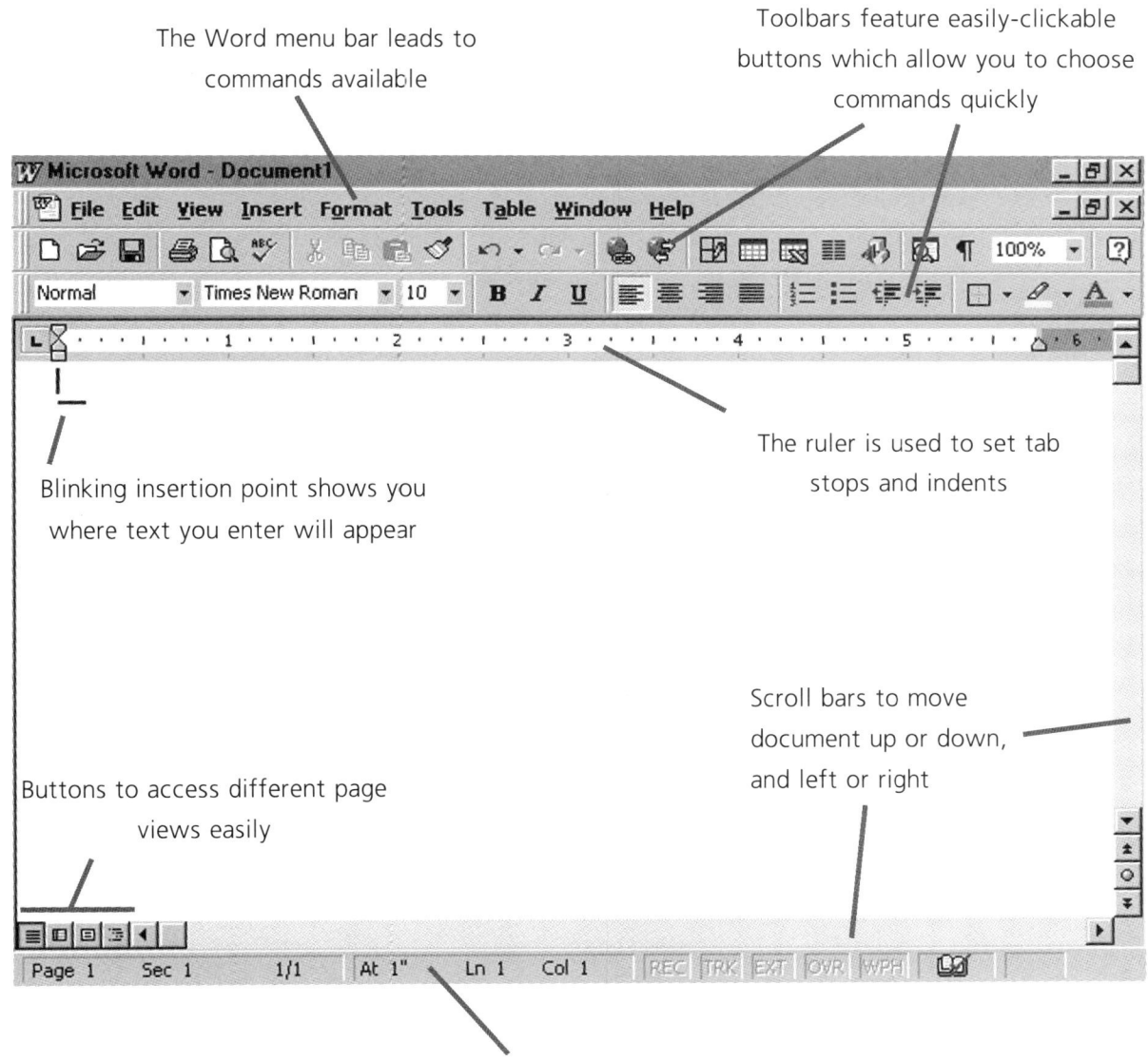

The Word menu bar leads to commands available

Toolbars feature easily-clickable buttons which allow you to choose commands quickly

The ruler is used to set tab stops and indents

Blinking insertion point shows you where text you enter will appear

Scroll bars to move document up or down, and left or right

Buttons to access different page views easily

The status bar along the bottom gives details about the document in the window (see pages 28–29 for more details)

Word menus

Word has nine menus in its menu bar. They hold all the commands and tools available to any user of Word. While you don't (and that's just as well!) need to know what all these commands and tools are to get good results from Word, it's worth looking at all the menus to get an overall feel for what they are about — use this page as a reference.

The menu bar itself looks like this:

Basic steps:

1 To display a menu, click on its name in the menu bar
2 Alternatively, enter Alt + the menu's underlined letter
3 To remove a displayed menu, click anywhere else in the window

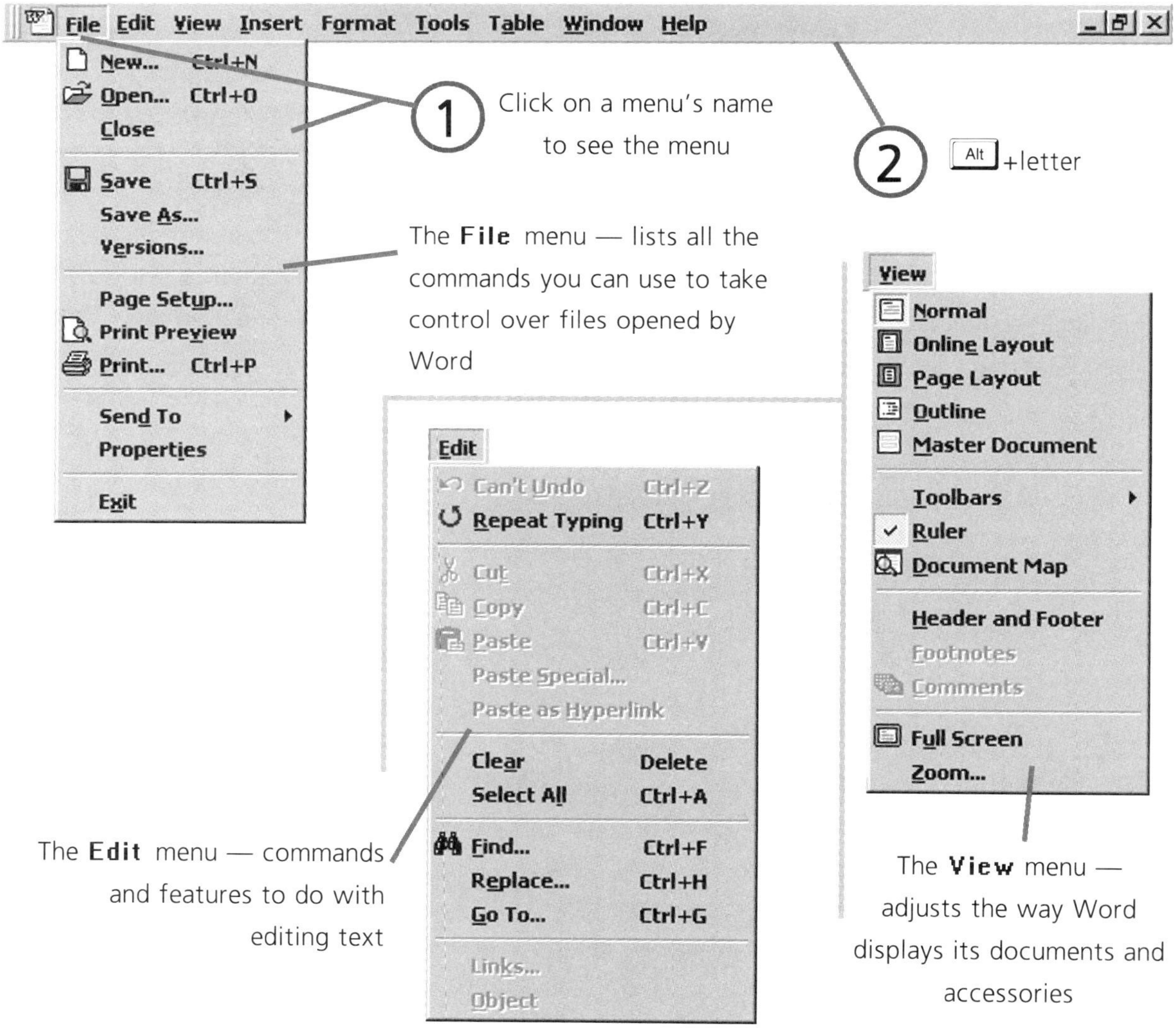

① Click on a menu's name to see the menu

② Alt +letter

The **File** menu — lists all the commands you can use to take control over files opened by Word

The **Edit** menu — commands and features to do with editing text

The **View** menu — adjusts the way Word displays its documents and accessories

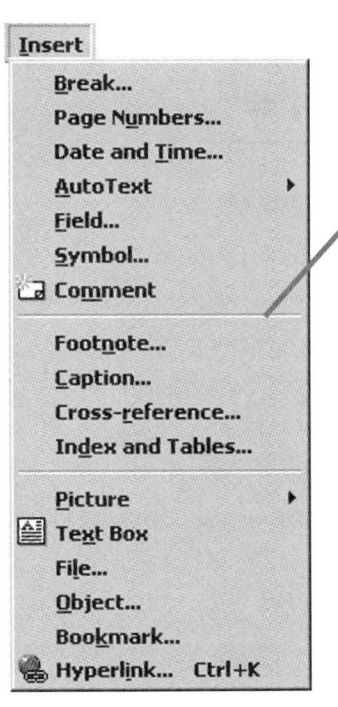

The **Insert** menu — used to place certain features over and above ordinary text into a document

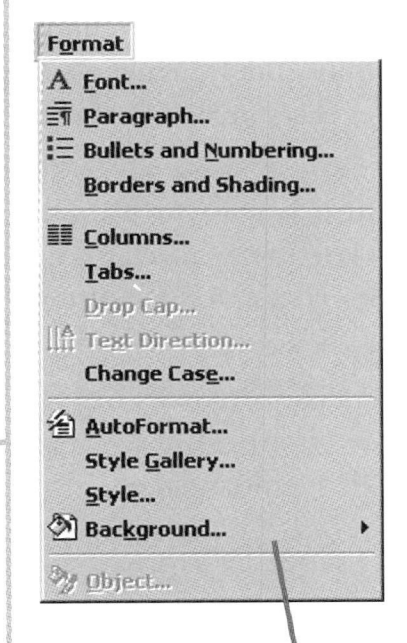

The **Format** menu — the menu you use to apply styles and so on to your document

The **Tools** menu — special features and controls

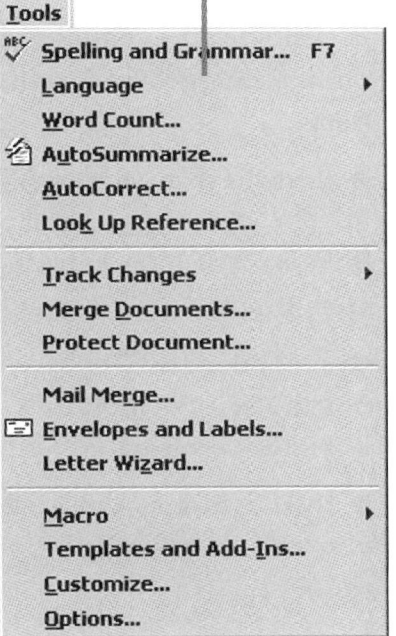

The **Table** menu — controls aspects of tables within a document

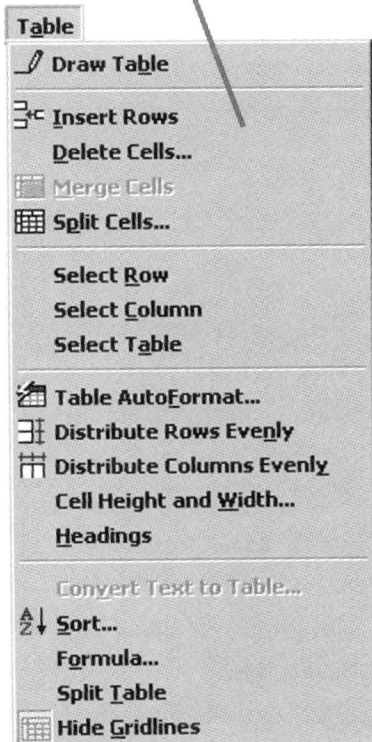

The **Window** menu — choose between documents and control how they are displayed

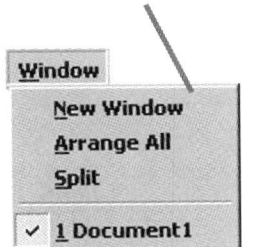

The **Help** menu — how to how to?

5

Help me, I'm drowning!

Inevitably you will find there are times you don't know what you are doing. This happens whenever you are new (and, sometimes not-so-new) to a complex program like Word. Fortunately, Word has an incredibly useful — and even-more-incredibly comprehensive — on-line help system built-in to it. This comes in three parts:

● first there are ScreenTips — little labels which show up (1) when you point over any of the myriads of buttons Word has in its many toolbars, and (2) at other specific places

● second is the Office Assistant — a sort of electronic dogsbody that monitors where you are within Word, and gives contextual help and advice if you need

● third is Help — an easily accessible system in which you can locate help about any feature, command or topic in Word.

Basic steps:

SCREENTIPS

1 Simply position your pointer over any button in any toolbar to see the button's name as a label

OFFICE ASSISTANT

1 If not already displayed, click the Office Assistant button [?] on the Standard toolbar, choose **Help→Microsoft Word Help**, type [Alt]+[H] then [H], or (best) type [F1]. Once displayed, as you move around within Word, the Office Assistant will provide help

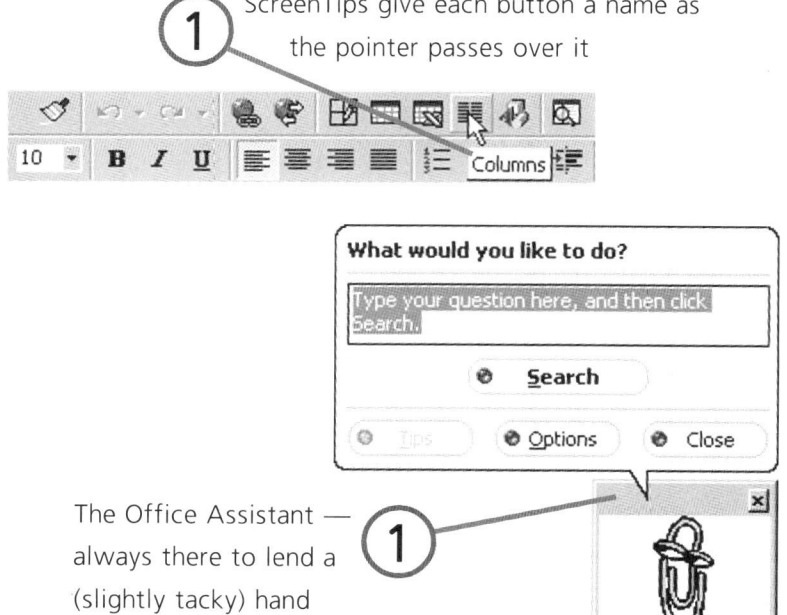

ScreenTips give each button a name as the pointer passes over it (1)

The Office Assistant — always there to lend a (slightly tacky) hand (1)

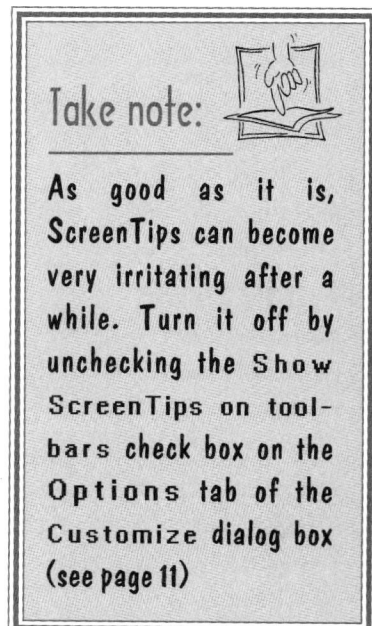

Take note:

As good as it is, ScreenTips can become very irritating after a while. Turn it off by unchecking the Show ScreenTips on toolbars check box on the Options tab of the Customize dialog box (see page 11)

Help is available through the Help system in several ways within Word. Knowing which method is best for you is largely a matter of experience. The four main ways — Help by topic, Help by Index, Help by Find, Help — What's This? are shown here.

HELP BY TOPIC

1 Choose **Help→Contents and Index** to call up the **Help Topics: Microsoft Word** window

2 Click the **Contents** tab

3 Click any topic then click **Open** (or simply double-click the topic) to get help

HELP BY INDEX

4 Click the **Index** tab

5 Type in a few letters of the topic you want help with — as you do, the list of entries jumps to the respective entry

6 Click **Display** (or double-click the entry) to display the topic

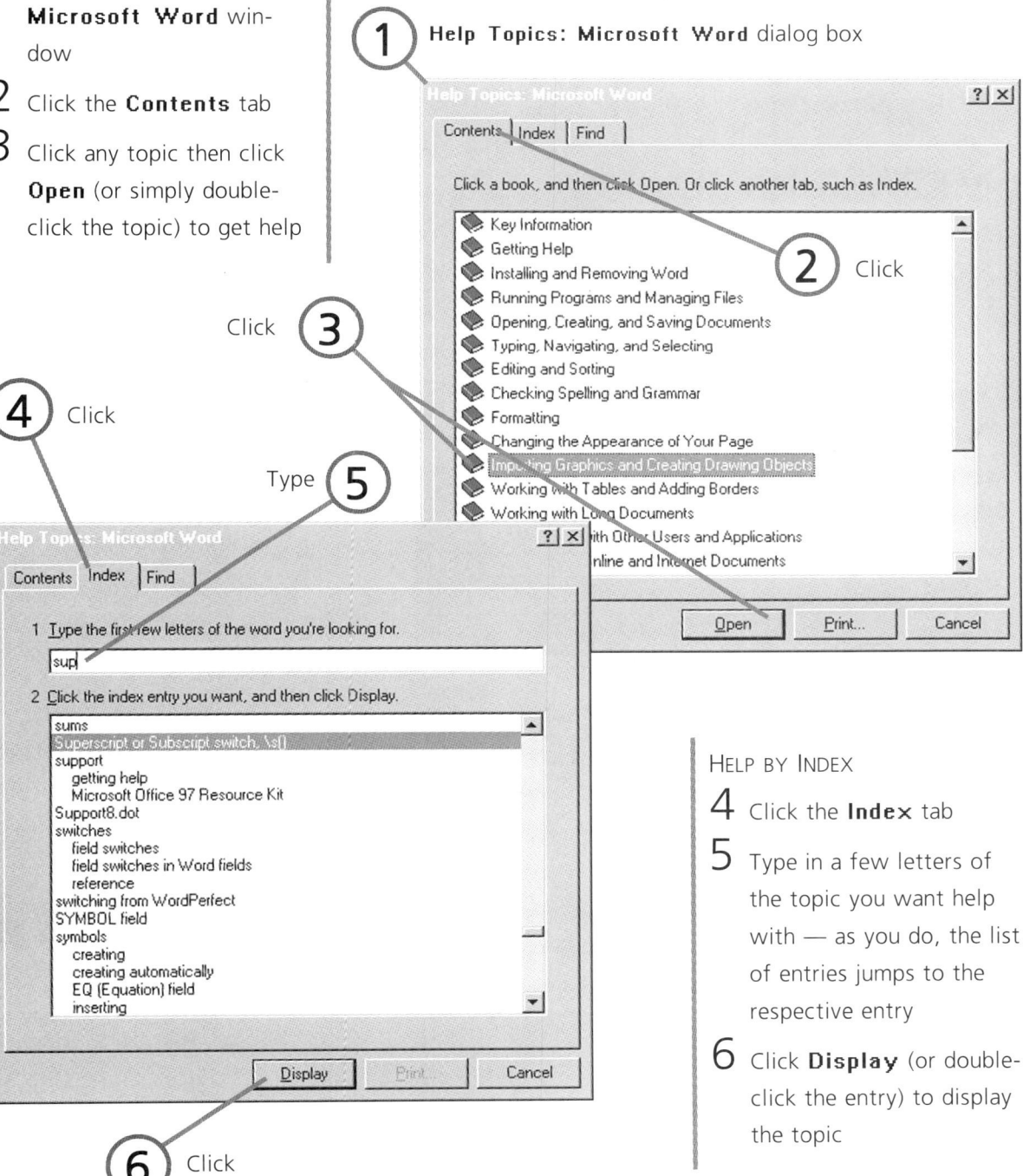

...still drowning (contd)!

Basic steps (contd):

HELP BY FIND

7 Click the **Find** tab

8 Type the words you want to find

9 Select words to narrow the search

10 Select a topic then click **Display**, or simply double-click the topic

HELP — WHAT'S THIS?

11 Choose **Help→What's This?**, or simply press Shift + F1. The pointer changes to the help pointer

12 Click the button, object, or even menu command you want help with, and the Help system, goes straight to the information you need, displaying it as a ScreenTip

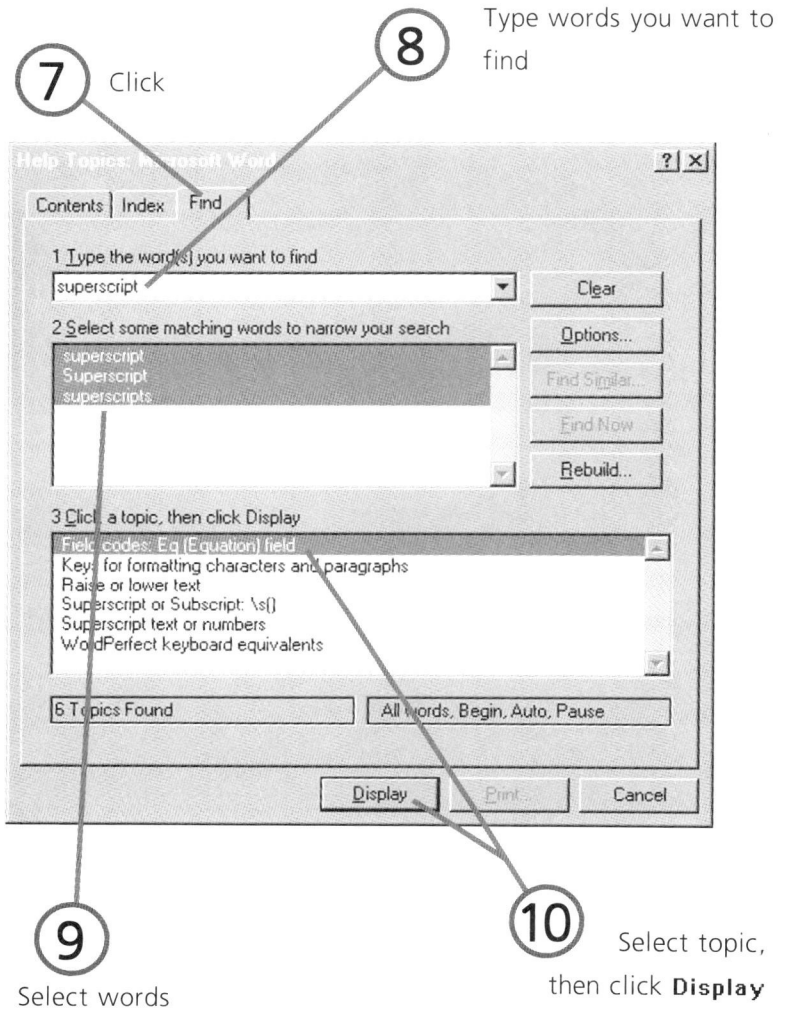

7 Click

8 Type words you want to find

9 Select words

10 Select topic, then click **Display**

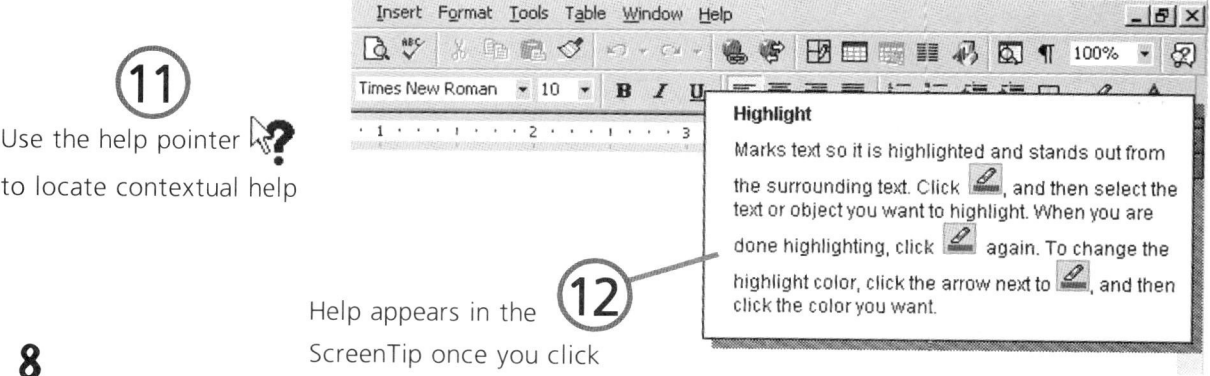

11 Use the help pointer to locate contextual help

12 Help appears in the ScreenTip once you click

Help – I'm not so Perfect!

If you've previously used WordPerfect as your word processor, then some of Word's features will probably be confusing to you.

Not to worry, though: help is at hand in the form of a system which correlates specific WordPerfect commands to those in Word.

Basic steps:

1 Type **Alt**+**H**, then **P**, or choose **Help→Word Perfect Help** — or more quickly — double-click the WordPerfect help button **WPH** on the status bar. This calls up the **Help for WordPerfect Users** dialog box

2 Select the WordPerfect command name in the command keys box

3 Read the information about the command

4 For a demonstration of the command, click **Demo**

The **Help for WordPerfect Users** dialog box

Select the WordPerfect command you are familiar with here

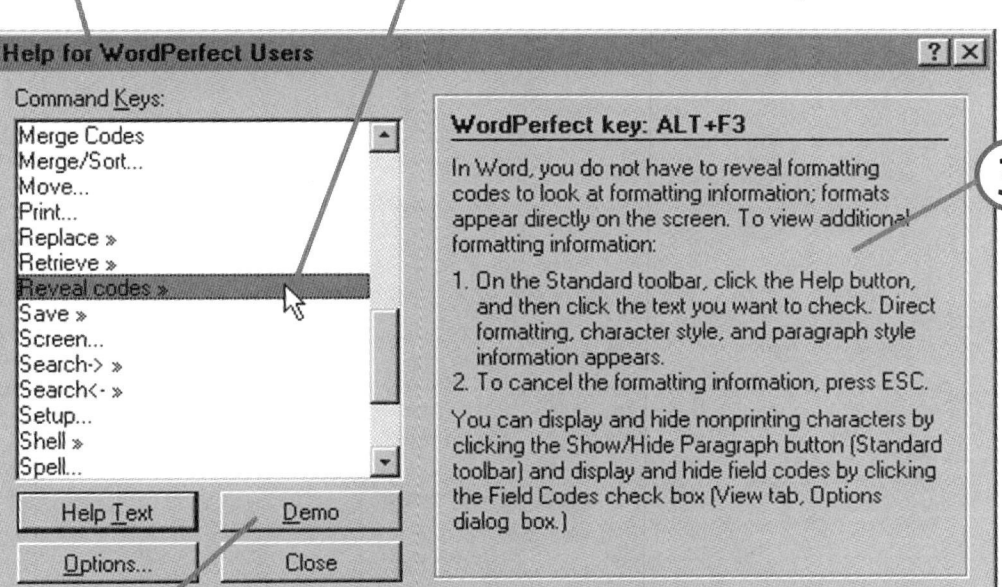

Read information about your selected command

Click for a demonstration

Toolbars

Basic steps:

Apart from choosing commands in menus, Word is controlled by on-screen buttons, found in toolbars. The two most obvious toolbars are at the top of a Word document but, as we'll see, there are others, too — and further — Word lets you customize them to your heart's content — see page 148 for more details.

1 To display any particular toolbar, choose **View ↪ Toolbars**

2 In the **Toolbars** pop-out menu, drag to the toolbar you want displayed, then click

The standard toolbar — buttons used for common everyday tasks

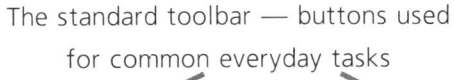

The formatting toolbar — containing buttons you use to stylise text within documents

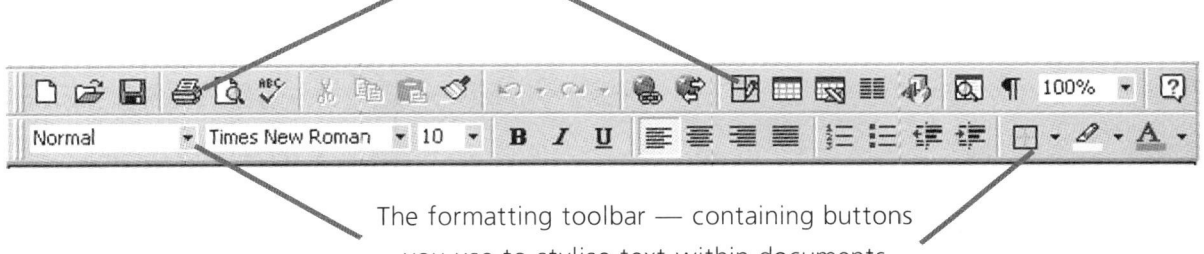

Choose **View ↪ Toolbars**, to see the pop-out menu

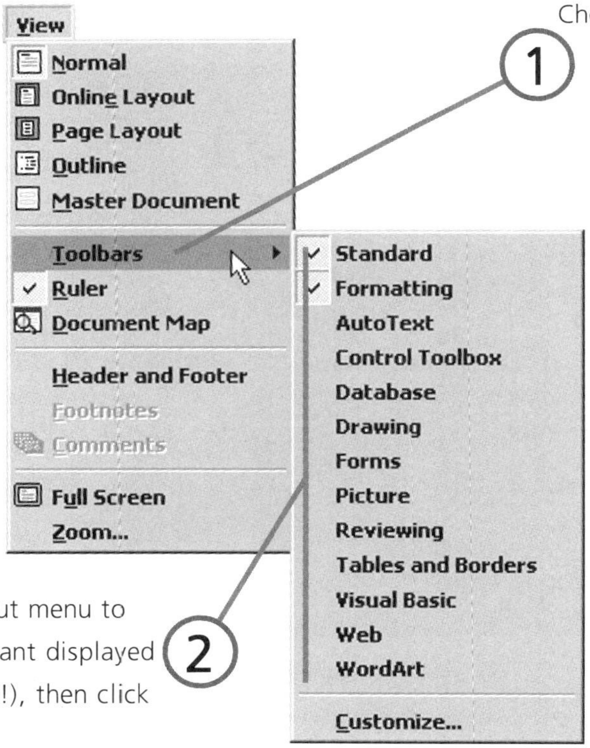

The toolbars displayed are those ticked. Tick more to see more toolbars, tick less to see less

Drag in the pop-out menu to the toolbar you want displayed (or to be removed!), then click

Toolbars (contd)

You can turn off any existing toolbar, or turn on any of the other toolbars (see previous page), on-the-fly in Word by clicking on any toolbar with the right mouse button. This calls up a drop-down menu from which you can choose the toolbar you want displayed.

Basic steps (contd):

4 Alternatively, use the mouse shortcut — click any toolbar with the right mouse button

5 Click the toolbar you want turned on or off

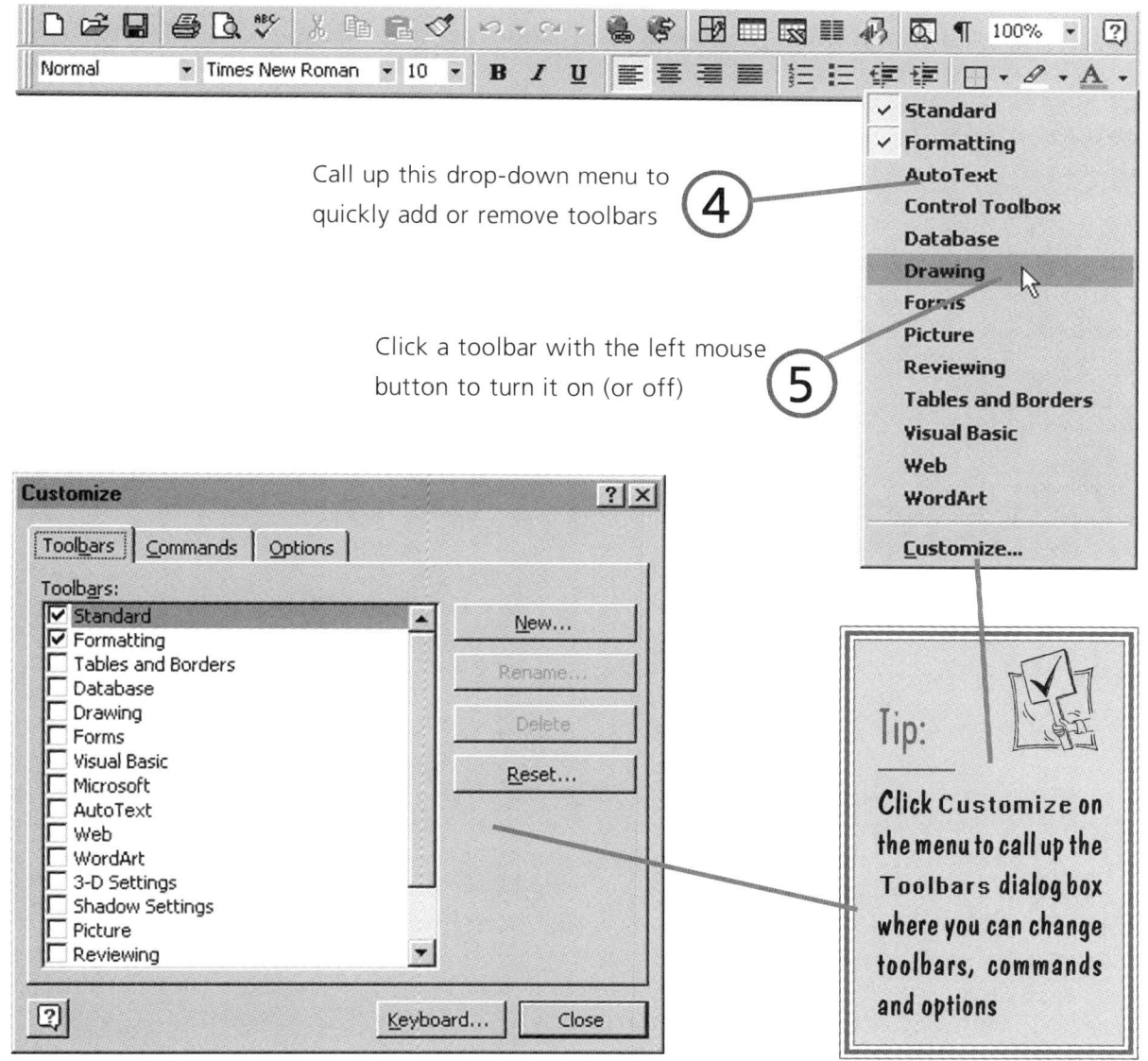

Call up this drop-down menu to quickly add or remove toolbars ④

Click a toolbar with the left mouse button to turn it on (or off) ⑤

Tip:

Click Customize on the menu to call up the Toolbars dialog box where you can change toolbars, commands and options

11

Other toolbars

All default toolbars in Word are displayed below. While most appear intitially fixed in position in the document window, you can move many of them by dragging them away from their initial positions — at which point they become floating toolbars, movable anywhere you might have some screen space suitable. Any new toolbars you create for yourself (page 149) float too.

As you work your way round Word 97, you'll find that other toolbars appear too, dependent on what you are attempting to do. When you have finished that particular task, or switch to another, these toolbars will disappear again.

Finally, remember that you can customize default toolbars, as well as any of your own creations, by moving, removing, adding, or creating buttons.

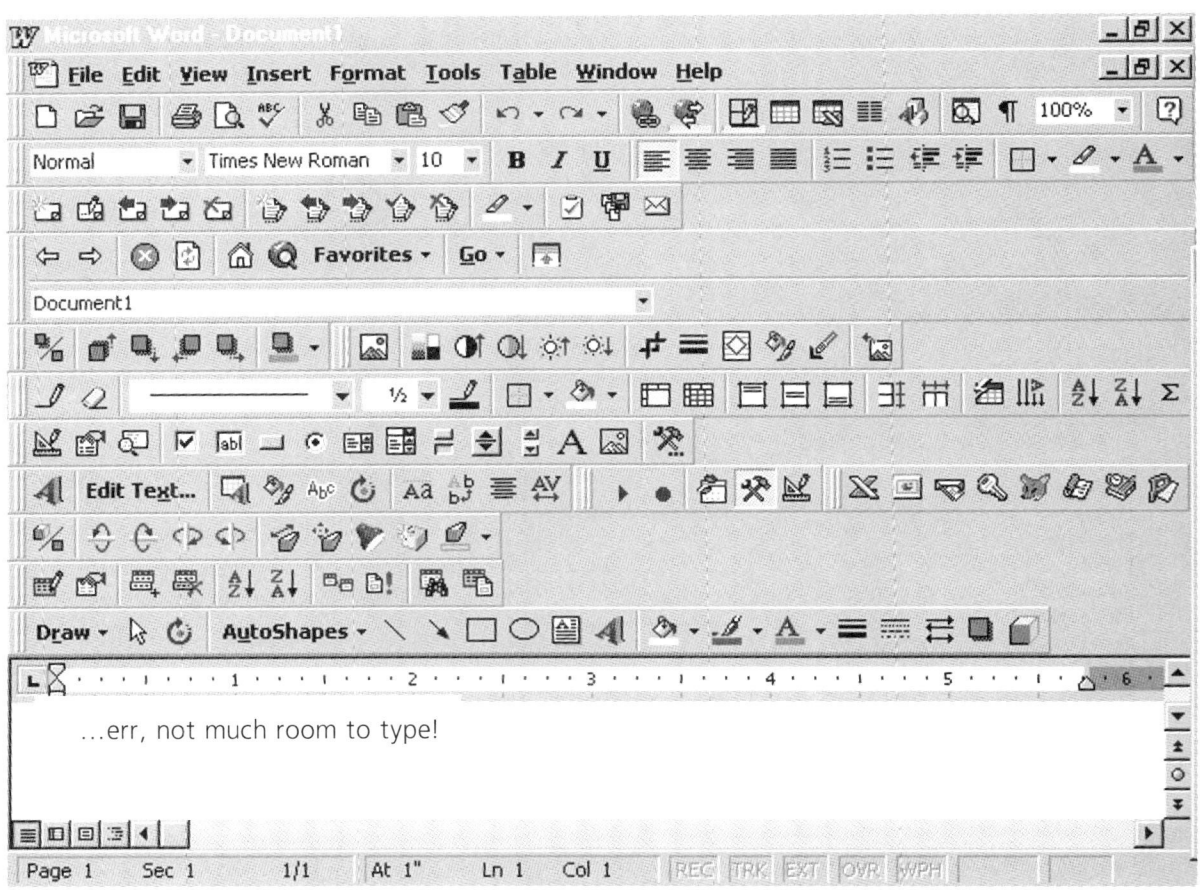

Buttons

Buttons on toolbars are graphically representative of their function. As a result it's easy to see what most of them do. However, some buttons are a little more obscure. Here the standard and formatting toolbar buttons are listed together with brief explanations.

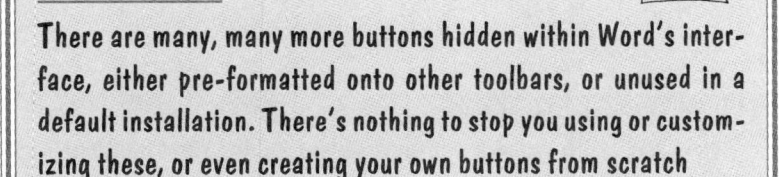

> **Take note:**
>
> There are many, many more buttons hidden within Word's interface, either pre-formatted onto other toolbars, or unused in a default installation. There's nothing to stop you using or customizing these, or even creating your own buttons from scratch

- — new document
- — open document
- — save document
- — print document
- — print preview
- — spelling
- — cut
- — copy
- — paste
- — format painter
- — undo
- — redo
- — insert hyperlink
- — Web toolbar

- — tables and borders
- — insert address
- — insert table
- — insert Excel worksheet
- — columns
- — drawing
- — document map
- — show/hide ¶
- — zoom control
- — TipWizard
- — Office Assistant
- — style
- — font
- — font size

- — bold
- — italic
- — underline
- — align left
- — align centre
- — align right
- — justify
- — numbering
- — bullets
- — decrease indent
- — increase indent
- — borders
- — highlight
- — font colour

Normal view

Basic steps:

Word allows a number of views of your document — normal view is simply the one new documents usually default to. It's important to remember, though, that each view of a document makes no difference to what's actually in the document — it's just one way of looking at it.

1 Your document is probably already in normal view (see below). If not, choose **View→Normal**, or type `Alt`+`V` then `N`, or (best) click the Normal view button at the bottom left of your document window

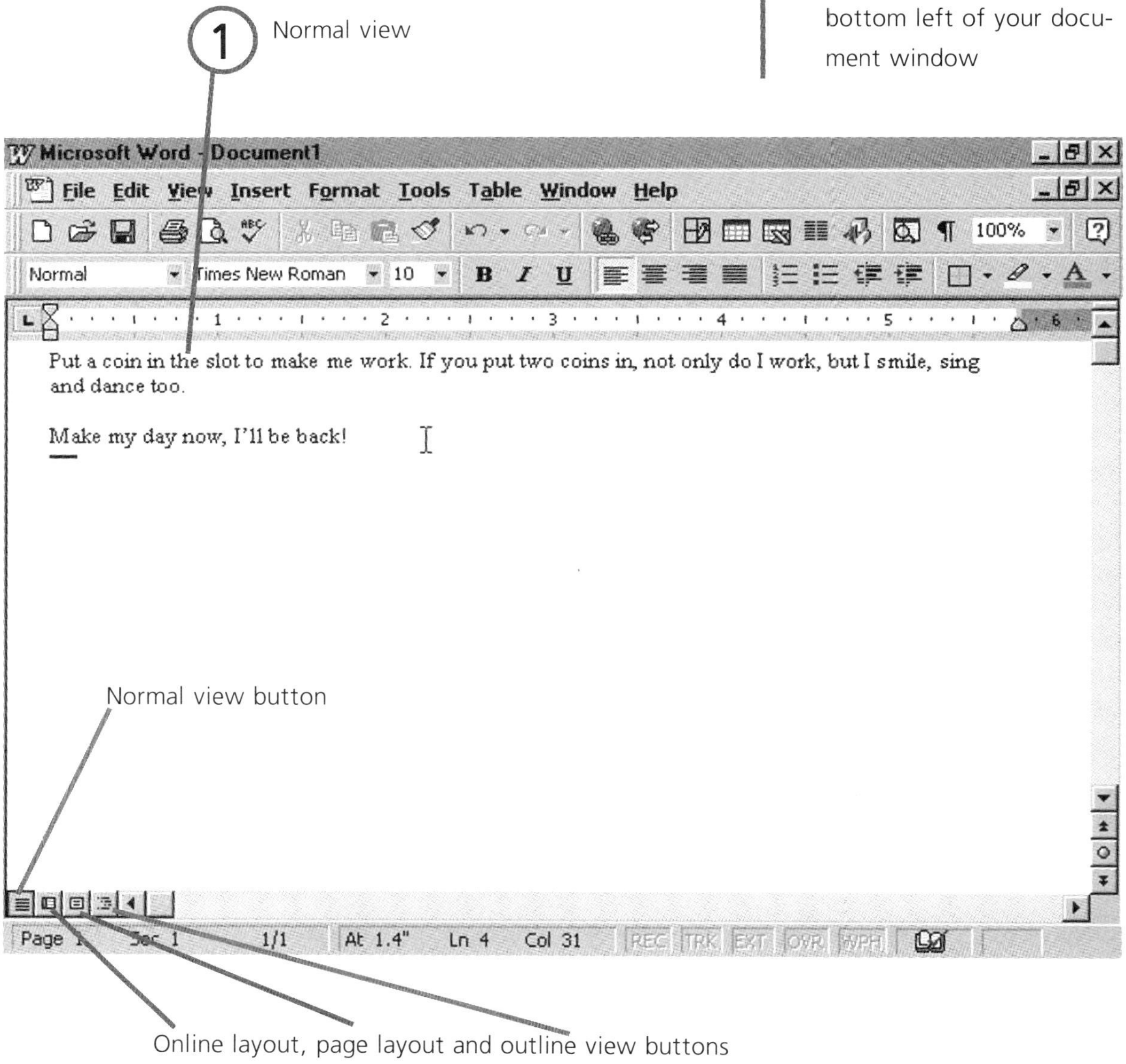

(1) Normal view

Normal view button

Online layout, page layout and outline view buttons

Online layout view

Basic steps:

One of the hottest things in computing these days is hypertext markup language (HTML). Hypertext is the way some documents allow you to access related information merely by clicking a link (sometimes called a hyperlink, because of this). Pages displayed on the part of the Internet known as the World Wide Web are all created with hypertext markup language. Word 97 allows you to create and view hypertext documents in online layout view.

1 Choose **View➔Online Layout**, or type `Alt`+`V` then `E`, or (best) click the Online Layout View button at the bottom left of the document window

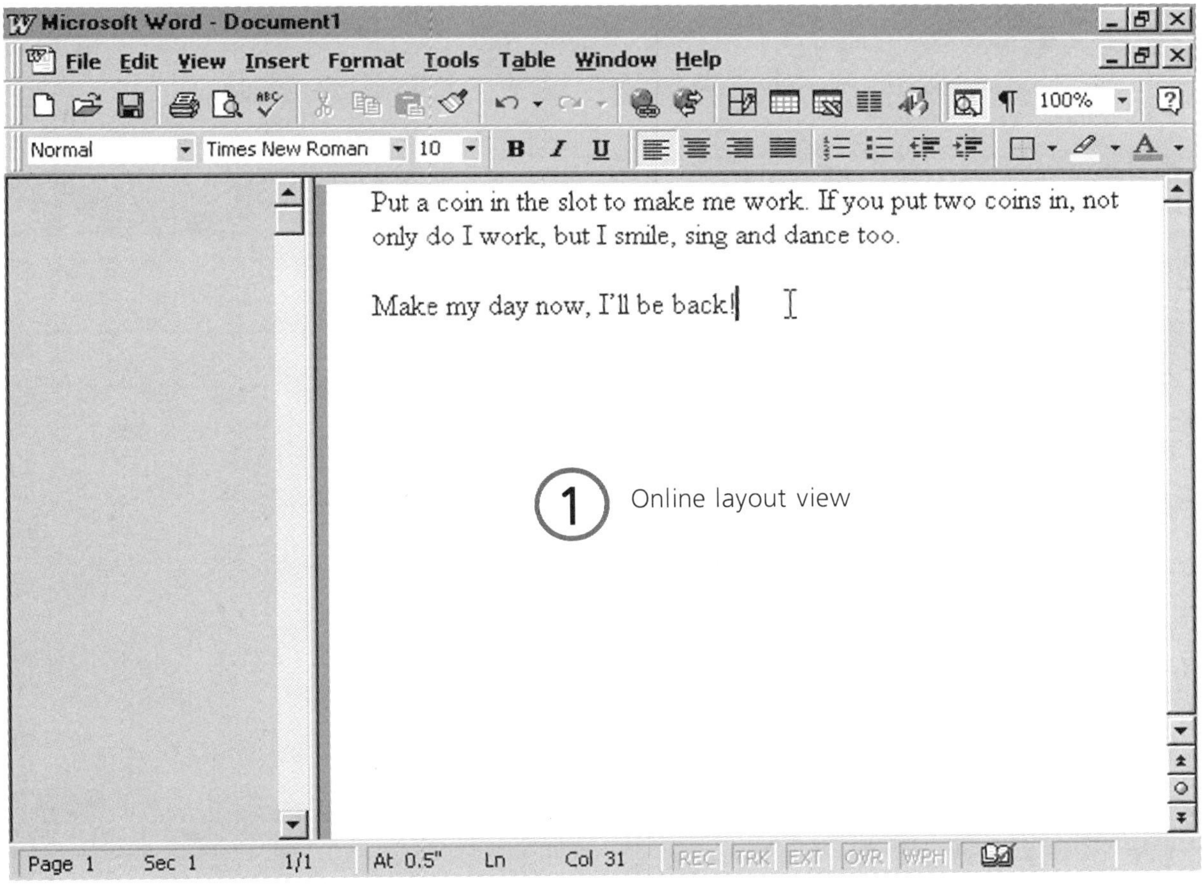

① Online layout view

Page layout view

This view lets you see how the printed page will appear — *what you see is what you get* (WYSIWYG). Margins and borders around text are shown, as well as positions of graphics. This is a useful view to check the final appearance of your document before printing.

However, general operation becomes a little slower.

Basic steps:

1 Choose **View→Page Layout**, or type `Alt`+`V` then `P`, or (best) click the Page Layout button at the bottom left of your document window

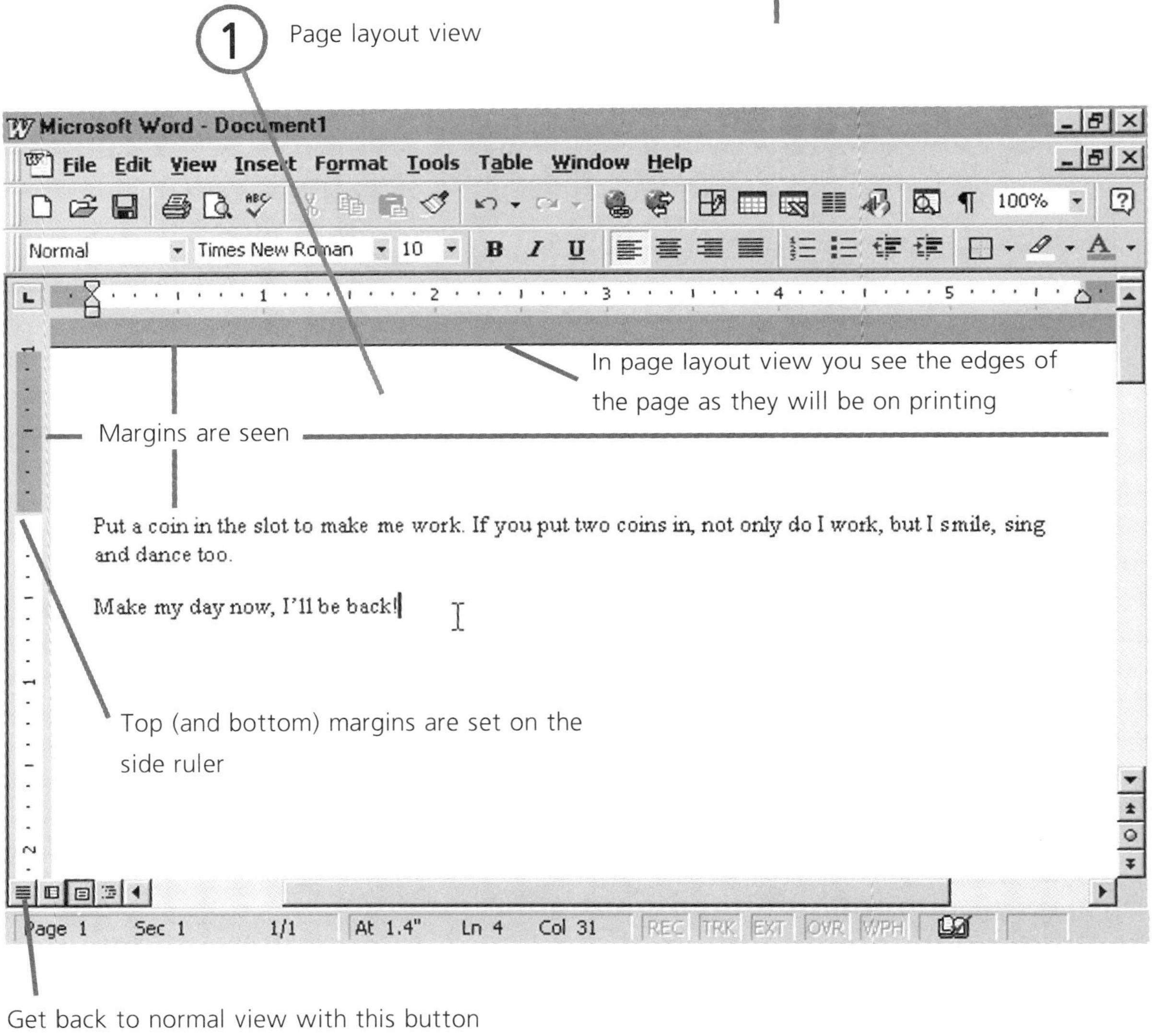

① Page layout view

In page layout view you see the edges of the page as they will be on printing

Margins are seen

Top (and bottom) margins are set on the side ruler

Get back to normal view with this button

Outline view

Outline view allows you to control how the various levels of heading and subheadings in your document are displayed (or not displayed) and organised. It is the ideal method of rearranging documents by moving parts of text long distances within the document, or changing the hierarchy of headings. See page 104 for fuller details of outlining.

Basic steps:

1. Choose **View→Outline**, or type [Alt]+[V] then [O], or (best) click the Outline button at the bottom left of your document window

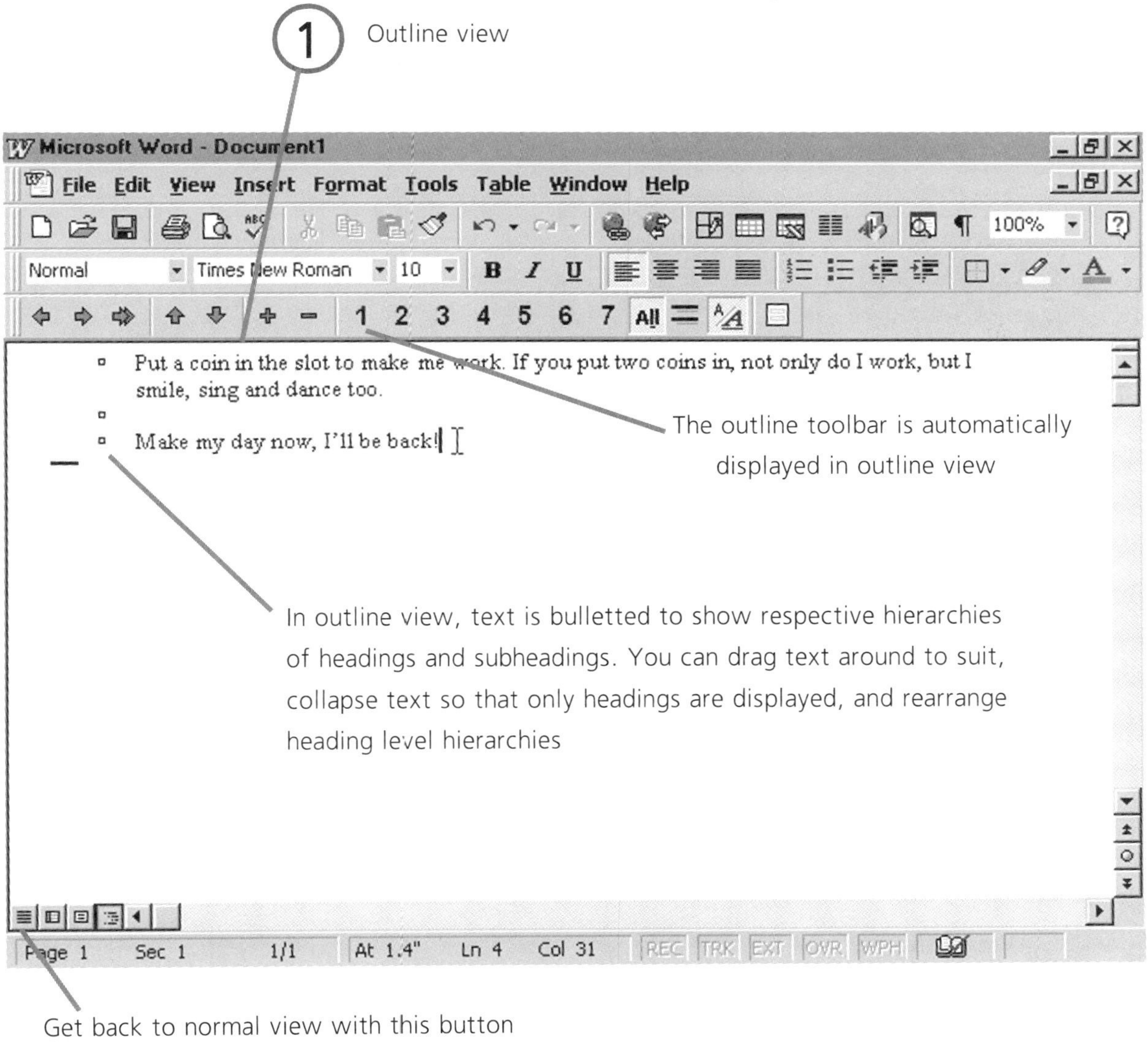

1 Outline view

The outline toolbar is automatically displayed in outline view

In outline view, text is bulletted to show respective hierarchies of headings and subheadings. You can drag text around to suit, collapse text so that only headings are displayed, and rearrange heading level hierarchies

Get back to normal view with this button

Full screen view

Basic steps:

Word has a neat facility to get rid of all the on-screen clutter such as toolbars, menu line, and scroll boxes.

1 Choose **View**➔**Full Screen**, or type `Alt`+`V` then `U`

Tip:

You can still access individual menus by moving the mouse pointer over the thick top edge of the window, or by typing `Alt`+the menu's underlined letter eg, `Alt`+`F` displays the File menu

① Full screen view

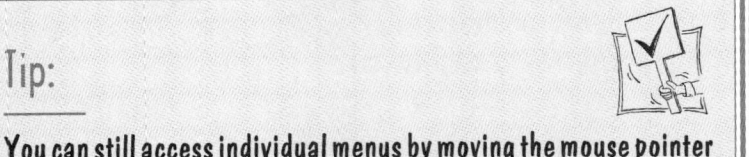

Put a coin in the slot to make me work. If you put two coins in, not only do I work, but I smile, sing and dance too.

Make my day now, I'll be back!

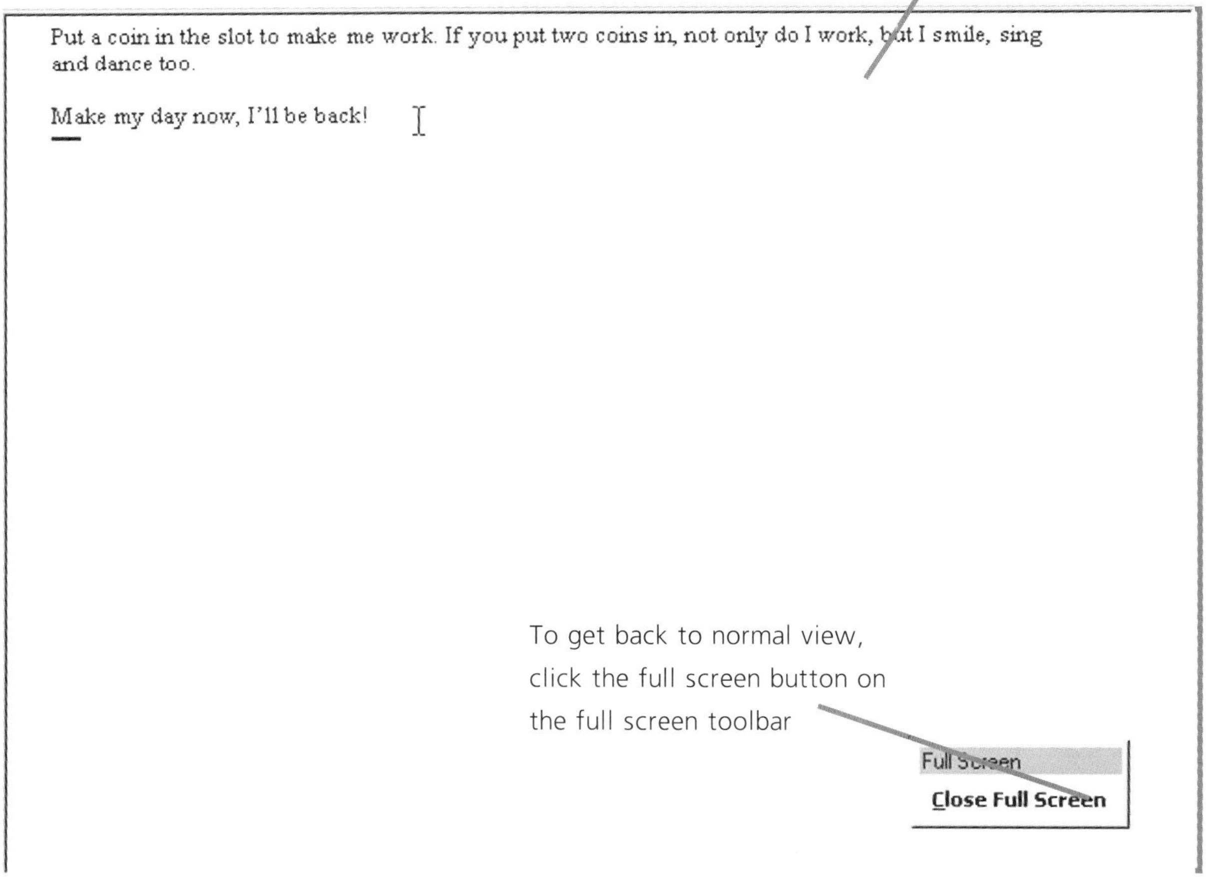

To get back to normal view, click the full screen button on the full screen toolbar

Full Screen
Close Full Screen

18

Zooming

Basic steps:

You can magnify or reduce part of a document page in Word, to get a close up or overall view of the page. This is known as zooming

1 Click on the down arrow of the zoom control button of the standard toolbar

2 From the resultant drop-down menu, choose your desired zoom percentage

3 As an alternative you can choose **View→Zoom**, to call up the **Zoom** dialog box, and select zoom value there

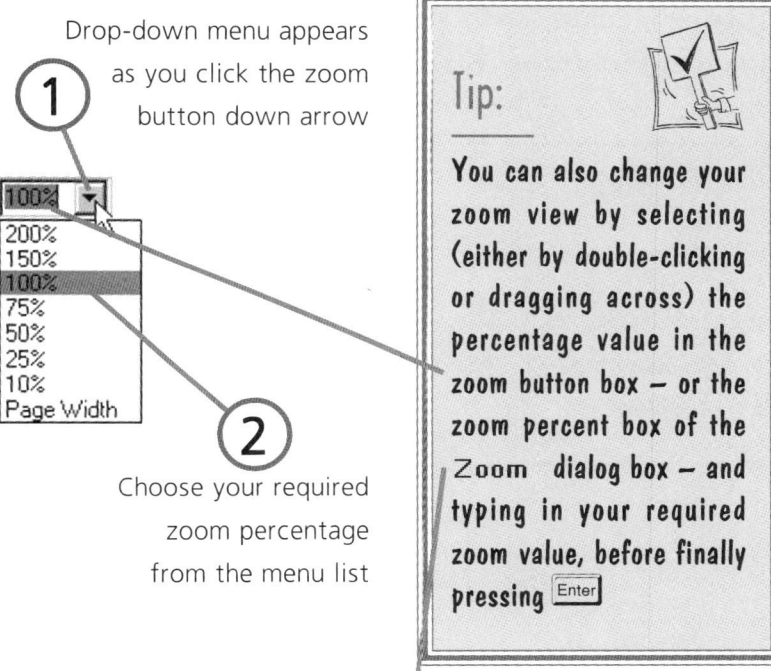

Drop-down menu appears as you click the zoom button down arrow

Tip:

You can also change your zoom view by selecting (either by double-clicking or dragging across) the percentage value in the zoom button box — or the zoom percent box of the Zoom dialog box — and typing in your required zoom value, before finally pressing Enter

Choose your required zoom percentage from the menu list

A preview gives you some idea of text size

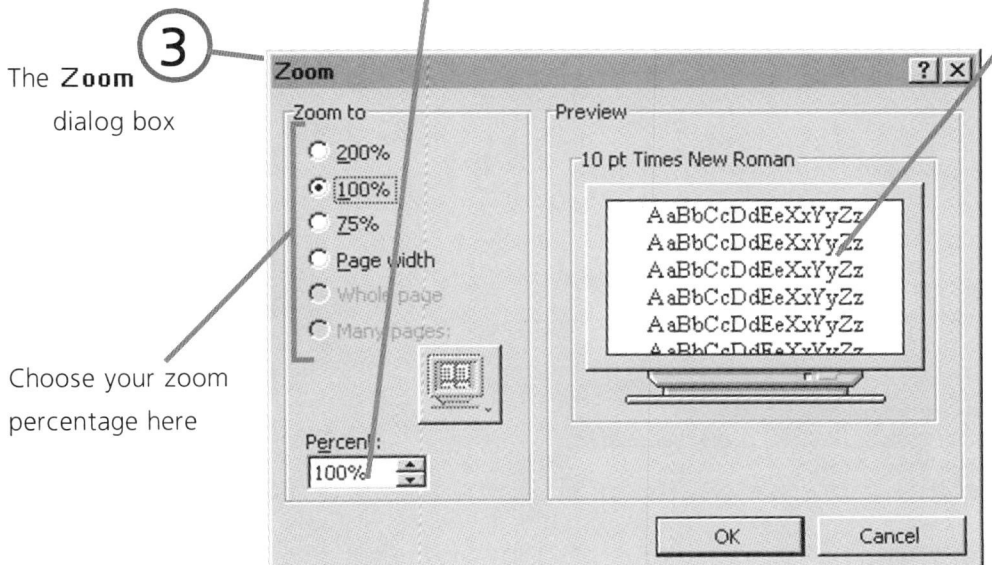

The **Zoom** dialog box

Choose your zoom percentage here

Saving a document

Basic steps:

Once you've worked on a document you need to save it onto disk:

- the document remains in computer memory only as long as Word is running
- if you quit Word, or turn off your machine without saving the document to disk it is lost forever — **RIP**

> **Take note:**
>
> **Save your document regularly, throughout working on it. That way, if your machine buckaroos — or you do something silly — your work is not lost — at least upto the last save operation**

1 Choose **File→Save**, or type `Alt`+`F` then `S`, or type `Ctrl`+`S`, or click the Save button 🖫, to call the **Save As** dialog box if this is the first time you have saved the document. If you have already saved the document the **Save As** dialog box isn't even called up — the document is simply saved over itself with the same file name

2 Enter a name in the **File Name** box

3 Locate the folder you want, then click **Save** to save the document

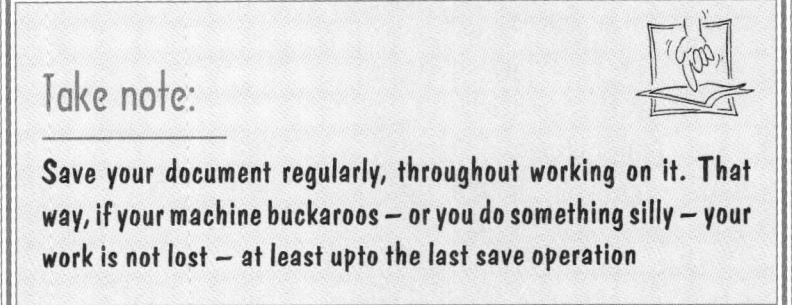

① The **Save As** dialog box

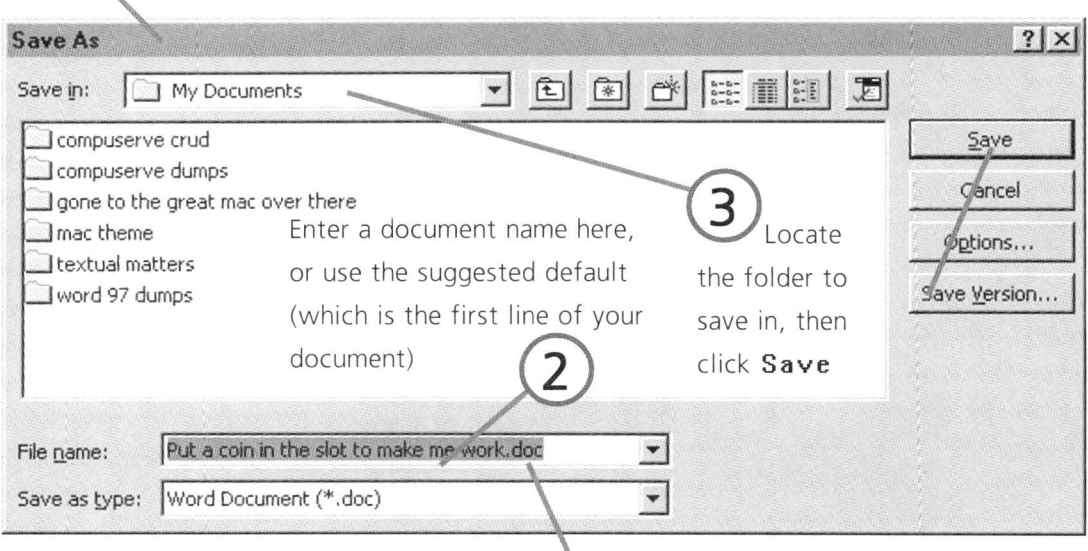

Enter a document name here, or use the suggested default (which is the first line of your document)

③ Locate the folder to save in, then click **Save**

Note: you don't need to enter the extension **.doc** as Word does that for you when you complete step 3

Opening documents

When you first startup Word a new document is created automatically for you, ready for you to enter text. Usually, this new document is of a standard form.

There are times, however, when you may need to open another style of document to use as your new one, or even just open existing documents you have previously saved. If you have worked on these documents recently, you might find them listed in the Documents folder of the **Start** menu, but if it's been a while since using them, you can open them from within Word.

Basic steps:

1. Choose **File→Open**, or type `Alt`+`F` then `O`, or type `Ctrl`+`O`, or click the Open button. The **Open** dialog box is shown

2. Locate the document you wish to open in its drive and folder

3. Click the Preview button to see a preview of any selected document

4. Click **Open**

(1) **Open** dialog box

(2) Find the document to open

(3) Clicking here allows you to view a preview of any selected document

(4) Click

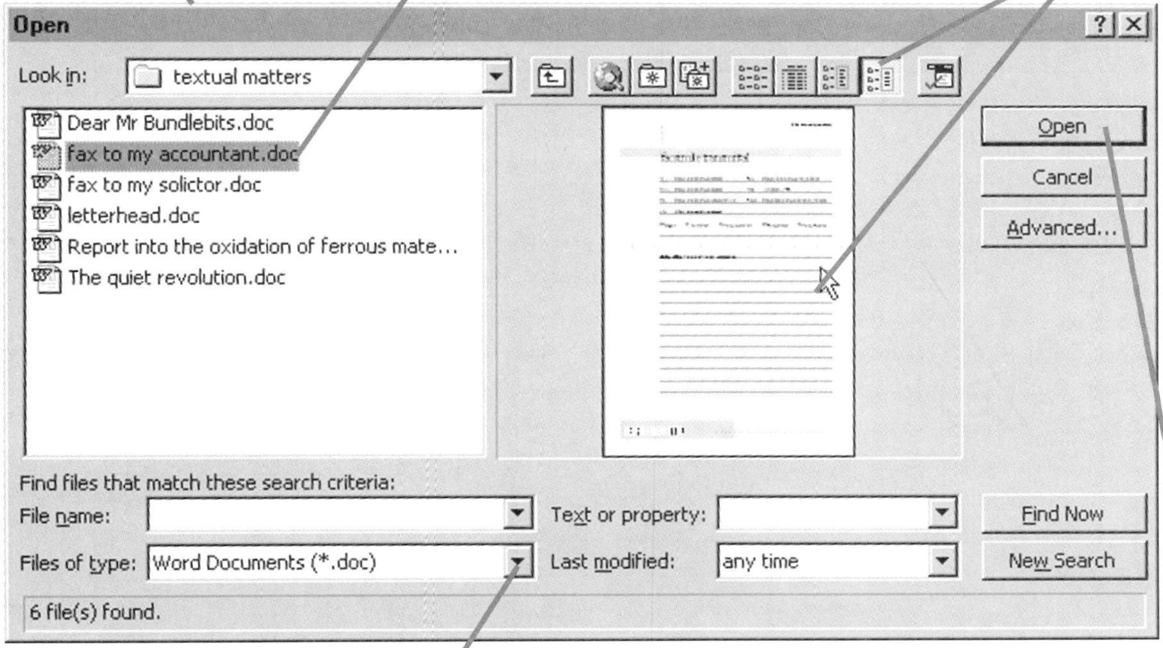

If the document isn't a Word document (with the **.doc** extension), this drop-down box lets you see other openable document types

Creating new documents

Basic steps:

Creating a new document is just as easy as opening an existing document. Word create a new document as the image of a template. Templates are ready-built and installed document *plans*, complete with styles and formats you might want to use for any particular appearance of document (see page 134 for further details of templates).

Templates are arranged in sections, accessed in the New **Office Document** dialog box with tabs.

CREATING A NEW DOCUMENT

1 Choose **Start** → **New Office Document**. The **New** dialog box is called up

2 Click a tab with the generic heading of the document type you want to create

3 Select a template

4 Click **OK**

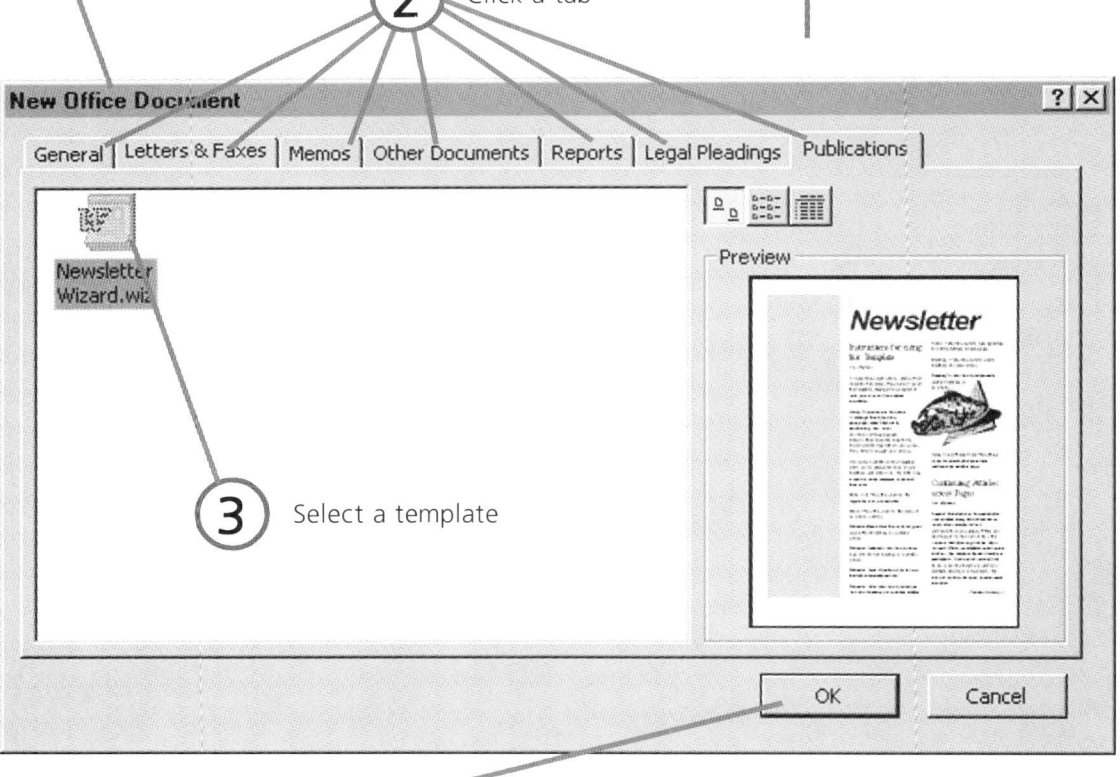

① **New Office Document** dialog box

② Click a tab

③ Select a template

④ Click **OK**

You can create new documents from other documents, too. If you have, say, a letter (or in this example, a fax) that you have previously written, and decide that it is in the same format as another you want to send, you can simply open it and change the details you need to change, saving considerable time.

Basic steps:

1 On the desktop, locate the folder holding the Word document you want to create a new copy from

2 Click the document with the right mouse button

3 In the shortcut menu, click **New** with your left mouse button — a copy of the document is opened

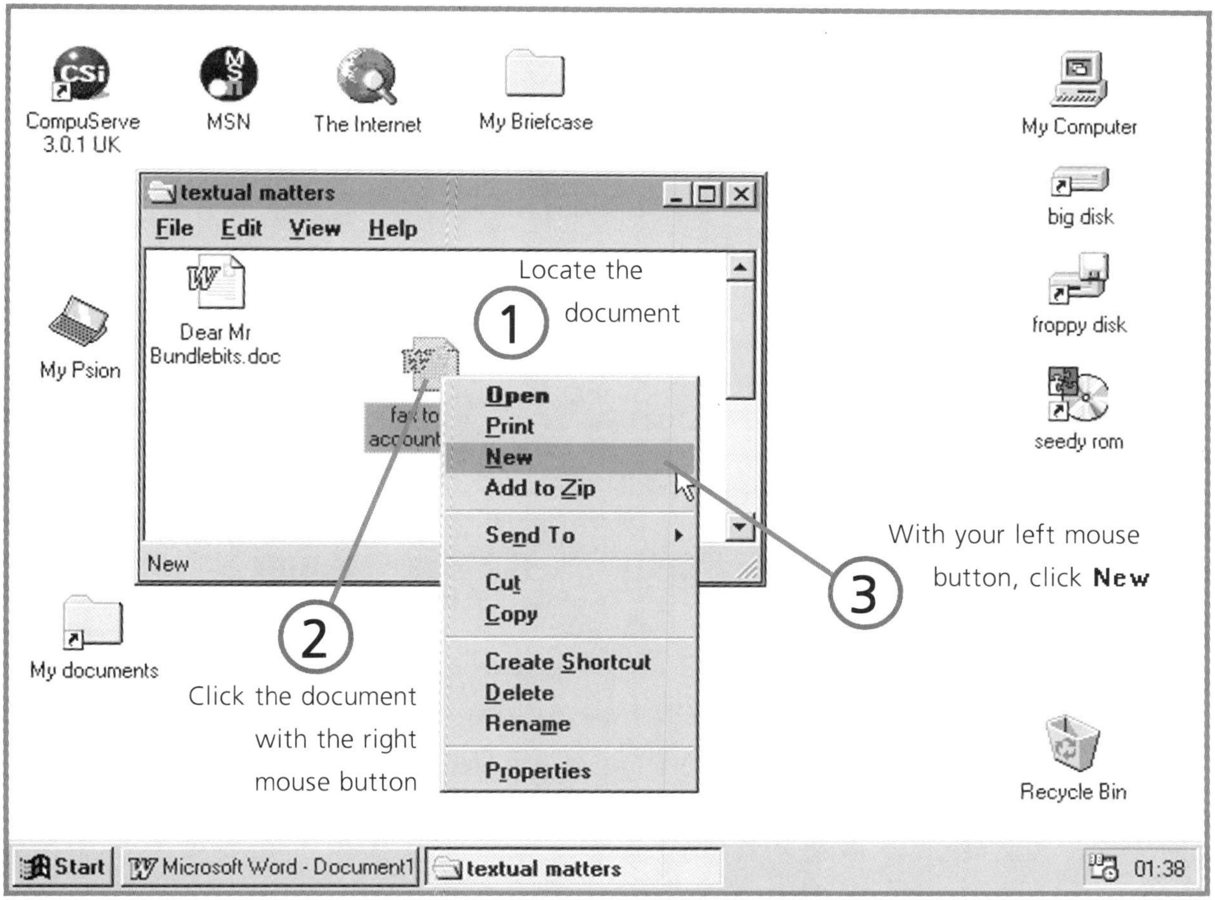

Tip:

This works even when you don't have Word running. As you create the new document, Word is automatically launched

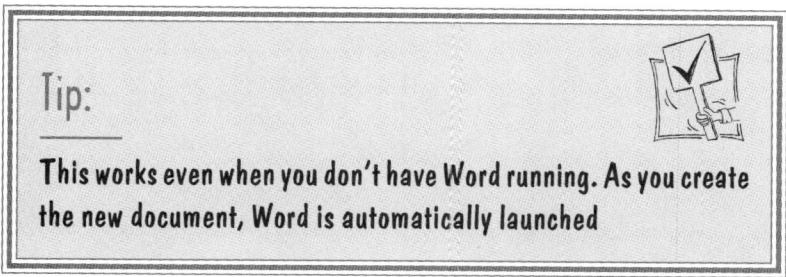

Locate the document

Click the document with the right mouse button

With your left mouse button, click **New**

Goodbye – or just au revoir?

After you've finished using a computer program it's usual to exit or quit it. If you're only trying to clear the screen for a short while, on the other hand, there are alternatives.

① **Save Changes** dialog box when the Office Assistant is not running

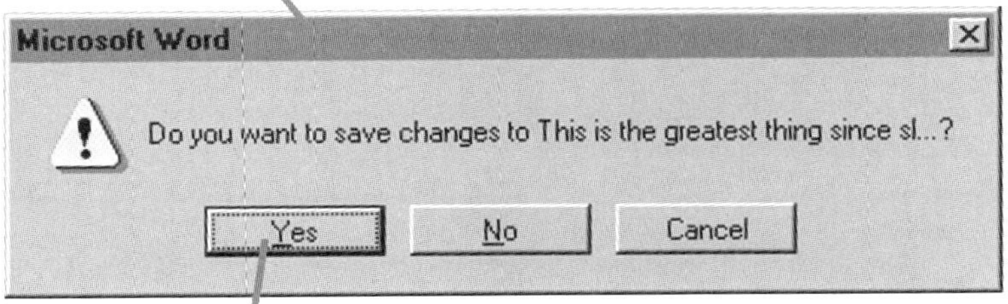

② Click to save. If you have not saved the document before this, the **Save As** dialog box will be displayed (see page 20)

Basic steps:

1 Choose **File→Exit**, or type [Alt]+[F] then [X]. If you have recently saved the document or documents you are working on and have not worked on them since, Word quits straightaway. If you have worked on a document since last saving it (or have not saved it at all) the **Save Changes?** dialog box is displayed. This varies depending on whether you have the Office Assistant running or not

① **Save Changes** dialog box when the Office Assistant is running

Tip:

You don't actually have to quit programs before you shut down your computer. Just choose [Start]→Shut Down, and the computer exits all your open programs correctly, presenting the required Save Changes dialog boxes to suit

Basic steps:

1 Click a window's **Minimize** button ▬, at the top right corner

2 Click the window's button created on the Taskbar, to restore the window to its previous size and position

Temporarily clearing your screen

If you're only trying to clear your screen for a short while — and you don't want to quit Word — click the **Minimize** button ▬ at the top-right of the Word program window. This minimizes the window as a button, left on the taskbar — showing the document name (as long as it's not too long) — as well as its creator (Microsoft Word). This is true for any minimized program window in Windows 95, of course, whether it's a window open within a program, or simply a desktop window.

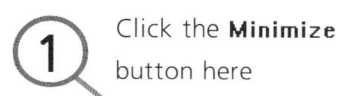

Click the **Minimize** button here

Take note:

While the technique here works for a document window, it also works for a complete program. In other words, clicking a program's Minimize button (that is, the Minimize button above a document window's Minimize button) minimizes the whole program as a Taskbar button. While this can be confusing for a new user, used properly it can help clear up your desktop. However, it's best to remember that programs should not be left long term in this mode — exiting them correctly clears up computer memory for other tasks

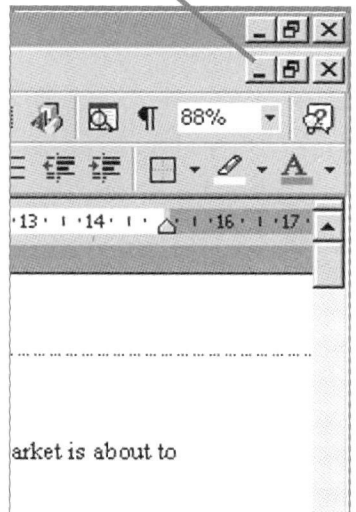

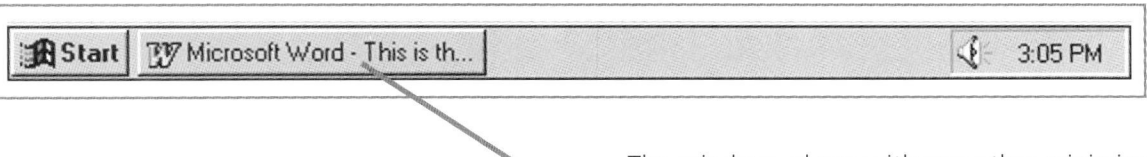

The window, along with any other minimized windows are displayed along the Taskbar. Click a button to restore its window

25

Summary for Section 1

- Startup Word by choosing **Start** ↪ **Programs** ↪ **Microsoft Word**, or **Start** ↪ **Programs** ↪ **Microsoft Office** ↪ **Microsoft Word** from the taskbar.

- Get on-line help by clicking the Office Assistant button [?] in the standard toolbar.

- Access toolbars by either clicking on any toolbar with the right mouse button then selecting the one you want, or choose **View** ↪ **Toolbars** to call up the **Toolbars** dialog box.

- Change document view between normal, online layout, page layout and outline to suit the way you work.

- Page layout view lets you see the page as it will be printed.

- Outline view lets you rearrange headings and their hierarchies, as well as dragging text large distances easily in the document.

- Remove all on-screen clutter with full screen view by choosing **View** ↪ **Full Screen**

- Open existing Word documents — or other applications' documents — from the **Open** dialog box.

- Create a new document — in the form of a selected template — in the **New** dialog box.

2 Text essentials

Entering text 28

Editing text 30

Selecting text 32

Ooops – a mistake! 36

Cut, copy and paste 38

Drag-and-drop editing 40

Entering symbols 42

Summary for Section 2 44

Entering text

As a word processor, of course, Word's main function is to store straightforward text. As you startup Word, or create a new document, you can begin to enter text immediately.

Basic steps:

1. Simply type something. It doesn't matter what — a few lines of rubbish will do nicely

2. If your document is important, remember to save it

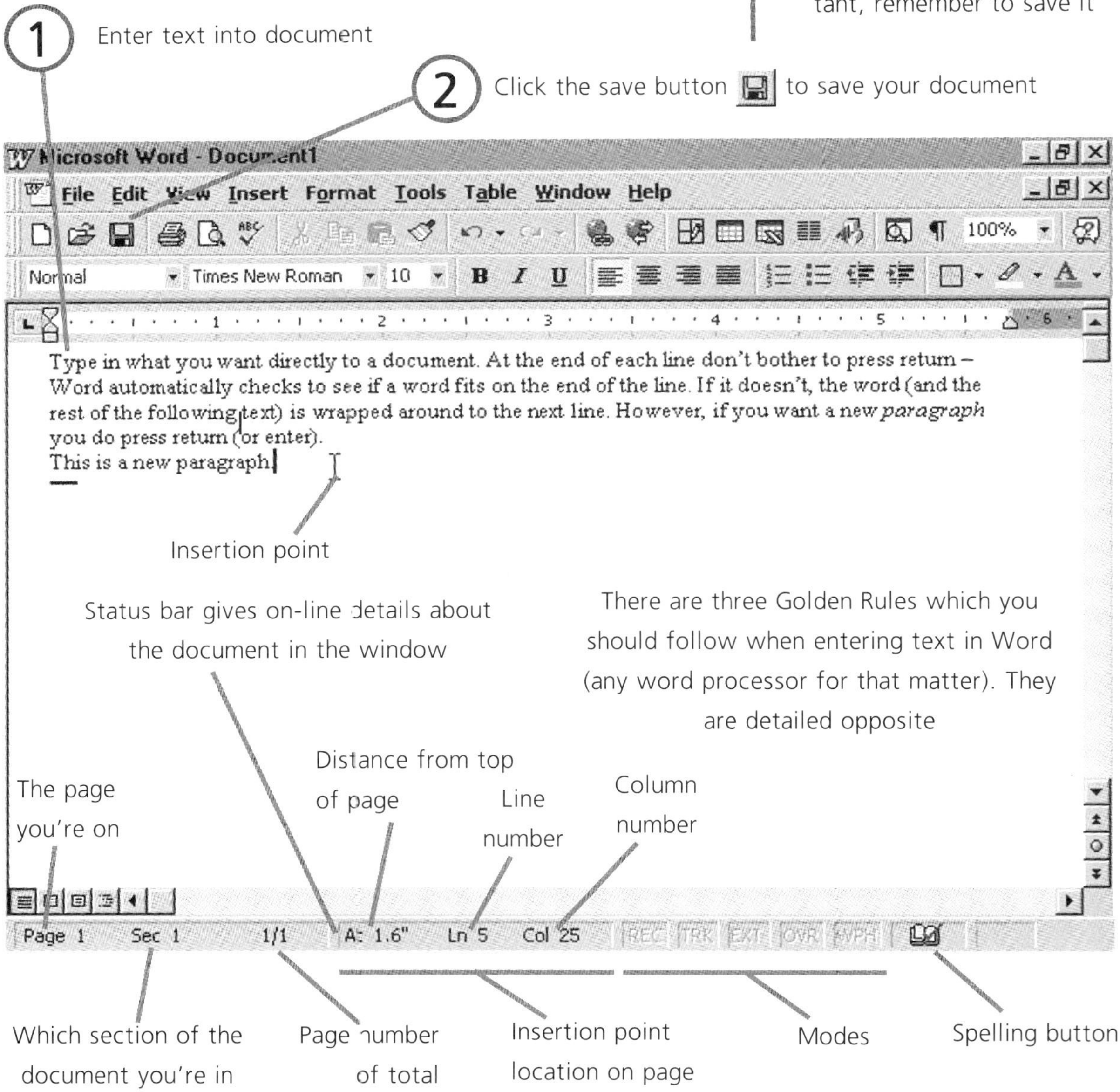

① Enter text into document

② Click the save button to save your document

- Insertion point
- Status bar gives on-line details about the document in the window
- The page you're on
- Which section of the document you're in
- Distance from top of page
- Page number of total
- Line number
- Column number
- Insertion point location on page
- Modes
- Spelling button

There are three Golden Rules which you should follow when entering text in Word (any word processor for that matter). They are detailed opposite

The status bar

Get into the habit of looking at the status bar. It gives some explicit information about what's happening within your Word document, such as:

- page number, section (you can break your document up into smaller sections, to make it more manageable — see page 74) number, and total number of pages

- location of the insertion point (that is, the point within text where your keyboard entries appear on screen)

- mode buttons — accessed by double-clicking — of these only two are of importance here, and are:

- `WPH` — on-line help for ex-WordPerfect users. See page 9 for details

- `OVR` — active when blacked (that is, not greyed). See over for details

- spelling button — if the button displays an ✘ mark, Word has detected a spelling error

Take note:

The Golden Rules of Word

1 Never, never, never, never, never, never, never, never, never, never (get the message?) put two spaces together. The old typists' routine of putting two spaces at the end of a sentence should not be done in a word processor because spaces aren't generally of a fixed width. A program like Word adjusts spaces to ensure the text fits its given column width and looks good. Two or more spaces together may be adjusted in width to give ridiculously wide spaces between words. For the same reason, text which is formed into tabular columns mustn't be created by inserting spaces to line columns up — it might look aligned on screen, but when it prints you can't guarantee it — use proper tabs instead (see page 60)

2 Never, never, never, never (oh, here we go again) put two carriage returns together. Actually, this isn't quite so critical as Golden Rule number 1, but important nevertheless. Spaces between paragraphs are best controlled by creating styles for each paragraph type (see section 6) which incorporate spaces before and after them

3 Never (once is enough this time, I'm sure) press ⏎ or `Enter` at the end of a line of text — unless the end of the line is also the end of a paragraph. There is simply no need — and carriage returns fix the text to those line lengths. Use Word's word-wrapping facility to do it automatically — then any textual style changes will automatically create consequent new word-wraps, too

Editing text

Inevitably you will make mistakes in your work. This is where a word processor like Word shows its forté. On a typewriter, mistakes have to be erased and retyped, usually resulting in a shoddy document. In a word processor, on the other hand, mistakes are simply edited on-screen before printing. Even if a mistake slips by you, and you only see it after printing, you can correct it and reprint the document.

Even if your required corrections aren't due to mistakes, but are straightforward editorial changes, Word has some unbeaten facilities for making any kind of textual change necessary in a document.

There are several ways you can edit text. The simplest — covered here — is overtyping.

All editing procedures, on the other hand, rely on the principle of placing the insertion point at the point which requires editing! If you learn nothing else from this page, learn this fact.

Basic steps:

OVERTYPE EDITING

1 If you spot a mistake which requires you to retype part or all of a word or sentence, position the insertion point at the beginning of the mistake

2 Look at the [OVR] button on the status bar. If it is greyed, you are in insert edit mode, if it is black you are in overtype edit mode. Double-click it to toggle between the two modes. Make sure you are in overtype edit mode (the button should be in blackface (ie [OVR])

As you move the mouse pointer over text it changes to the I-beam pointer ⊺. When you position the pointer over the point to edit then click, the insertion point of Word becomes active at that point. This whole process of pointing and clicking with the I-beam pointer ⊺ is known as *positioning the insertion point*.

Remember it — because all editing relies on it!

(1)

> There was a cow stupefied on a hill. If it hasn't gonn it will be their still.
> Now is the time for all good men to come to the aid of the party

3 Retype the section of text — this overtypes text already there

4 Move to any other areas you need to overtype as in Step 1

5 When you have finished overtyping double-click the overtype button `OVR` again, to return to insertion mode

> **Take note:**
>
> Editing in any word processor worth its salt is most often a combination of techniques — not just one. In other words: find out about all techniques — these shown here, as well as those shown over following pages — to take full advantage of Word. Word is an immensely powerful computer program. If you don't take advantage of its power you're not using your computer efficiently

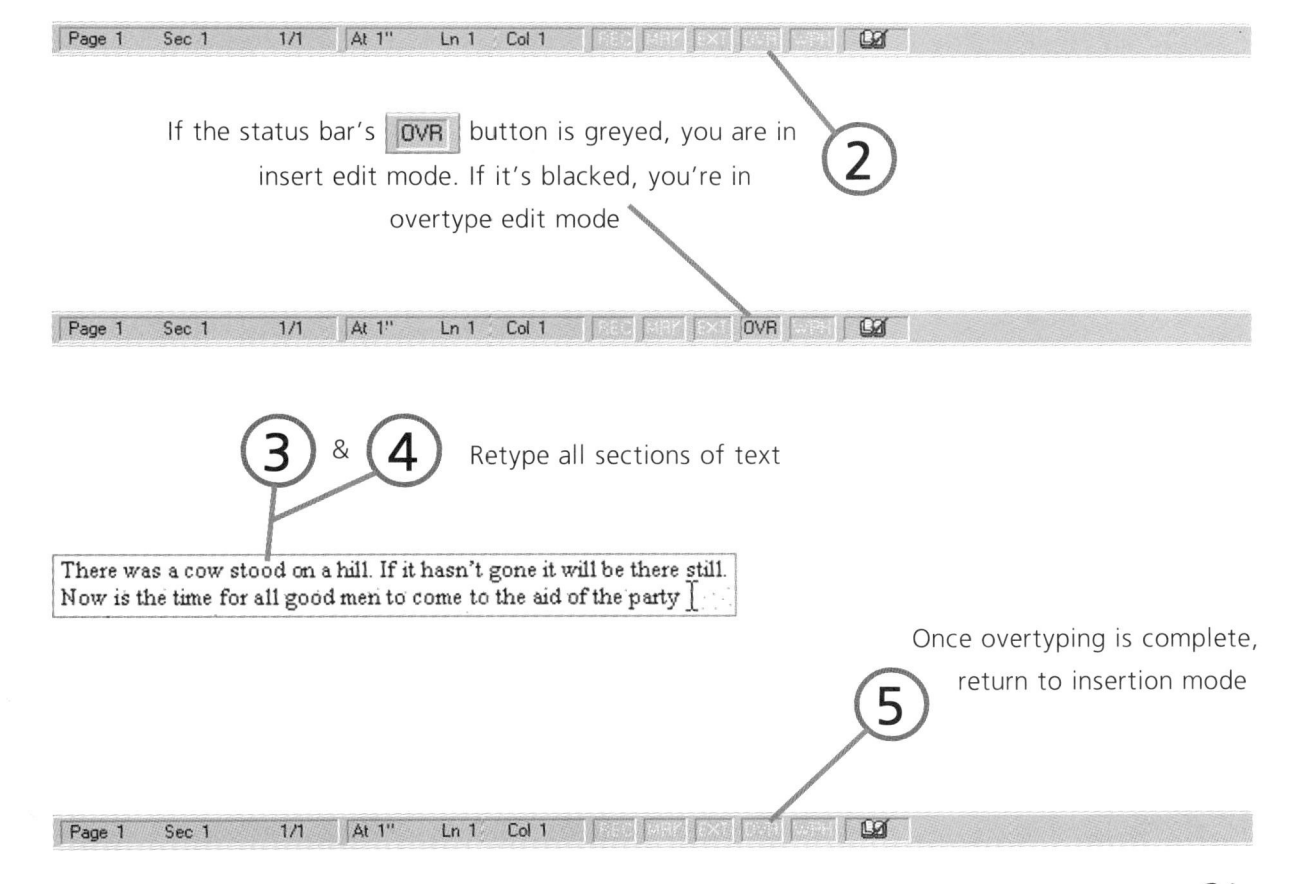

If the status bar's `OVR` button is greyed, you are in insert edit mode. If it's blacked, you're in overtype edit mode ②

③ & ④ Retype all sections of text

There was a cow stood on a hill. If it hasn't gone it will be there still. Now is the time for all good men to come to the aid of the party

Once overtyping is complete, return to insertion mode ⑤

Selecting text

Whenever you want to edit text (that is, apart from when you overtype — see previous page) you need to select the particular text you want to change:

- Word allows you to do this in various ways
- no single way is best
- instead, a combination of selecting techniques — depending on what is to be selected — should be used
- selection of text is sometimes known by different names such as blocking or highlighting. These names are often merely descriptive of the selection process — text which is selected becomes highlighted or blocked and that's how you know the text happens to be selected!

Basic steps:

1 You can select any letter, word, sentence, paragraph, or any part of these by dragging over the required text

2 To select a single word, double-click the word

3 To select more than one word, drag from one word across to the next, or further if you want more words to be selected

4 To select a whole line of text, click in the selection bar to the left of the line

---

1 Drag the I-beam pointer I over the letters, or words, or sentences, or paragraphs you want to be selected

No, no, no, said the Giant. There can be no suggestion of a compromise. I am going to eat you all up, because that's the sort of thing giants are known to do.

As you drag over your selected text and release the mouse button, the selected text becomes highlighted.

Highlighted text is simply the visible sign that the text is selected

2 You can select a single word most quickly by double-clicking the word

No, no, no, said the Giant. There can be no **suggsetion** of a compromise. I am going to eat you all up, because that's the sort of thing giants are known to do.

③ Drag over words to select them. As you drag over each new part of a word the whole word becomes selected automatically

> No, no, no, said the Giant. There can be no suggsetion of a compromise. I am going to eat you all up, because that's the sort of thing giants are known to do.

Tip:

When you begin selecting in the middle of a word, then drag to include part of another word, Word automatically selects both words (and any subsequent ones too), as well as any space after the words

④ Select whole lines of text by clicking in the selection bar

> No, no, no, said the Giant. There can be no suggsetion of a compromise. I am going to eat you all up, because that's the sort of thing giants are known to do.

The selection bar is to the left of text on any Word document page

Take note:

All of these selection techniques can be used to select graphic items, such as pictures, as well as text

Selecting text (contd)

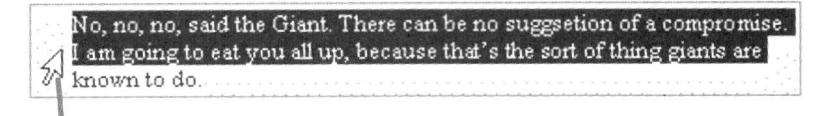

Basic steps:

5 To select multiple lines of text, drag in the selection bar to the left of the lines

6 To select a sentence, hold down `Ctrl` and click anywhere in the sentence

7 To select a paragraph, either double-click in the selection bar to the left of the paragraph, or triple-click anywhere in the text

8 To select multiple paragraphs, drag in the selection bar to the left of the paragraphs

9 To select an entire document, triple-click in the selection bar

10 Select text which is neither a whole word, sentence, or paragraph by positioning the insertion point at the beginning of the text, then holding down `Shift` while you click at the end of the text

⑤ Select multiple lines of text by dragging in the selection bar

⑥ Select a single sentence by holding down `Ctrl` and clicking in the sentence

⑦ Double-click in the selection bar (or triple-click in the text) to select a paragraph

⑧ Drag across paragraphs in the selection bar to select multiple paragraphs

Select an entire document's text by triple-clicking in the selection bar ⑨

Tip:

Cancel a selection by clicking outside of it, or pressing any arrow key

By clicking at the starting point, then holding down `Shift` and clicking at the finishing point, a complete block of text can be selected ⑩

Tip:

Whatever you do in Word — writing, editing, stylising, formatting and so on — relies on being able to select text.

No single selection method is best for all purposes. Depending on what you want to select, you should choose the preferred method. Sometimes you should use the mouse, sometimes you should use the keyboard.

The only way you can make sure you use the preferred method for any particular purpose is to learn how to use all methods

KEYBOARD SHORTCUTS

You can select text with the keyboard too:

One character right	`Shift` + `→`
One character left	`Shift` + `←`
To the end of a word	`Ctrl` + `Shift` + `→`
To the beginning of a word	`Ctrl` + `Shift` + `←`
To the end of a line	`Shift` + `End`
To the beginning of a line	`Shift` + `Home`
One line down	`Shift` + `↓`
One line up	`Shift` + `↑`
To the end of a paragraph	`Ctrl` + `Shift` + `↓`
To the start of a paragraph	`Ctrl` + `Shift` + `↑`
One screen down	`Shift` + `Page Down`
One screen up	`Shift` + `Page Up`
To end of document	`Ctrl` + `Shift` + `End`
To beginning of document	`Ctrl` + `Shift` + `Home`
Entire document	`Ctrl` + `A`
To a specific location	`F8` + arrow keys

Ooops – a mistake

Word processors are meant to make the correction of mistakes as simple as possible. Apart from the proper editing facilities of Word we've already seen, however, are extra goodies which make the correction of simple typing errors almost as easy as making the mistakes in the first place — but not qwite, if you see what I mean!

It's as well to know all these goodies to get the best out of Word. The mistakes we're concerned with here are those which you notice almost as you make them:

- obvious spelling errors
- mis-hit keys
- style changes which shouldn't have been made

and so on.

Basic steps:

1 If you have just a few letters you want to delete, a quick result can be to press ⌫, or ⌦:

❑ ⌫ deletes the character before the insertion point

❑ ⌦ deletes the character after the insertion point

❑ Ctrl + ⌫ deletes the word before the insertion point

❑ Ctrl + ⌦ deletes the word after the insertion point

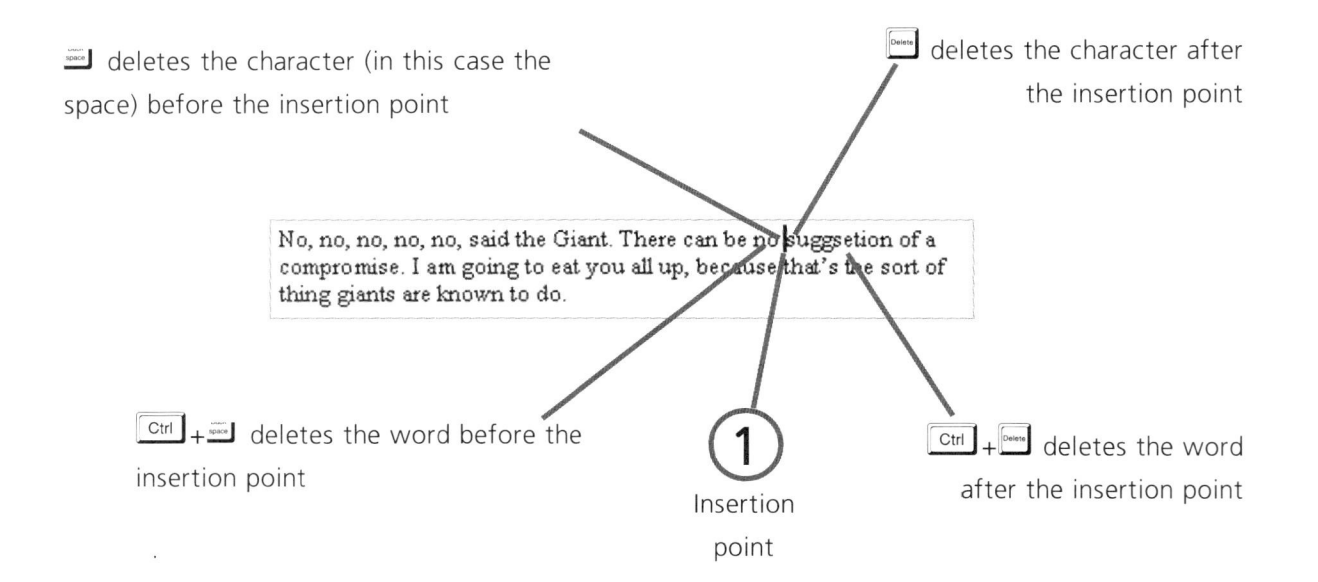

⌫ deletes the character (in this case the space) before the insertion point

⌦ deletes the character after the insertion point

No, no, no, no, no, said the Giant. There can be no suggsetion of a compromise. I am going to eat you all up, because that's the sort of thing giants are known to do.

Ctrl + ⌫ deletes the word before the insertion point

① Insertion point

Ctrl + ⌦ deletes the word after the insertion point

2 You can very often *undo* a mistake or change you make in a Word document, because Word features a multiple undo facility. Just click the Undo button after you have made a mistake or change you want to undo and a drop-down box lists all your recent actions in reverse order — your most recent action at the top of the list

Take note:

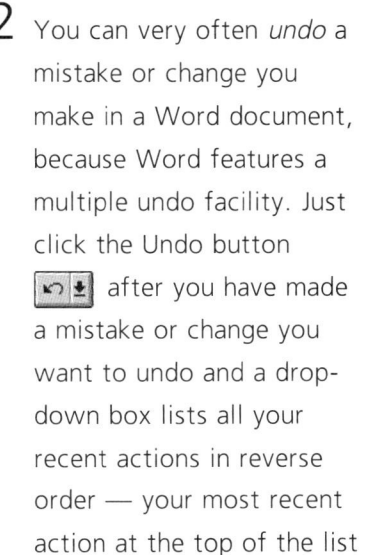

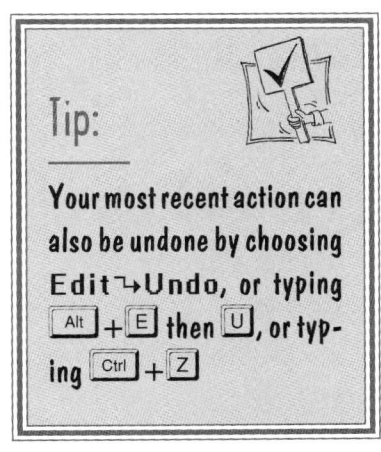

Actions can only be undone in strict order — if you want to undo the action 48 places down the list, the most recent 47 actions have to be undone also!

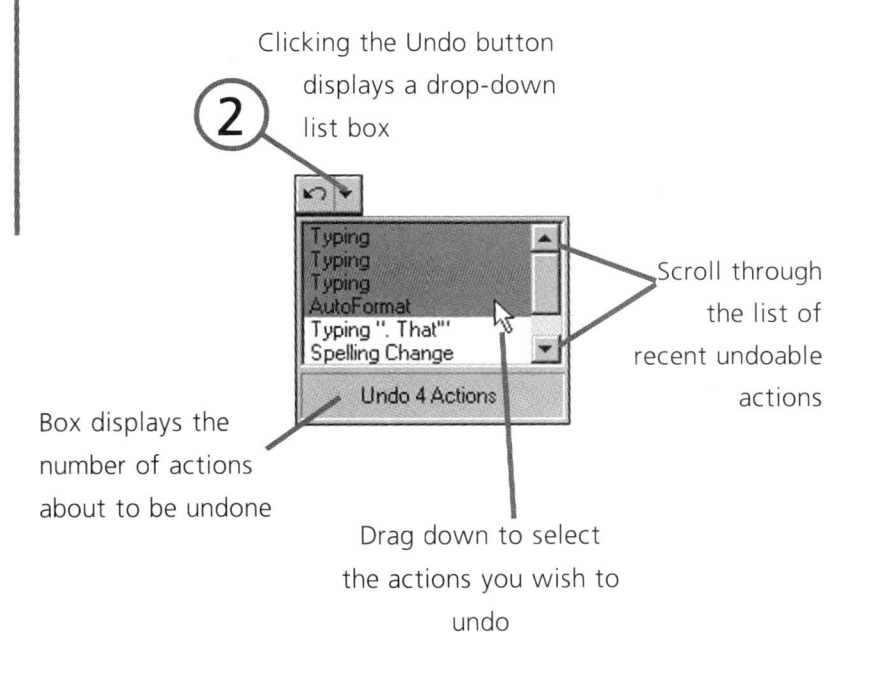

Clicking the Undo button displays a drop-down list box

Scroll through the list of recent undoable actions

Box displays the number of actions about to be undone

Drag down to select the actions you wish to undo

Tip:

Your most recent action can also be undone by choosing Edit→Undo, or typing Alt + E then U, or typing Ctrl + Z

Tip:

If you undo an action by mistake, click the Redo button to undo the undo!

Take note:

While Word's undo feature is a boon for those of us who make mistakes — that is, anyone who uses a computer — you should remember that some actions are not undoable

37

Cut, copy and paste

Word (like any Windows application) uses a temporary storage area known as the Clipboard to keep items you want to move or copy within a Word document. These items can be of text or graphic forms (or a mixture of both). Using the Clipboard to do this is known as cutting, copying and pasting:

- you *cut* an item onto the Clipboard when you want to remove it from one place in a document and move it to another place

- you *copy* an item onto the Clipboard when you want it to occur at more than one place in your document

- taking an item from the Clipboard and putting it in your document is known as *pasting*.

Basic steps :

CUTTING

1 Select the item or items you want to cut onto the clipboard. This can be a selection of text, a graphical item, or a combination of the two

2 Choose **Edit→Cut**, or type [Alt]+[E] then [T], or type [Ctrl]+[X], or simply click the Cut button [✂] to cut the selected item — it disappears from your Word document and is moved onto the Clipboard

Come and see the show

On the other hand, this is a boring part of this document. Let's liven it up by moving the graphic down here!

① & ③ Select the item or items to be cut or copied

Use whichever selection method is appropriate for the text (or graphic in this case) to be copied or cut. To select this graphic, clicking in the selection bar is fastest

② Cut the item or items (now you see it — now you don't!)

Come and see the show

On the other hand, this is a boring part of this document. Let's liven it up by moving the graphic down here!

Position the insertion point before pasting ⑤

38

COPYING

3 Select the item or items you want to copy

4 Choose **Edit→Copy**, or type `Alt`+`E` then `C`, or type `Ctrl`+`C`, or click the Copy button — the selection stays in your document but is copied onto the Clipboard too

PASTING

5 Position the insertion point where you want the item or items stored on the Clipboard to be pasted

6 Choose **Edit→Paste**, or type `Alt`+`E` then `P`, or type `Ctrl`+`V`, or click the Paste button to paste the item or items into your document

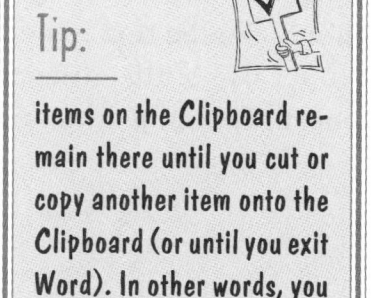

Tip:

items on the Clipboard remain there until you cut or copy another item onto the Clipboard (or until you exit Word). In other words, you can paste an item into your document over and over again if you want

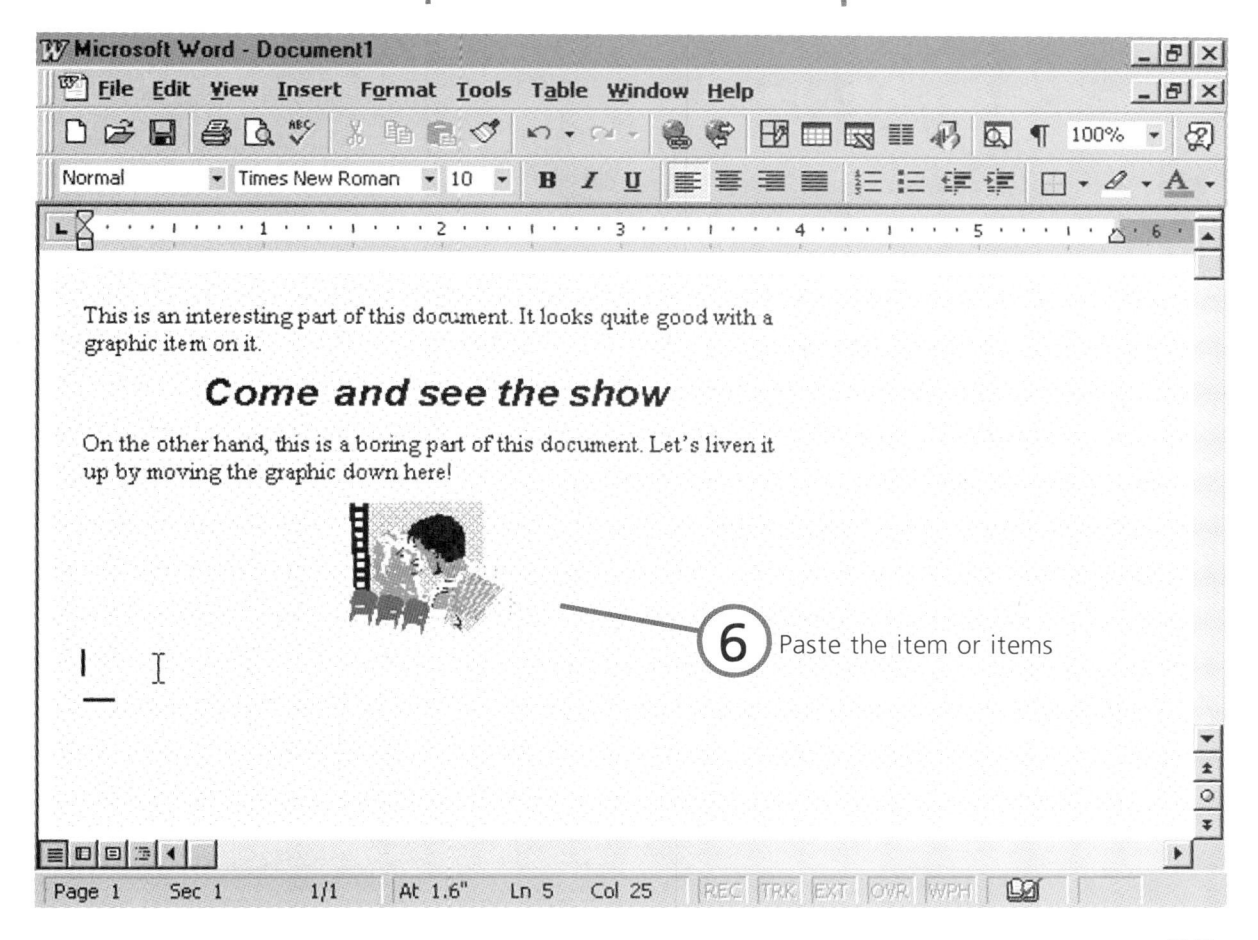

6 Paste the item or items

Drag-and-drop editing

Word has an extremely useful feature in its ability to allow selected text to be moved or copied by dragging. Proper use of this drag-and-drop editing can speed up incorporation of revisions in a document.

① Select the text

Take two aspirins and call me in the mroning. The dogs sat on the mat.
When the Queen of Hearts had no tea the Knave of Hearts stole the tarts.
Instead she beat the Knave of Hearts soundly and sent him to bed.

② The arrow pointer replaces the I-beam pointer over selected text

Take two aspirins and call me in the mroning. The dogs sat on the mat.
When the Queen of Hearts had no tea the Knave of Hearts stole the tarts.
Instead she beat the Knave of Hearts soundly and sent him to bed.

③ As you drag the selected text, the drag-and-drop pointer is displayed

Take two aspirins and call me in the mroning. The dogs sat on the mat.
When the Queen of Hearts had no tea the Knave of Hearts stole the tarts.
Instead she beat the Knave of Hearts soundly and sent him to bed.

④ The dotted insertion point tells you where the text will be moved to

⑤ The text moves as you let go the mouse button

Take two aspirins and call me in the mroning. The dogs sat on the mat.
When the Knave of Hearts stole the tarts the Queen of Hearts had no tea.
Instead she beat the Knave of Hearts soundly and sent him to bed.

Basic steps:

MOVING SELECTED TEXT

1 Select the text to be moved

2 Position the pointer over the selected text (the I-beam pointer I changes to the arrow pointer

3 Click on the selected text and drag the pointer — it changes to the drag-and-drop pointer

4 As you drag the drag-and-drop pointer to a new position, the dotted insertion point follows incicating where the selected text will be dragged to

5 When you have located the dotted insertion point where you want, release the mouse button. The selected text moves to the new location

COPYING SELECTED TEXT

6 Select text as before

7 Drag the selected text as before

8 Locate the position you wish to copy text to as before (with the dotted insertion point)

9 Before you let go the mouse button, press and hold down `Ctrl` (the drag-and-drop pointer changes to show a plus symbol indicating Word is ready to copy (that is, not just move) text

10 Let go the mouse button. The selected text is copied to the new location

Tip:

Drag-and-drop editing is really just an extension of the cut, copy and paste principle. As a result, you can drag-and-drop graphical items, or a combination of graphical *and* text items, as well as just text

6 Select text to be copied

No, no, no, said the Giant. There can be no suggsetion of a compromise. I am going to eat you all up, because that's the sort of thing giants are known to do.

7 Drag selected text with drag-and-drop pointer

8 Locate the dotted insertion point where you want the text to be copied to

No, no, no, said the Giant. There can be no suggsetion of a compromise. I am going to eat you all up, because that's the sort of thing giants are known to do.

9 Hold down `Ctrl` to copy selected text (indicated by + symbol on drag-and-drop pointer)

No, no, no, said the Giant. There can be no suggsetion of a compromise. I am going to eat you all up, because that's the sort of thing giants are known to do.

10 As you release the mouse button, selected text is copied

No, no, no, no, no, said the Giant. There can be no suggsetion of a compromise. I am going to eat you all up, because that's the sort of thing giants are known to do.

Entering symbols

Although Word is a *word* processor, very often it's necessary to include symbols within text. Examples of such symbols are:

● mathematical or scientific symbols — Ω µ ß ∝ for example (however, if you want to include complete mathematical formulae or expressions into your work it is best to use Word's integral equation editor, which is beyond the scope of this book)

● dingbats — the blob or bullet (●) at the left of this list is an example of a dingbat. Others are ✂ ☞ ♣ ◻ ♠ which can be used to embellish text

● typographical symbols and marks — the most obvious examples of typographical marks are the curly quotes (' and ") which differentiate properly typeset text from typewritten (with straight quotes — ' and ") text together with en dashes (–) and em dashes (—)

● foreign letters with accents — é ü å õ ç

and so on.

The ability to enter such symbols rapidly greatly enhances a word processor. Word has a special Symbol command which simplifies the task.

> **Tip:**
>
> Use typographer's symbols and marks to give your work that professional edge. Automatically include curly quotes using Word's AutoCorrect feature (page 100). Use an en dash to combine number ranges (eg, pages 44–56) and use an em dash to separate emphasising text – just like that!

Basic steps:

1. Position the insertion point where you want the symbol to be (if you are typing in text and want to enter the symbol as you go, the insertion point is already positioned correctly). Now choose **Insert→Symbol**, or type [Alt]+[I] then [S]. This calls up the **Symbol** dialog box which automatically displays symbols available in fonts

2. Click a symbol and it is displayed enlarged. Click Insert if you want the symbol in your text. Alternatively, double-click the symbol you want. It is placed in text at the position of the insertion point

3. Display and choose a different font if you want with the **Font** drop-down list box

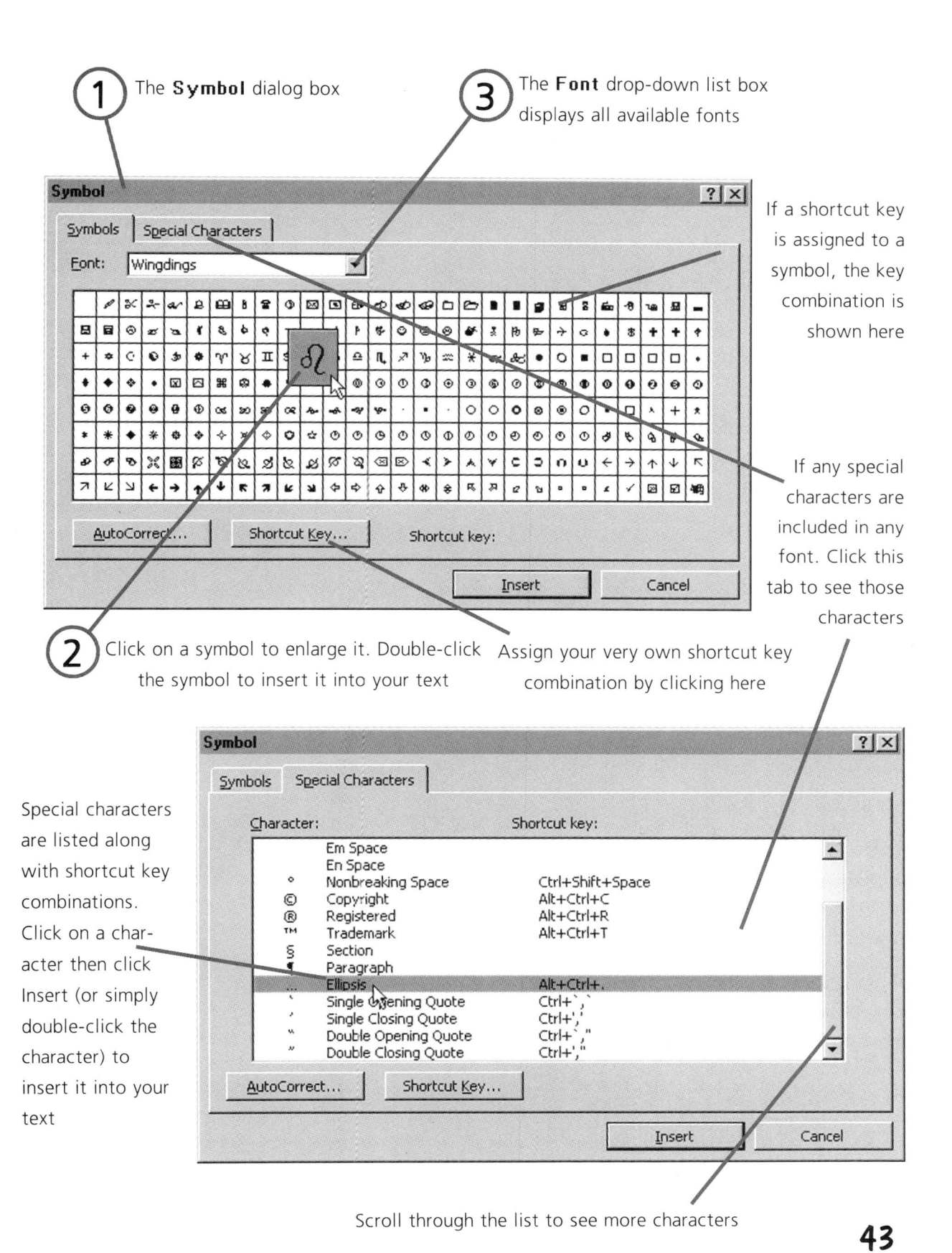

① The **Symbol** dialog box

③ The **Font** drop-down list box displays all available fonts

If a shortcut key is assigned to a symbol, the key combination is shown here

If any special characters are included in any font. Click this tab to see those characters

② Click on a symbol to enlarge it. Double-click the symbol to insert it into your text

Assign your very own shortcut key combination by clicking here

Special characters are listed along with shortcut key combinations. Click on a character then click Insert (or simply double-click the character) to insert it into your text

Scroll through the list to see more characters

43

Summary for Section 2

- Follow the three Golden Rules:
  1. never put two spaces together
  2. never put two carriage returns together
  3. never press ⏎ or Enter at the end of a line of text — unless it is also the end of a paragraph.

- Get into the habit of checking the status bar regularly.

- If you're an ex-WordPerfect user (and who wouldn't be now that Word 97 for Windows is here), remember to access Word's on-line help system for WordPerfect users.

- Learn how to select text using *all* of the available methods — no one method is best for all cases, and you really need to know them all.

- Use the cut, copy and paste facility to speed up your work. Learn the keyboard shortcuts (Ctrl+X to cut, Ctrl+C to copy, Ctrl+V to paste), or use the buttons (✂, 📋, and 📋).

- Use drag-and-drop editing — although a little tricky to get the hang of, it's an extremely good editing aid.

- Word's multiple undo feature can save you hours of work if you make a mistake.

- Access symbols and special characters with the **Symbol** dialog box.

- Use typographer's special marks and symbols to give your work a truly professional look.

3 Formatting text

About formatting 46

Character formats 48

Painting a format 53

Paragraph formats 54

Tabs 60

Simple tables 62

More about tabs 64

Borders and shading 66

Summary for Section 3 72

About formatting

When you first enter text at the keyboard in Word it is generally unformatted. That is, it is plain, unembellished, with no changes applied to alter its appearance. Generally, it will be in the default font (say, Times New Roman) and a default size (say, 10 point).

Making alterations to text's appearance is known as formatting the text. There are several ways this can be done in Word:

- formatting can be applied by the user to individual or grouped characters — this is known as *character formatting*

- formatting can be applied by the user to whole paragraphs — called (fancy that) *paragraph formatting*

- formatting can be applied automatically by Word — either as you enter text or afterwards, and either across a whole document (using Word's *AutoFormat* feature), or to paragraphs (using *paragraph styles*).

While character and paragraph formatting are both very powerful tools and can give you the visual effects you might require in a document, the *real* power of a word processor like Word lies in its ability to apply automatic formatting.

Take note:

Use character and paragraph formatting by all means — and they're going to be described over the next few pages so you can get to grips with them — but bear in mind that only when you use them to build *automatic* formatting features do they *really* become useful

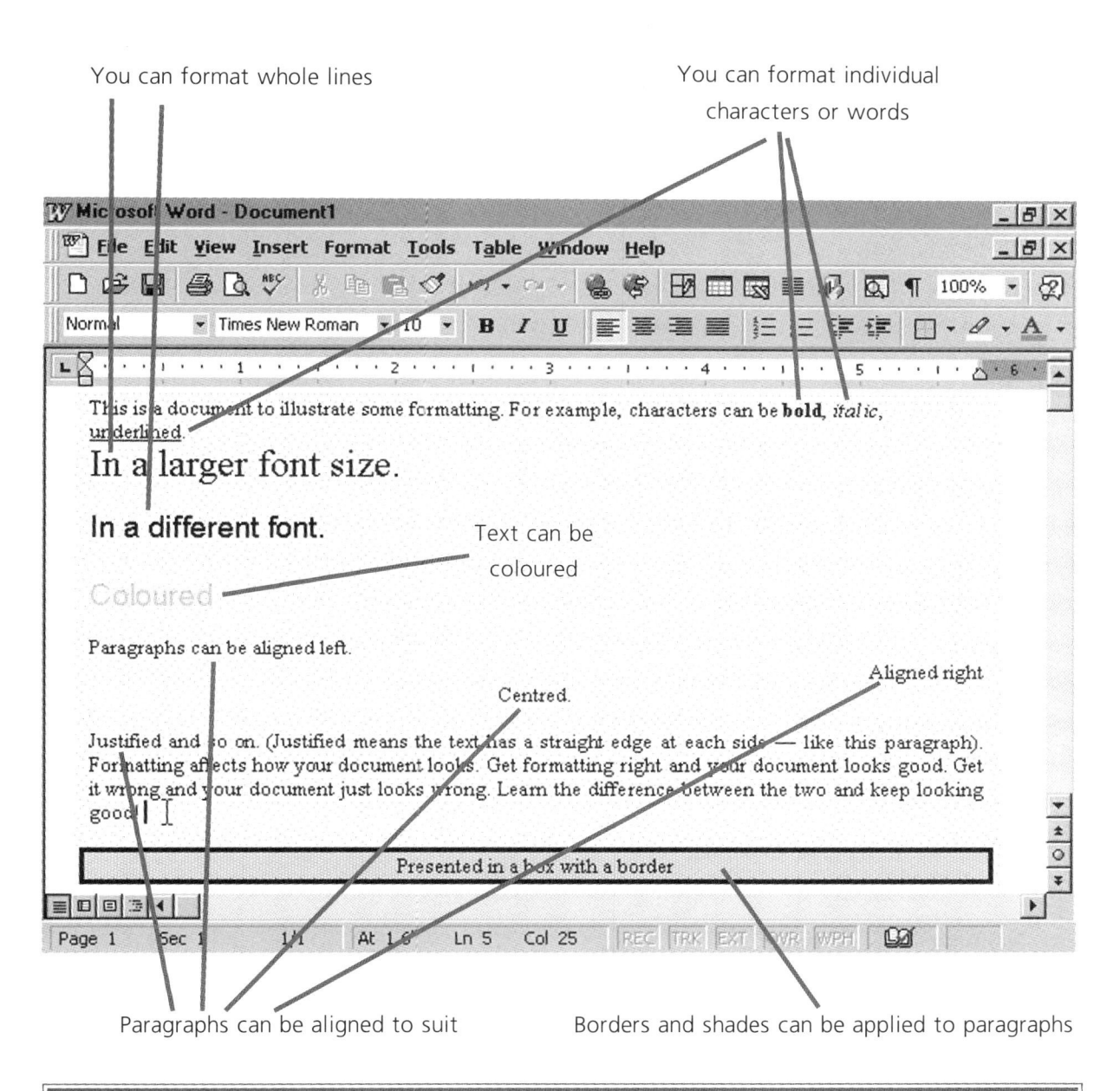

You can format whole lines

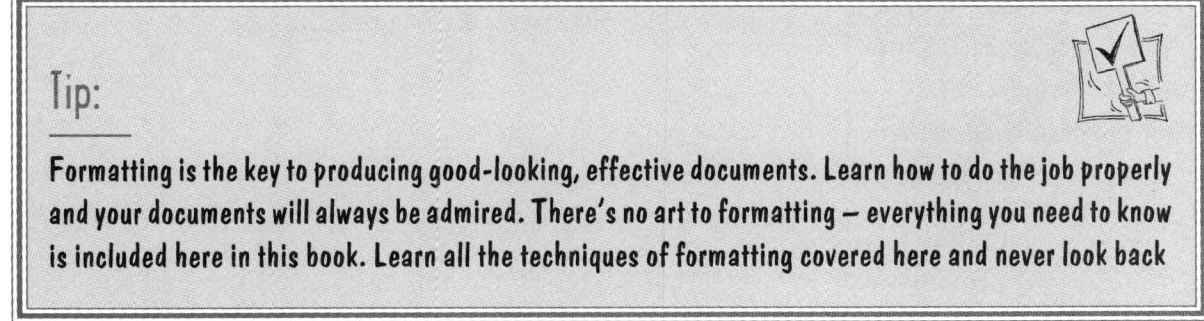

You can format individual characters or words

Microsoft Word - Document1 window showing:

This is a document to illustrate some formatting. For example, characters can be **bold**, *italic*, underlined.

In a larger font size.

In a different font.

Text can be coloured

Coloured

Paragraphs can be aligned left.

Centred.

Aligned right

Justified and so on. (Justified means the text has a straight edge at each side — like this paragraph). Formatting affects how your document looks. Get formatting right and your document looks good. Get it wrong and your document just looks wrong. Learn the difference between the two and keep looking good.

Presented in a box with a border

Paragraphs can be aligned to suit

Borders and shades can be applied to paragraphs

Tip:

Formatting is the key to producing good-looking, effective documents. Learn how to do the job properly and your documents will always be admired. There's no art to formatting — everything you need to know is included here in this book. Learn all the techniques of formatting covered here and never look back

Character formats

Basic steps:

Character formatting is a matter of selecting the text you wish to format, then applying the format change you want.

Many of the most common formats are available as buttons or options on the formatting toolbar. Some, however, are accessed by menu choice.

1 Select the text to be formatted
2 Apply the new format or formats

① Select the text to be formatted — this can be an individual letter, a word, group of words, sentence, paragraph, or even the whole document

> This is a sample of text in Times New Roman font at 10 point. It will be used to **illustrate character formatting**.

② Format the selected text to suit — this example shows the selected text emboldened

> This is a sample of text in Times New Roman font at 10 point. It will be used to **illustrate character formatting**.

Text you format is displayed formatted on screen. There are no formatting codes (as in some — let's say — lesser-capable word processors). What-you-see on-screen is more-or-less what-you-get on printout

Tip:

To format a single word you don't need to select the word in the usual manner — all you have to do is click anywhere in the word, then apply the format changes you want

Basic steps:

There are three main ways you can apply formatting to text:

1 From the formatting toolbar — buttons or options

The formatting toolbar gives the easiest options to change common formats

①

Click buttons to apply (or remove) bold, italic, and underline

Change font with this drop-down list box

Change font size with this drop-down list box

If you have many fonts in your system you can jump in the list by entering the font's initial letter in the font name box — the list jumps directly to fonts with that initial letter for you to select

If the font size you want isn't listed, just enter your desired size at the keyboard — if you are using a TrueType or PostScript font it will display and print correctly for just about any size you want

The fonts you've used most recently are listed in the top of the list, above this line

A TrueType font

A font available on the printer currently selected

All fonts are listed alphabetically below the line

49

Character formats (contd)

Basic steps:

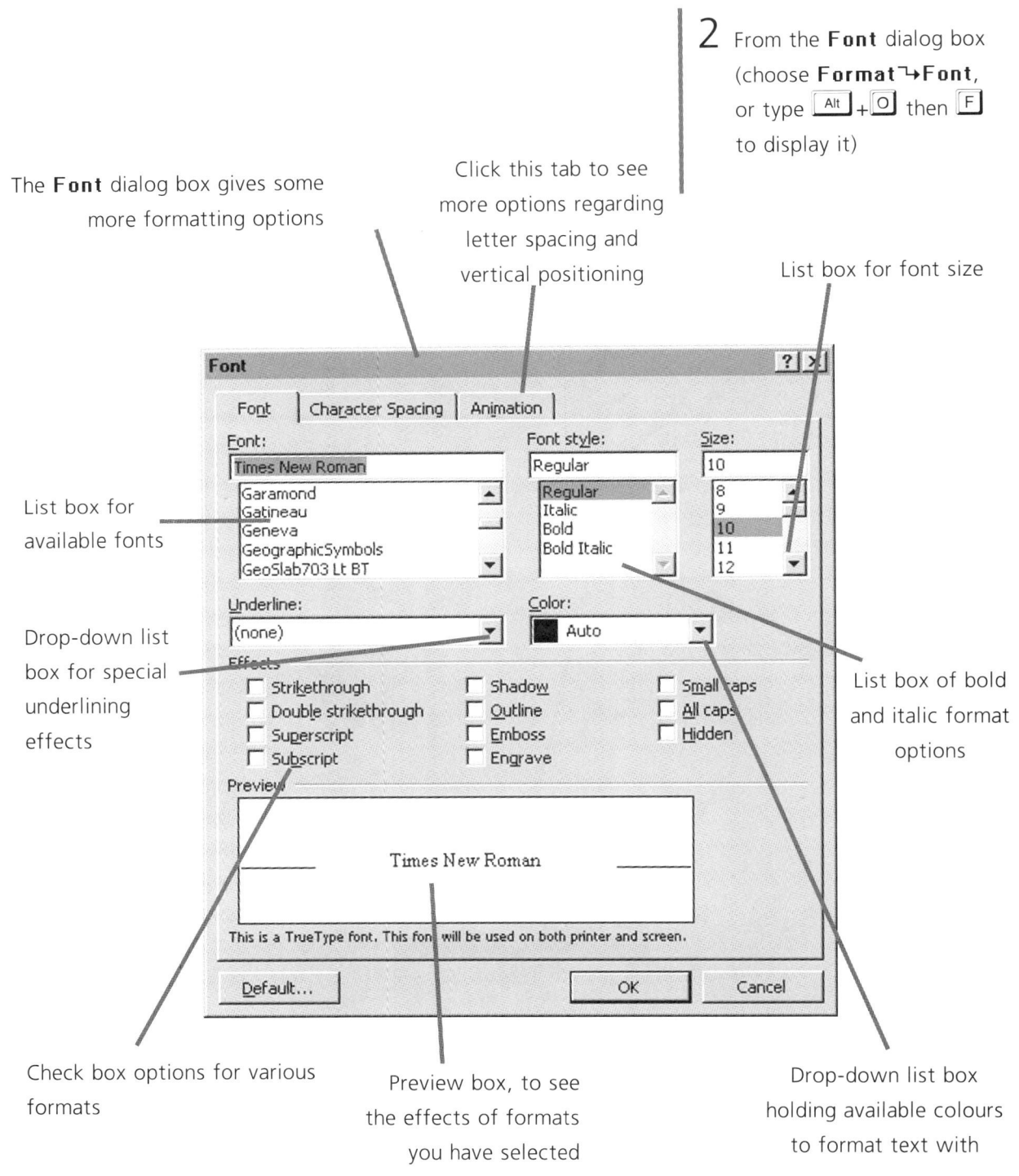

2 From the **Font** dialog box (choose **Format→Font**, or type `Alt`+`O` then `F` to display it)

The **Font** dialog box gives some more formatting options

Click this tab to see more options regarding letter spacing and vertical positioning

List box for font size

List box for available fonts

Drop-down list box for special underlining effects

List box of bold and italic format options

Check box options for various formats

Preview box, to see the effects of formats you have selected

Drop-down list box holding available colours to format text with

50

3 With keyboard combinations. These can very often provide the quickest methods of applying formats

KEYBOARD SHORTCUT COMBINATIONS

Many formatting options can best be applied with a keyboard shortcut:

Bold	Ctrl + B
Italic	Ctrl + I
Underline	Ctrl + U
Word underline	Ctrl + Shift + W
Double underline	Ctrl + Shift + D
Subscript	Ctrl + =
Superscript	Ctrl + Shift + =
Small caps	Ctrl + Shift + K
All caps	Ctrl + Shift + A
Change case	Shift + F3
Hidden text	Ctrl + Shift + H
Copy formats	Ctrl + Shift + C
Paste formats	Ctrl + Shift + V
Remove formats	Ctrl + spacebar
Font	Ctrl + Shift + F
Symbol font	Ctrl + Shift + Q
Point size	Ctrl + Shift + P
next up	Ctrl + >
next down	Ctrl + <
up one point	Ctrl +]
down one point	Ctrl + [

Tip:

You can apply a format to the insertion point too. This way, anything you type after the format is applied has that format, until you change it again. This is useful for, say, italicising a single word for emphasis as you type it — just apply the italic format before you type the word, then remove the italic format (hence returning to regular text) after the word is finished

Character formats (contd)

There's a few points worth remembering about character formatting in Word. These are shown here as tips for you to use as reference.

> **Tip:**
>
> Your last formatting action can be repeated by choosing Edit↪Repeat Formatting, or typing `Alt`+`E` then `R`, or typing `Ctrl`+`Y`.
>
> Note that all formats applied via the Font dialog box will be reapplied as one, whereas only the last individual formatting action applied with, say, buttons on the Formatting toolbar is reapplied

> **Tip:**
>
> Removing a character format follows the same procedure as applying it in the first place. You first select the character, characters, word, words, sentence, paragraph and so on, then you go through the same steps you took to originally apply it. If a word is emboldened, for example, you simply select it then click the Bold button `B` on the formatting toolbar to remove the format

> **Tip:**
>
> You can remove *all* formatting applied by the methods shown over these last few pages to text, by first selecting the text then typing
>
> `Ctrl`+spacebar
>
> Note, though, that this does not remove formatting applied as part of styles (see page 120)

Painting a format

If you see text which is formatted the way you want another selection of text to be formatted, you can copy the formatting onto further text with the Format Painter button on the Standard toolbar.

① Select the text with the format you want to copy (in this case an italicised word)

> Take it from me. There's no *point* in trying to pass your driving test. Within ten years at most — more likely five — there'll be so many cars on the road that no-one will be able to drive more than 35 miles per hour anyway. And where's the fun in that?

③ Select the text to be formatted

> Take it from me. There's no *point* in trying to pass your driving test. Within ten years at most — more likely five — there'll be so many cars on the road that no-one will be able to drive more than 35 miles per hour anyway. And where's the fun in that?

Once selected, the text is automatically formatted

> Take it from me. There's no *point* in trying to pass your driving test. Within ten years at most — more likely five — there'll be so many cars on the road that no-one will be able to *drive more than 35 miles per hour* anyway. And where's the fun in that?

Tip:
You don't even need to select a single word if you want to paint another word's format onto it with the format painter pointer. Just click anywhere inside the word and the format is painted over the whole word

Basic steps:

1. Select the text, part of text, or simply position the insertion point anywhere inside the text you wish to copy the formatting from

2. Click the Format Painter button on the Standard toolbar. The pointer changes to the format painter pointer

3. Select the text you want to be formatted with that format

Tip:
If you double-click the Format Painter button after selecting text with the format you want to copy, the format painter pointer remains active after you have painted the format to further text. You can continue to paint the format for as long as you want onto more selections of text. Click the Format Painter button again to de-activate the format painter pointer

53

Paragraph formats

Whereas character formats affect just the *characters* you select, paragraph formats control the — you've got it — *paragraphs*. In other words, complete blocks of text and their line spacings, indents or alignments for example, are affected by paragraph formats. Paragraph formats *do not just affect* single characters, words, or sentences.

Paragraph marks (¶) indicate where a paragraph ends

This is a left-aligned paragraph.¶

This is a right-aligned paragraph.¶

This is a centred paragraph.¶

This paragraph has single line-spacing and is indented by a small amount on its first line. Lines are close together, set by Word itself. This is a standard setting unless you change the default style (covered later in the book).¶

This paragraph has double line-spacing and is indented on its first line by a slightly larger amount. Lines are obviously wider apart than the previous paragraph. It's possible to do this all in Word quite simply when you know what you're doing.¶

Note that while all these paragraphs in this screenshot of a Word document have the same character formats (they are all in the same font, size, and so on) they still *appear* different, because their paragraph formats are different

Paragraph marks (¶) are used by Word to store a paragraph's formatting

Take note:

A paragraph is defined as any block of text — no matter how short, or how long — ending with a paragraph mark ¶. A paragraph mark is added to your text each time you press `Enter` or ⏎.

Paragraph marks *may* be hidden — to display them (or hide them if they are currently displayed) click the Show/Hide ¶ button ¶ on the Standard toolbar

Basic steps:

1. First select the paragraph or paragraphs you intend to format
2. Apply the new paragraph format or formats

To apply a paragraph format to a paragraph you use the same techniques you use to apply a character format to a character.

① Select the paragraph or paragraphs (in this example there are two paragraphs) you want to format

> Here we go, here we go, here we go. It's another fine, fine day down at the ranch. The brunch is cooking and the horses are lively. After we've eaten we'll get going and round-up the cattle. Never in the field of human conflict has so much been eaten by so few. ¶
> Inevitably, there will be a cut in resources. There's now so little money to go round that it's just a question of jobs or the tools to do those jobs. If we want to maintain current levels of employment, we'll all just have to do with less to spend. ¶

Take note:

You don't have to select a whole paragraph before you apply paragraph formatting to it. If you position the insertion point *anywhere* within the paragraph then apply paragraph formatting the *entire* paragraph is formatted

Tip:

If you are currently typing text into a formatted paragraph, then press Enter or ↵, the new paragraph so created continues with the format of the preceding paragraph. In other words, if you have formatted a paragraph to the paragraph style you want, each subsequent paragraph has the same format

② Apply the paragraph formats — here the paragraphs have been indented on their first lines and justified

>   Here we go, here we go, here we go. It's another fine, fine day down at the ranch. The brunch is cooking and the horses are lively. After we've eaten we'll get going and round-up the cattle. Never in the field of human conflict has so much been eaten by so few. ¶
>   Inevitably, there will be a cut in resources. There's now so little money to go round that it's just a question of jobs or the tools to do those jobs. If we want to maintain current levels of employment, we'll all just have to do with less to spend. ¶

Paragraph formats (contd)

Like character formats, paragraph formats can be applied to text in three main ways.

Basic steps:

1 Paragraph formats can be applied from the Formatting toolbar (some are applied from the ruler, too)

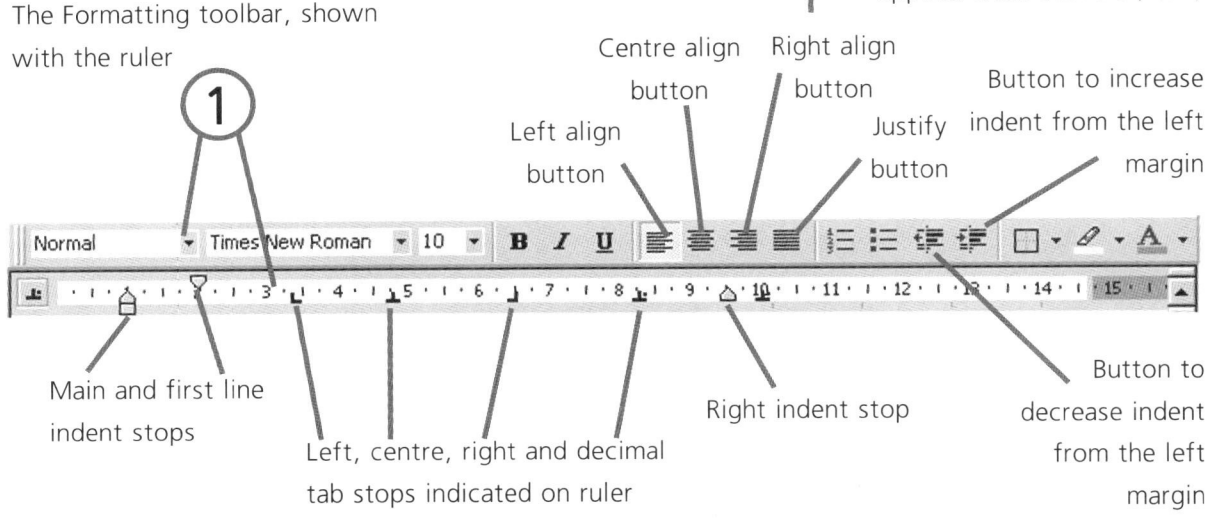

The Formatting toolbar, shown with the ruler

- Centre align button
- Left align button
- Right align button
- Justify button
- Button to increase indent from the left margin
- Main and first line indent stops
- Left, centre, right and decimal tab stops indicated on ruler
- Right indent stop
- Button to decrease indent from the left margin

Tip:

Unlike some word processors, Word does not use formatting codes. The formats you apply are visible directly on-screen, so you can see what they will print like. If, however, you want to see the particular paragraph (or character) formats applied, choose Help → What's This?, or type Shift + F1, then click in the paragraph.

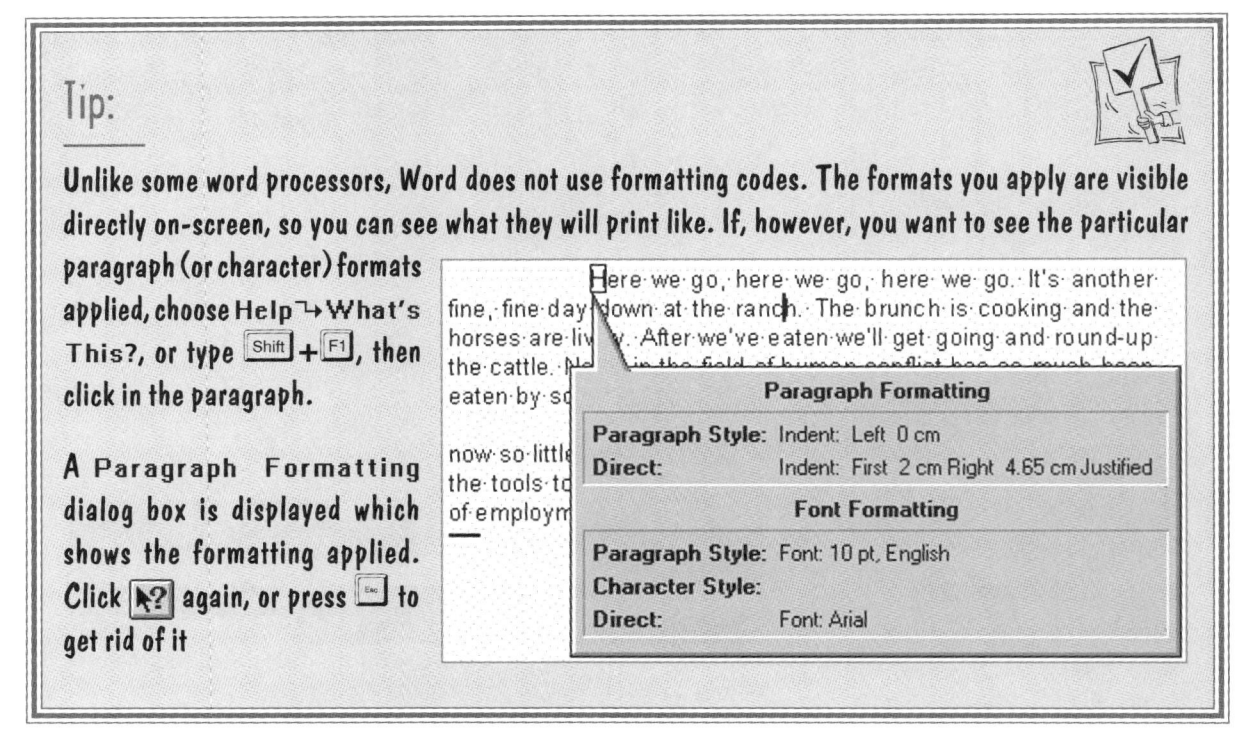

A Paragraph Formatting dialog box is displayed which shows the formatting applied. Click again, or press Esc to get rid of it

Paragraph Formatting

Paragraph Style:	Indent: Left 0 cm
Direct:	Indent: First 2 cm Right 4.65 cm Justified

Font Formatting

Paragraph Style:	Font: 10 pt, English
Character Style:	
Direct:	Font: Arial

2 Formats can be applied from the **Paragraph** dialog box (to display it choose **Format ↳ Paragraph**, or type `Alt`+`O` then `P`)

(2) The **Paragraph** dialog box, from which many paragraph formatting options can be set as one step

Click this tab for special text flow options (see over)

Alignment drop-down list box

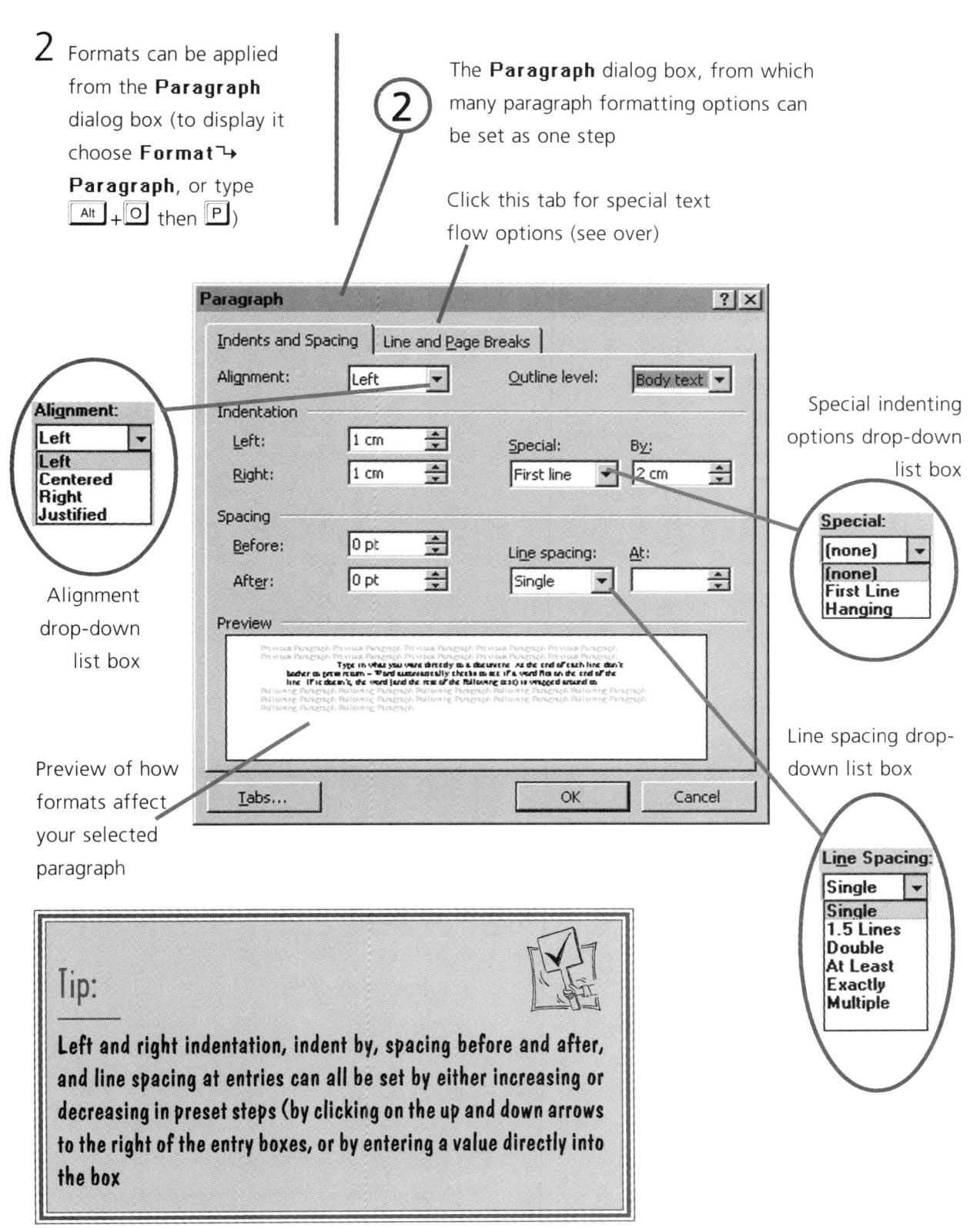

Preview of how formats affect your selected paragraph

Special indenting options drop-down list box

Line spacing drop-down list box

Tip:

Left and right indentation, indent by, spacing before and after, and line spacing at entries can all be set by either increasing or decreasing in preset steps (by clicking on the up and down arrows to the right of the entry boxes, or by entering a value directly into the box

Paragraph formats (contd)

Special paragraph formatting attributes are available from the **Text Flow** tab option of the **Paragraph** dialog box. These attributes affect the way text flows between pages of a document. Main ones are labelled and described.

Checking this check box prevents the last line of a paragraph from being printed at the top of a page (a widow), or the first line of a paragraph from being printed alone at the bottom of a page (an orphan)

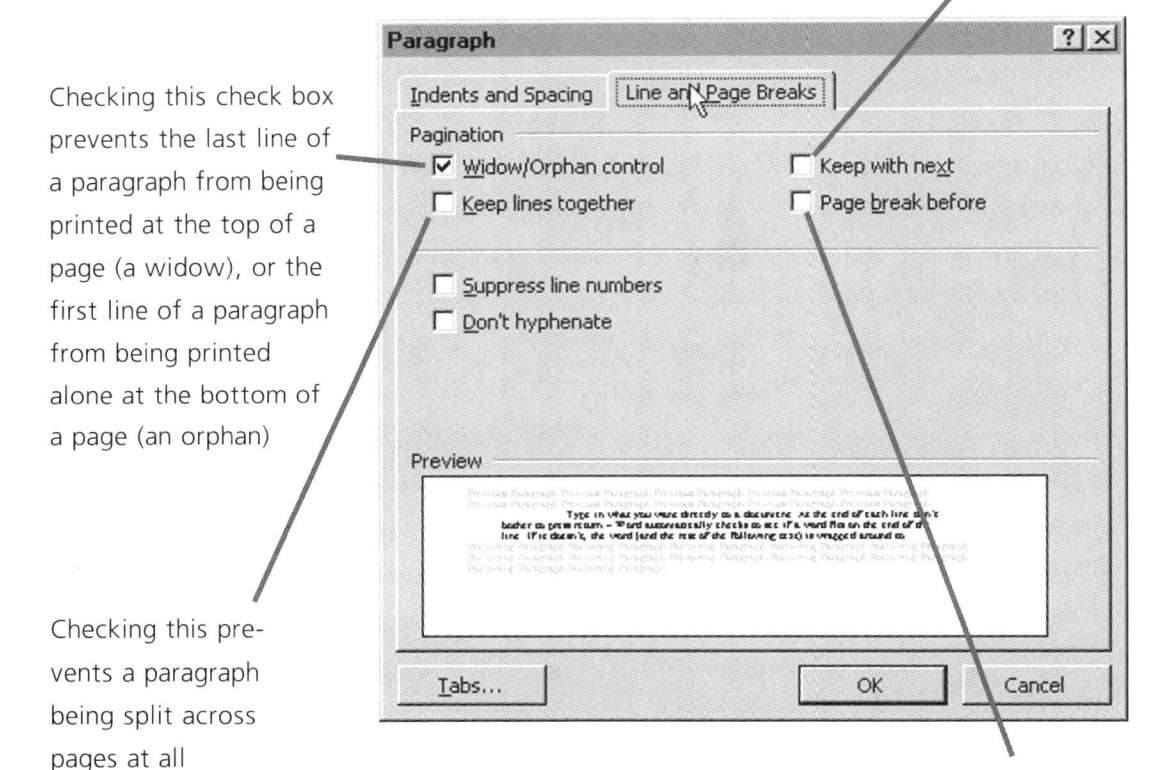

Checking this prevents a paragraph from being split from the following paragraph

Checking this prevents a paragraph being split across pages at all

Checking this inserts a page break before a paragraph (in other words, the paragraph will be at the top of a new page)

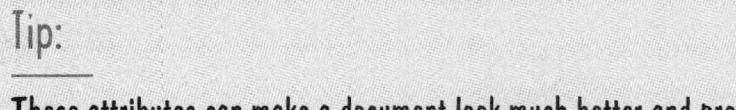

Tip:

These attributes can make a document look much better and prevent anomalies. If the Keep with Next option is checked for a paragraph formatted as a heading which by chance falls at the bottom of a page, for example, it will be forced onto the next page along with its accompanying text

Basic steps:

3 Paragraph formats can be applied directly with keyboard shortcut combinations. Like character formatting keyboard combinations, these are very often the quickest ways of applying certain formats.

KEYBOARD SHORTCUT COMBINATIONS

Left-align text	Ctrl + B
Centre align text	Ctrl + E
Right-align text	Ctrl + R
Justify text	Ctrl + J
Indent from left margin	Ctrl + M
Decrease indent	Ctrl + Shift + M
Create a hanging indent	Ctrl + T
Decrease a hanging indent	Ctrl + Shift + T
1 line space	Ctrl + 1
1.5 line space	Ctrl + 5
2 line space	Ctrl + 2
Add or remove 12 points of space before a paragraph	Ctrl + 0
Remove paragraph formats not applied by a style	Ctrl + Q
Restore Normal style	Ctrl + Shift + N
Display or hide nonprinting characters (¶ and so on)	Ctrl + *

Tip:

You can most quickly indent selected paragraphs using either the keyboard shortcut combinations above right, or (even better) using the Decrease Indent or Increase Indent buttons on the Formatting toolbar.

While changes due to either of these methods are in fixed increments you can always later change them by dragging indent markers on the ruler

Take note:

While character and paragraph formats are all very nice, and very good, and used properly can greatly improve the look of a document, bear in mind you have to apply every one of them individually.

On the other hand, you can apply formats automatically by using styles (page 120). Automatic formatting is much quicker and, because you can use both methods across documents, ensures that documents you create can have a unified style, or set of styles, giving a much more professional appearance to your work

Tabs

As a typewriter, any word processor has the ability to define tab stops. These are used to help align text, such that tables or columns of figures, say, can be neatened up and aligned underneath each other.

Better than a typewriter, on the other hand, word processors usually have more than just one type of tab stop. Where typewriters only align text so that text is left-aligned after the tab stop, Word allows text to be:

● left-aligned — as on a typewriter, with text aligned after the tab stop

● centre-aligned — with text centred around the tab stop

● right-aligned — where text is aligned-right to the tab stop

● decimal-aligned — with monetary figures, say, aligned so their decimal point is aligned directly on the tab stop

● bar-aligned — Word creates a vertical line in your document, the height of the text line, at the tab stop.

> **Tip**
>
> **You move to a tab stop when you're typing simply by pressing [Tab]. This action moves the insertion point to the next tab stop, after which you can carry on typing. Note (see illustration below) that a character → indicates a tab entry in text. These are special characters which are not printed (like paragraph marks ¶) and can be hidden or displayed (just like paragraph marks) by clicking the Show/Hide ¶ button [¶] on the Standard toolbar**

Tab character displayed when the Tab key is pressed

Left-align tab
Centre-align tab
Right-align tab
Decimal-align tab
Bar tab
Ruler

→ oranges → bananas → apples → £21.67¶
→ hammers → forks → spoons → £34.88¶
→ wellies → macs → hats → £1234.56¶

Text aligns left to tab
Text centres on tab
Text aligns right to tab
Decimal point aligns on tab
Vertical line aligns on tab

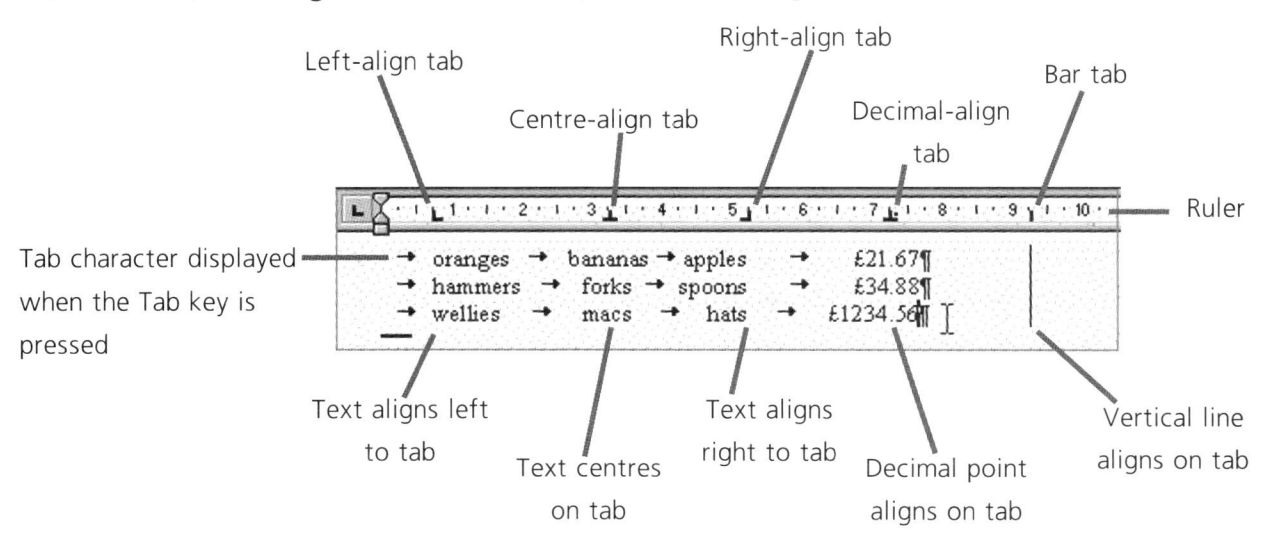

Basic steps:

The most straightforward way of setting tabs is with the ruler:

1 Repeatedly click the Tab Alignment button (preset as ▣) until the type of tab you require is displayed

- ▣ — align left
- ▣ — align centre
- ▣ — align right
- ▣ — align to decimal point

2 Click in the ruler at the position you want the tab stop. It is displayed in the ruler as a symbol (according to which tab stop type you selected

3 Adjust the tab stop if you need, by dragging it along the ruler to its new position

Take note:

Tabs are a paragraph format. In other words, they are set for and remain in force for a paragraph — no matter how many lines the paragraph runs to

Take note:

As you insert a new tab stop, any default tab stops to its left – literally – disappear

1 The Tab Alignment button — keep clicking it until the tab stop you want is selected (align left is default)

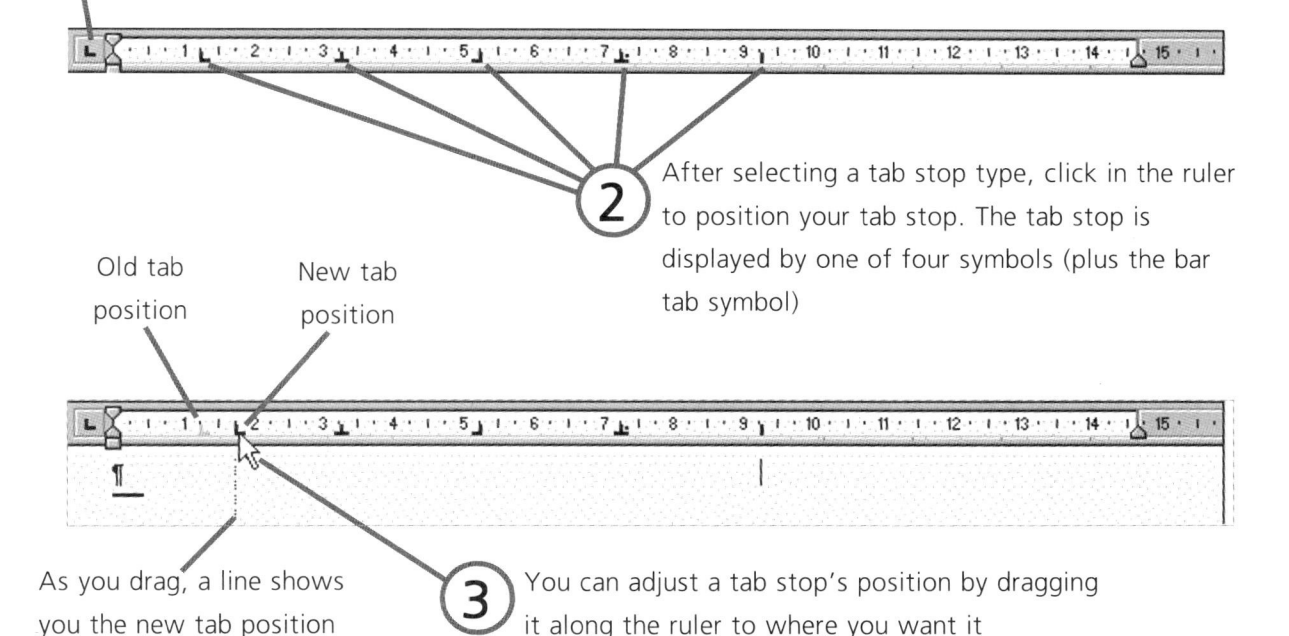

2 After selecting a tab stop type, click in the ruler to position your tab stop. The tab stop is displayed by one of four symbols (plus the bar tab symbol)

Old tab position

New tab position

As you drag, a line shows you the new tab position in the document

3 You can adjust a tab stop's position by dragging it along the ruler to where you want it

Simple tables

To tabulate a simple table you can use tabs. Because tabs are a paragraph format, you need to select the paragraphs which form the table before setting the tabs — in exactly the same ways described when we selected text previously. Once the paragraphs forming the table are selected, the tab changes you make affect all those paragraphs.

Basic steps:

1 After you've typed in the paragraphs you want to be tabulated, select them

2 Set your tabs (don't worry if they're not exact — just set them approximately)

3 Adjust the tabs (by dragging them along the ruler to suit) until the text tabulates as you want — by typing text in first using the default tab stops, followed by setting your own tabs then adjusting them, you can see the effects of adjustment on-screen

4 Make any changes to character or other paragraph formats you want

Take note:

Never, never, never, never, never (enough to make you see the importance?) press [Tab] more than once to align text. It doesn't matter if text doesn't align as you want while you're entering it (see Tip below) — it's still better to change the tabs later to suit your layout requirements. That way you can see the affects of changes you make to the text directly. If you set the tab stops *before* you enter the text, you're just guessing where they need to be, and you'll almost certainly have to change them anyway!

Tip:

Where tab stops have to be set prior to text entry on a typewriter, this is not the case with Word. In fact, it is better simply to enter the text which is to be tabulated before setting tabs at all. The default tabs in a Word document (set at every half inch — or 1.27 centimetre) will let you tabulate the text initially (it probably won't align at all as you type it in — but don't worry). Once the text is completely entered you can select it, then put the tab stops where you want. Even once you've set the tab stops you can change them to suit, until you've got the text looking as you want it

① Select the paragraphs you want — note the heading of the table isn't selected here

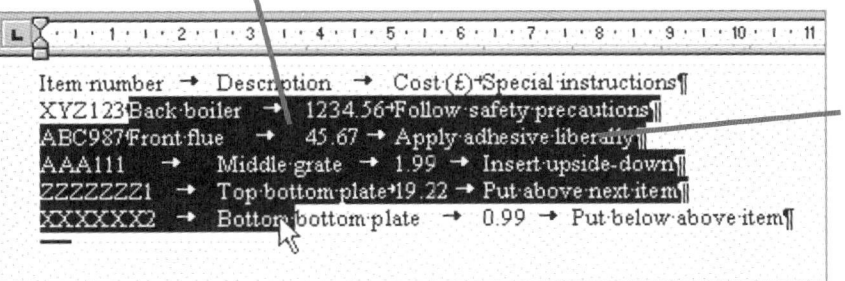

Note how the default tab stops render the table somewhat unattractive — it doesn't matter at this stage because step 3 tidies it up

② Set the tabs you want for each column of the table (see pages 60–61)

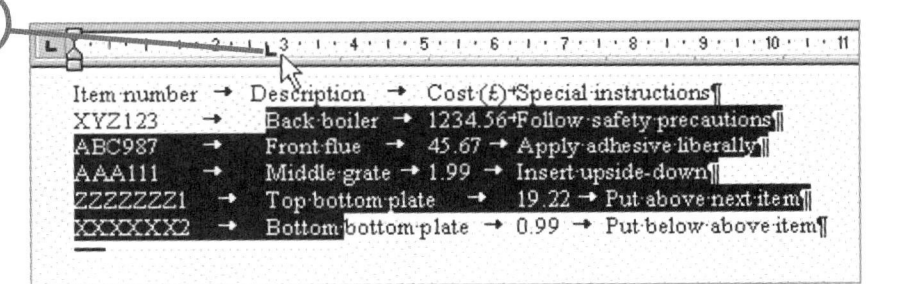

③ Adjust the tabs to suit the table and the appearance you want

Now the heading can be tabulated to suit

④ Make character and other paragraph formatting changes you want

More about tabs

While the ruler affords by far the easiest method of setting and adjusting tabs, it is actually quite inexact and some tab options aren't available from it. Total control over tabs (both setting and adjusting) is available from the **Tabs** dialog box.

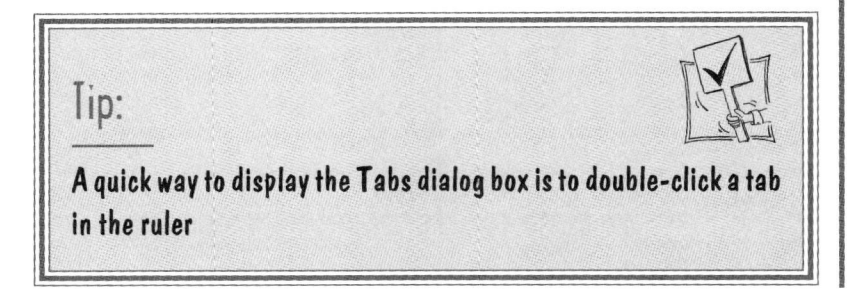

> **Tip:**
>
> **A quick way to display the Tabs dialog box is to double-click a tab in the ruler**

Basic steps:

1. Display the **Tabs** dialog box by choosing **Format→Tabs** or by typing [Alt]+[O] then [T] (or by clicking the **Tabs** button in the **Paragraph** dialog box — see page 57)

2. Set tab stop positions, alignment types, and leaders (if required)

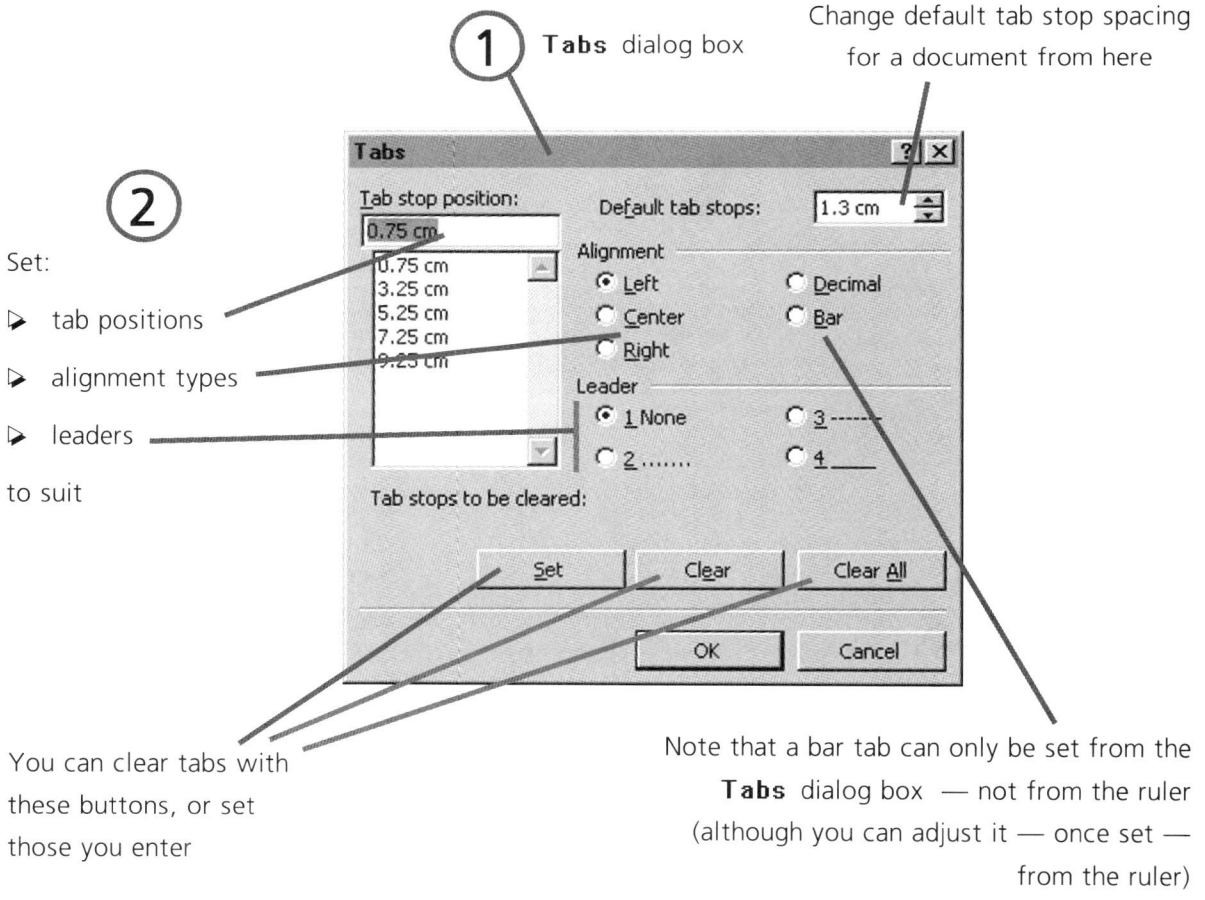

① **Tabs** dialog box

Change default tab stop spacing for a document from here

②

Set:

- tab positions
- alignment types
- leaders

to suit

You can clear tabs with these buttons, or set those you enter

Note that a bar tab can only be set from the **Tabs** dialog box — not from the ruler (although you can adjust it — once set — from the ruler)

64

There are two options to clear tabs:

1. You can use the clear buttons in the **Tabs** dialog box (see below left)
2. You can literally drag the tabs off the ruler so they disappear. This is by far the faster method where only a few tabs are to be cleared

Tip:

Tabs – as we've already seen – are paragraph formats. Like all the other paragraph formats they remain in operation after each paragraph, until you change them.

If you want tab settings to remain in operation for a few paragraphs you can set them before you start, then type away. As you press Enter or ↵ to begin a new paragraph the formats (including tab settings) are carried over

Tip:

You can fill the empty space before a tab stop with dotted, dashed, or solid lines called leaders. They can give a professional finish to contents pages, say, where a contents list is separated from its page number list by some considerable space

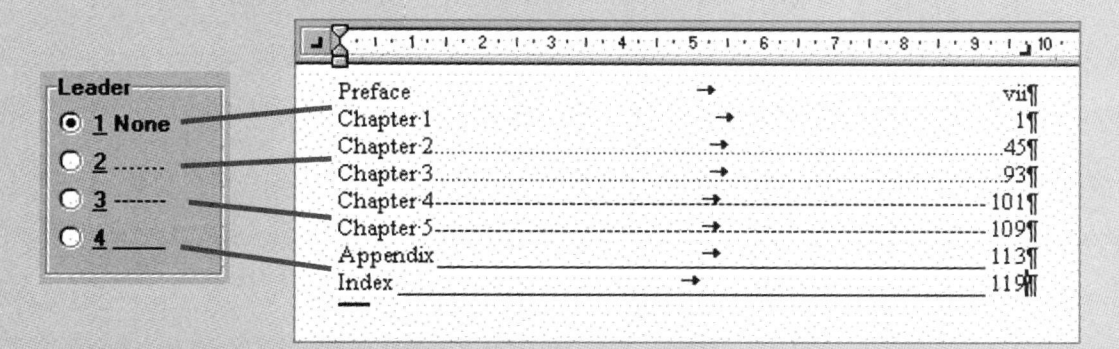

Take note:

You can only set or clear leaders from the Tabs dialog box

Borders and shading

Two other paragraph formats which can be used to create a professional appearance to Word documents are paragraph borders and shading.

Borders are rules around a paragraph (which may, or may not, be thick enough to see — a border of zero thickness is still there, albeit not visible). Shadings are the background shades of colours or greys which go inside borders.

Borders are set up and adjusted in one of three ways:

- with the Borders button on the Formatting toolbar
- through the Tables & Borders toolbar
- with the **Paragraph Borders and Shading** dialog box.

Basic steps:

The best way to apply borders and shading is with the Tables & Borders toolbar

1 If it's not already displayed, call up the Tables & Borders toolbar by clicking the Borders button on the Standard toolbar (or right-click any toolbar and check the **Tables & Borders** checkbox)

How the paragraph is formatted is very important to how the bordered and shaded paragraph will look. Justified or centred text always looks better than left- or right-aligned text, simply because the borders (and resultant shading) are evenly placed around the text

Borders can be:
- thinner
- thicker
- nonexistent

Here is a bordered paragraph — I think it looks really smart. If text is justified — which this is, or centred, it gives a tidy appearance at each side.

Here is another bordered paragraph — this time though aligned left to see the difference. Not so good, hmm? I agree. However, what do you think of the shading?

Here is a paragraph with no border but some shading. As the shading is quite dark (60%) the text colour has been reversed to white creating a nice effect.

For a paragraph you intend to shade darkly, consider reversing text to create a pleasant effect

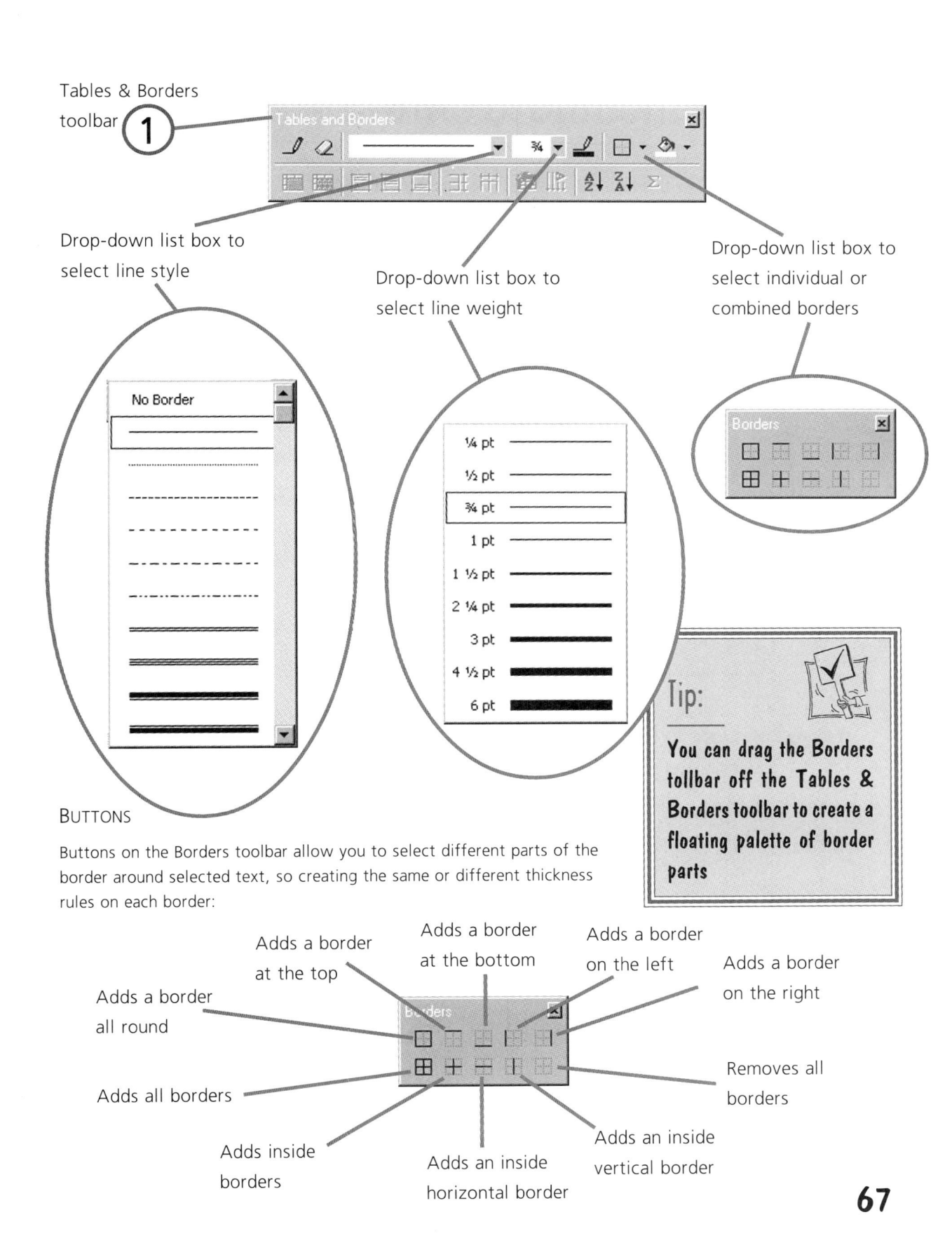

Tables & Borders toolbar ①

Drop-down list box to select line style

Drop-down list box to select line weight

Drop-down list box to select individual or combined borders

No Border

¼ pt
½ pt
¾ pt
1 pt
1 ½ pt
2 ¼ pt
3 pt
4 ½ pt
6 pt

Tip:

You can drag the Borders tollbar off the Tables & Borders toolbar to create a floating palette of border parts

BUTTONS

Buttons on the Borders toolbar allow you to select different parts of the border around selected text, so creating the same or different thickness rules on each border:

- Adds a border all round
- Adds a border at the top
- Adds a border at the bottom
- Adds a border on the left
- Adds a border on the right
- Adds all borders
- Adds inside borders
- Adds an inside horizontal border
- Adds an inside vertical border
- Removes all borders

67

Borders & shading (contd)

When you add a border to text it extends around the full size of the paragraph the text is formatted to. In other words, whatever the width and height of the paragraph will be the width and height of the border — regardless of whether the text itself totally fills the border. This can result in unusual (and unattractive) borders.

Basic steps:

1. Click in the paragraph to be bordered
2. Select the style and weight of border, and shading colour required
3. Apply the border
4. Adjust the right indent of the paragraph to be the same width as the text itself

1. Select the text to have a border — remember (as borders and shades are paragraph formats) you only need to click in the paragraph to select the whole paragraph

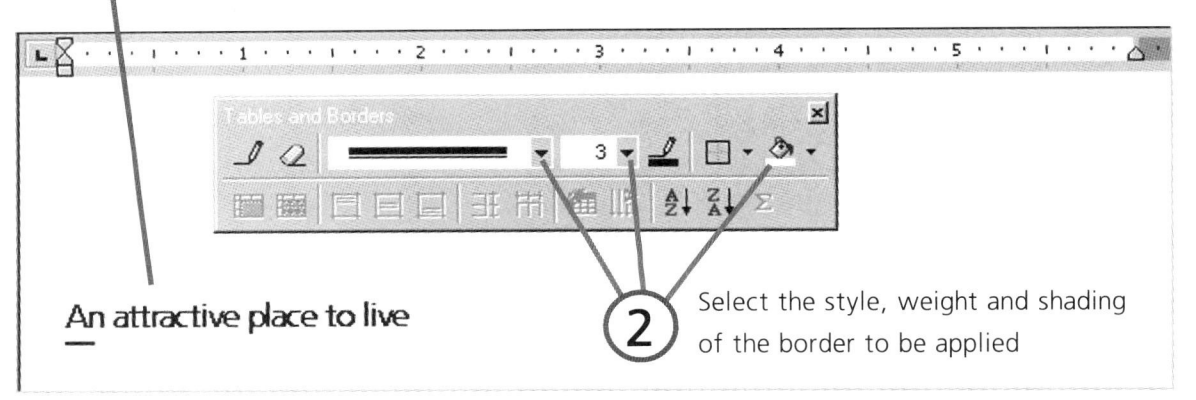

An attractive place to live

2. Select the style, weight and shading of the border to be applied

3. Apply the border — this one is a boxed border, applied with the boxed border button

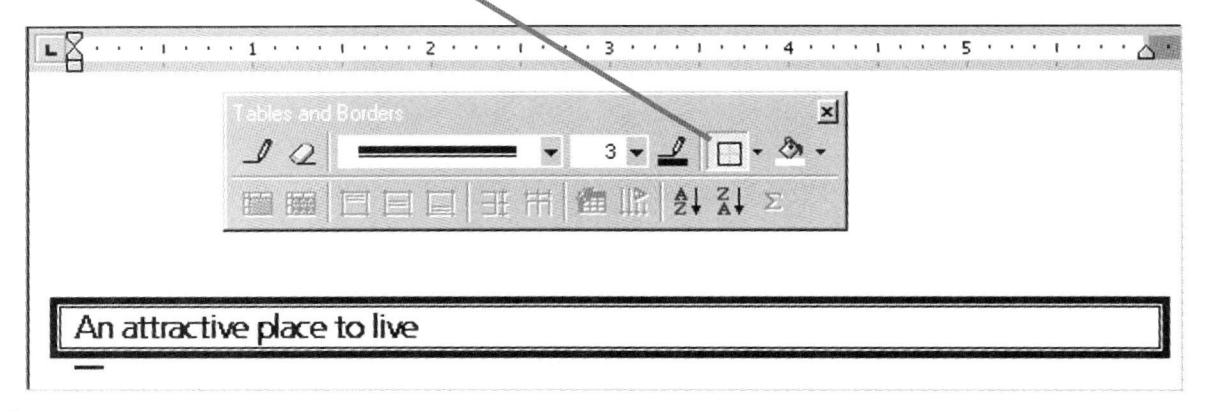

An attractive place to live

(4) Drag the right indent marker of the ruler in, until the indent is just to the right of the text in the paragraph

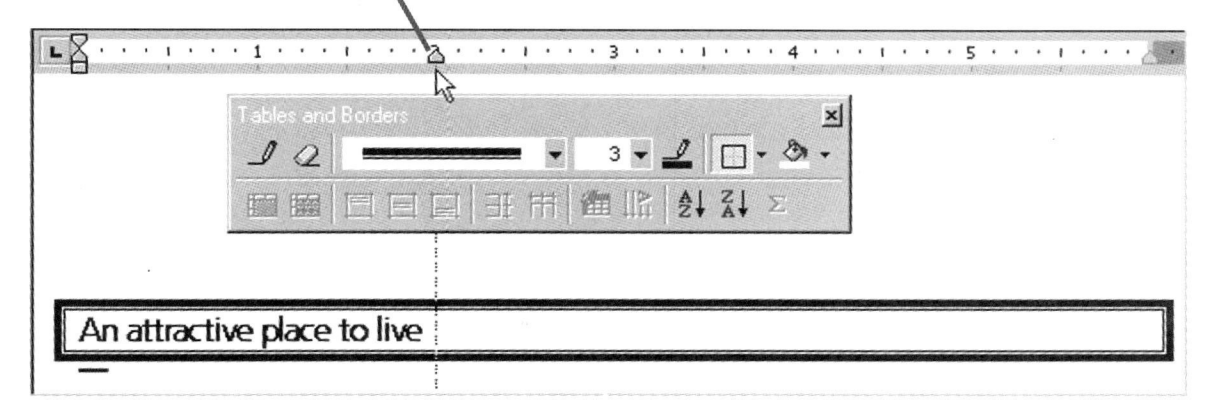

The paragraph is now boxed properly and attractively — note that if you now add to the text in the bordered paragraph the border will still be the correct width as the text simply overflows onto the next line which is of the same width. The border's bottom rule remains below the bottom line of the paragraph however many lines it has

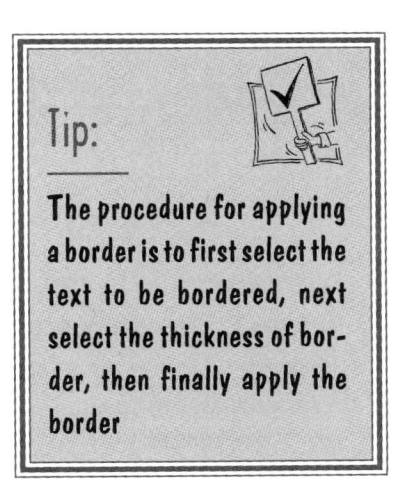

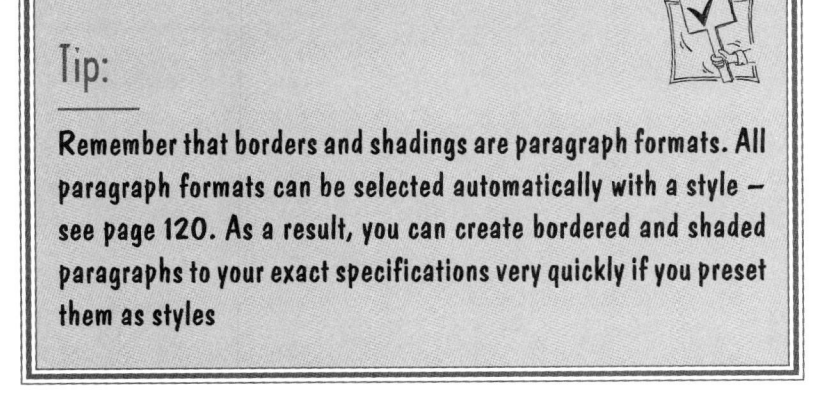

Tip:

The procedure for applying a border is to first select the text to be bordered, next select the thickness of border, then finally apply the border

Tip:

Remember that borders and shadings are paragraph formats. All paragraph formats can be selected automatically with a style — see page 120. As a result, you can create bordered and shaded paragraphs to your exact specifications very quickly if you preset them as styles

Borders & shading (contd)

Basic steps:

You can create and adjust borders and shadings through the **Borders and Shading** dialog box too. While this isn't as quick as using the Borders toolbar it does provide some options not otherwise available.

1 To call up the **Borders and Shading** dialog box choose **Format → Borders and Shading**, or type `Alt`+`O` then `B`

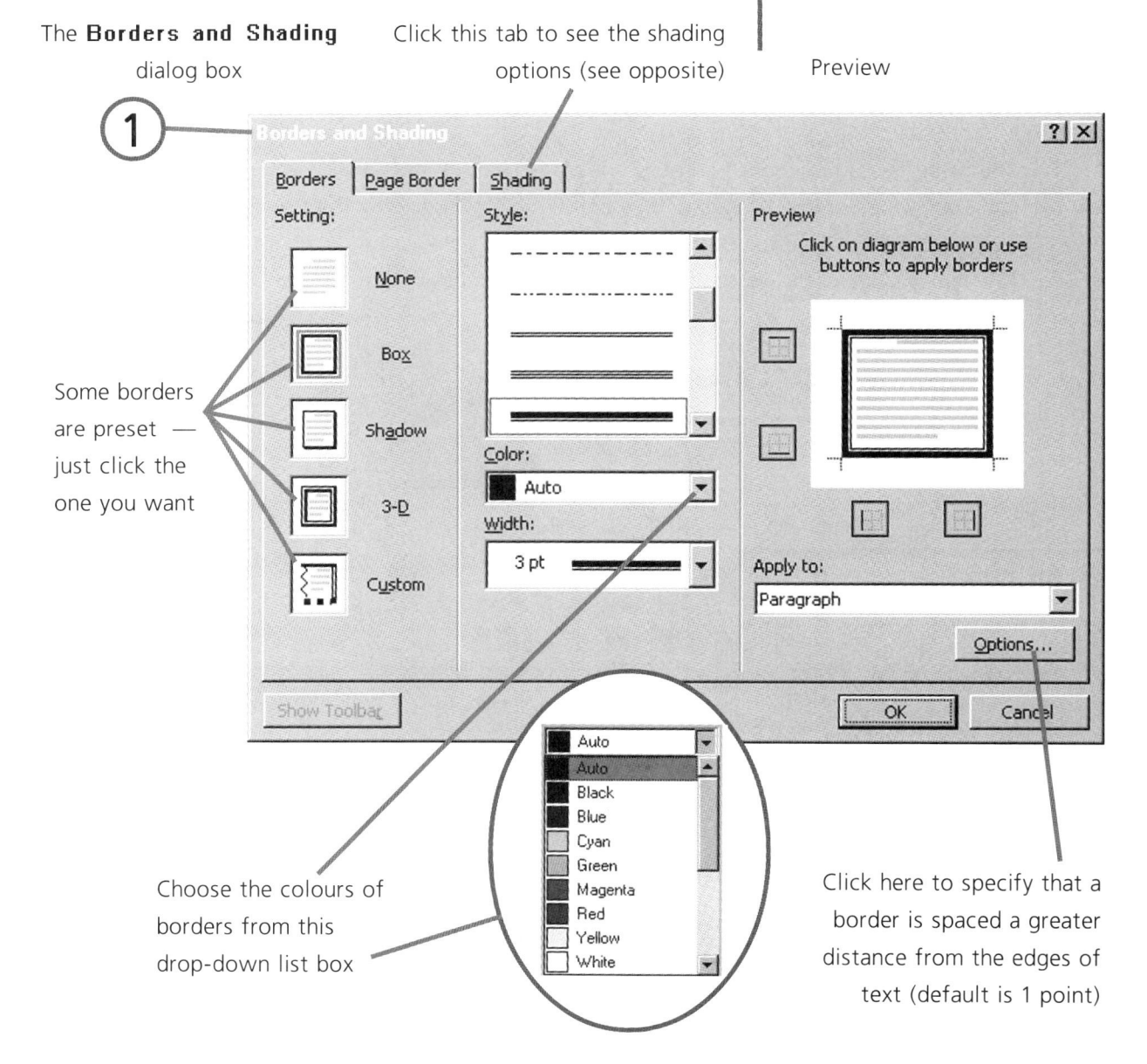

Preview

The **Borders and Shading** dialog box

Click this tab to see the shading options (see opposite)

Some borders are preset — just click the one you want

Choose the colours of borders from this drop-down list box

Click here to specify that a border is spaced a greater distance from the edges of text (default is 1 point)

70

Click this tab to get back to borders options

You can display the Borders toolbar (if it's not already displayed) by clicking this button

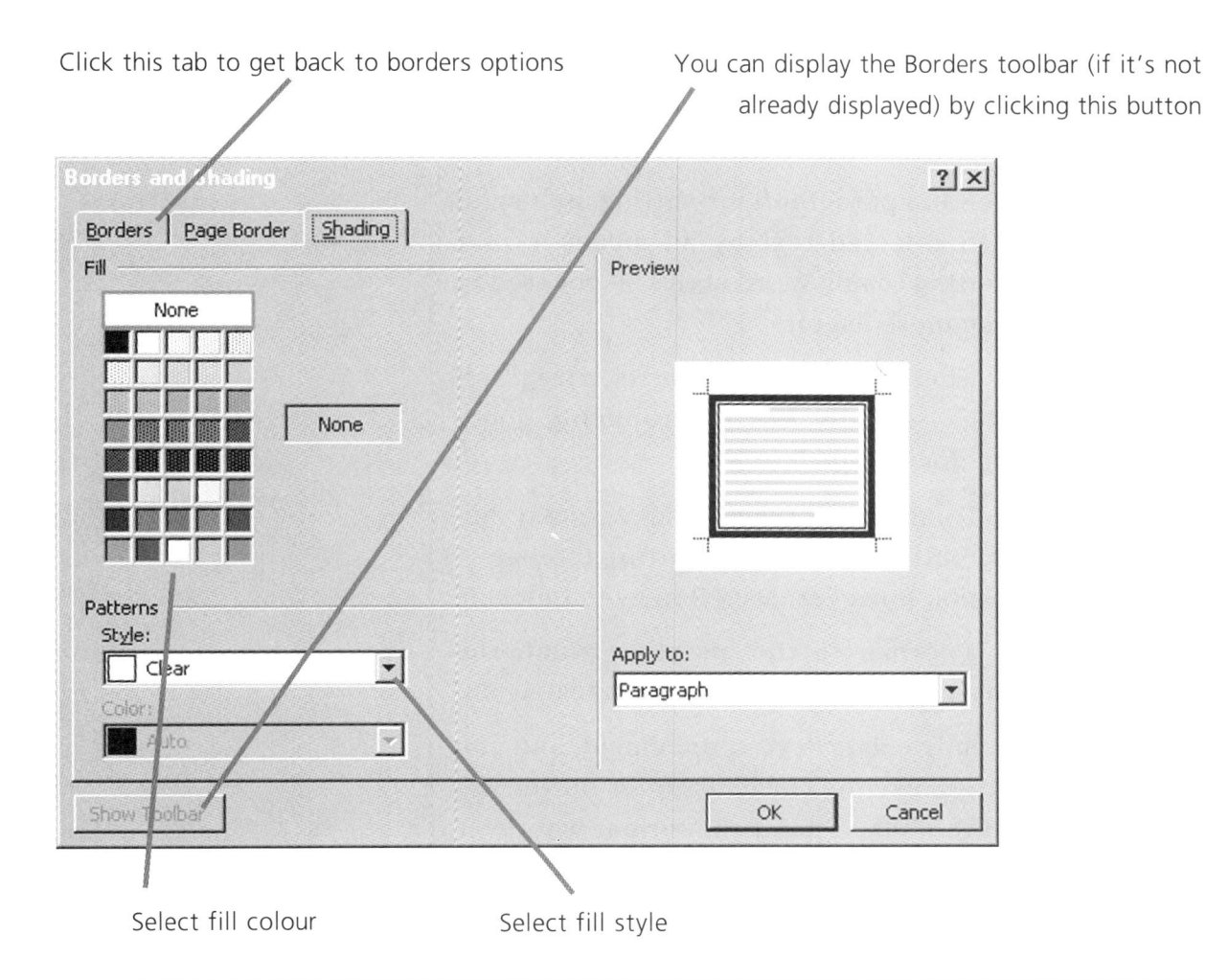

Select fill colour

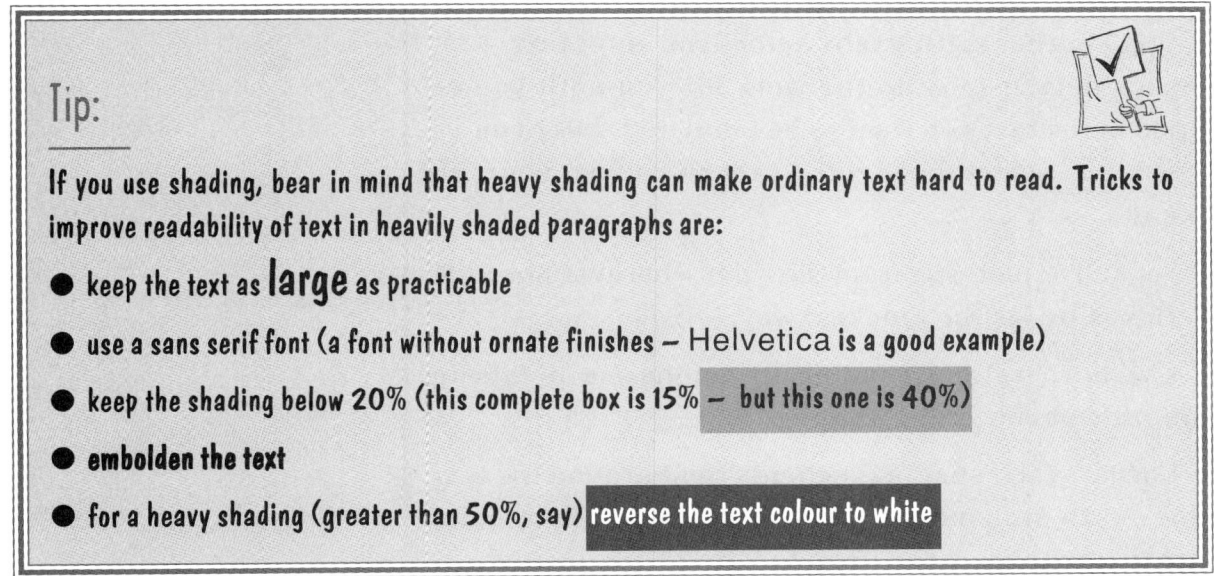

Select fill style

Tip:

If you use shading, bear in mind that heavy shading can make ordinary text hard to read. Tricks to improve readability of text in heavily shaded paragraphs are:

- **keep the text as large as practicable**
- **use a sans serif font (a font without ornate finishes –** Helvetica is a good example**)**
- **keep the shading below 20% (this complete box is 15% – but this one is 40%)**
- **embolden the text**
- **for a heavy shading (greater than 50%, say) reverse the text colour to white**

71

Summary for Section 3

- Both character and paragraph formatting are useful — apply them to selected text by all means — but automatic formatting (using Word styles — covered in Section 6) is even more useful.

- Formatting — whether character formats, paragraph formats or styles — is the key to producing good-looking effective documents.

- Character and paragraph formats are quickly applied by clicking buttons on the Formatting toolbar — keyboard shortcuts, however, are often even quicker

- If you apply a format to the insertion point, the format continues as you type until you change it again.

- If a format already exists in your document, and you want to use it again, use the Format Painter button on the Standard toolbar to paint the format wherever you want.

- Paragraph formats are all stored in a paragraph's paragraph marker ¶.

- Don't bother setting tabs *before* you enter text — let Word's default tabs do the work for you until you've typed in the text you want to be tabulated. After you've typed it in, select the text then set and adjust your tab to suit.

- Set and adjust tabs from the ruler wherever possible — this is by far the quickest way.

- Use borders and shading to emphasise points in your document.

- Borders (and shading) extends right around the text block — to each indent. If you want the border around *just* the text, bring the indents in to those positions.

4 Sections and pages

About sections 74

Setting up a document 76

Margins 77

Headers and footers 80

Line numbers 84

Columns 86

Summary for Section 4 90

About sections

Sometimes when you are working on a document, you need to split it up into smaller parts, without splitting it up into totally different documents. These smaller parts are called *sections*.

You only need to create sections if you want to change the appearance of parts of your document in certain ways. The changes you can make within a document which require that sections have to be created include:

- a different page size
- different margins (page 77)
- a different number of columns (page 86)
- a different header or footer (page 80)
- different line numberings (page 84).

In normal view (and in page layout view if the Show/Hide ¶ button [¶] on the Standard toolbar is clicked), a section end is displayed as shown below.

> **Take note:**
>
> **You only need to split your document up into sections if *part* of your document needs to have one or more of these changes applied. If the *whole* document needs to have the change applied there's no need to use sections at all**

A section break, indicated by a dotted line. This does not print

---

The quiet revolution
The personal computer world is in a state of limbo as Intel's domination of the market is about to be challenged.
································Section Break (Next Page)································

Things move pretty quickly where personal computers are concerned. From the dawn of the personal computer era just twelve years ago several generations of integrated circuits have come and gone, tens of computer manufacturers have made fortunes and bitten the dust, and just a handful of manufacturers now seems to survive. But that's by no means an end to the story. This year there's the start of what will come to be seen as the biggest shake-up ever know in the industry, with conventions overthrown and market percentages re-negotiated to an extent never seen before. Yet users could be forgiven for not even realizing what's going on. Most of the changes have occurred so far in the mainstream background, with little noise and a great deal of stealth.

Basic steps:

1 Position the insertion point in your document where you want the new section to be, then choose **Insert→Break**, or type `Alt`+`I` then `B`, to call up the **Break** dialog box

2 Click the button corresponding to the section break you want:

> **Next Page** — the section break causes the document to force following text to appear at the top of the next page

> **Even Page** — following text is forced to the top of the next even page of the document

> **Odd page** — following text is forced to the top of the next odd page of the document

> **Continuous** — following text occurs straight under the section break, wherever it occurs on a page

3 Click **OK**

Effectively, the changes listed are parameters you apply much like character and paragraph formats, except they affect the whole section (not just a few characters or paragraphs). Every time you want to change one or more of these parameters in just *part* of your document, you need a new section.

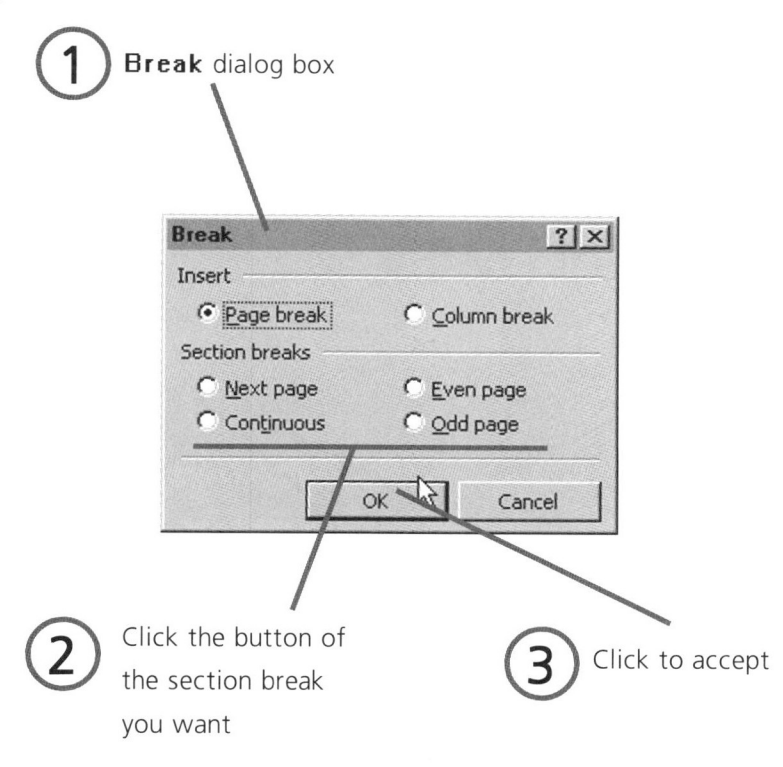

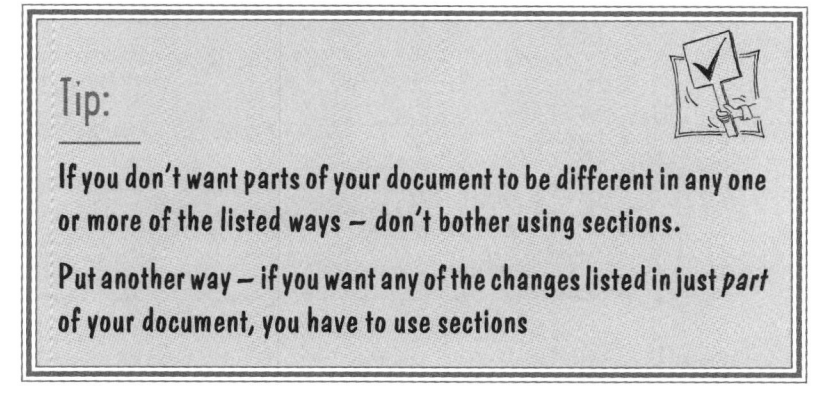

(1) **Break** dialog box

(2) Click the button of the section break you want

(3) Click to accept

Tip:

If you don't want parts of your document to be different in any one or more of the listed ways — don't bother using sections.

Put another way — if you want any of the changes listed in just *part* of your document, you have to use sections

Setting up a document

Apart from character and paragraph formats, a document has other parameters you can format. Where these are contained within a section (or selected sections) of a document they affect just that section (or sections). Where the document contains no section breaks (that is, the document comprises just one section), or where all sections of a document are selected before formatting, the whole document is affected.

Most of these parameters are adjusted from the **Page Setup** dialog box, although other methods are sometimes available.

Basic steps:

1. Choose **File→Page Setup**, or type `Alt`+`F` then `U`, to call up the **Page Setup** dialog box
2. Click tabs to see the different controls available to adjust parameters
3. If you make any changes to parameters, click **OK** to accept changes, or **Cancel** to ignore them

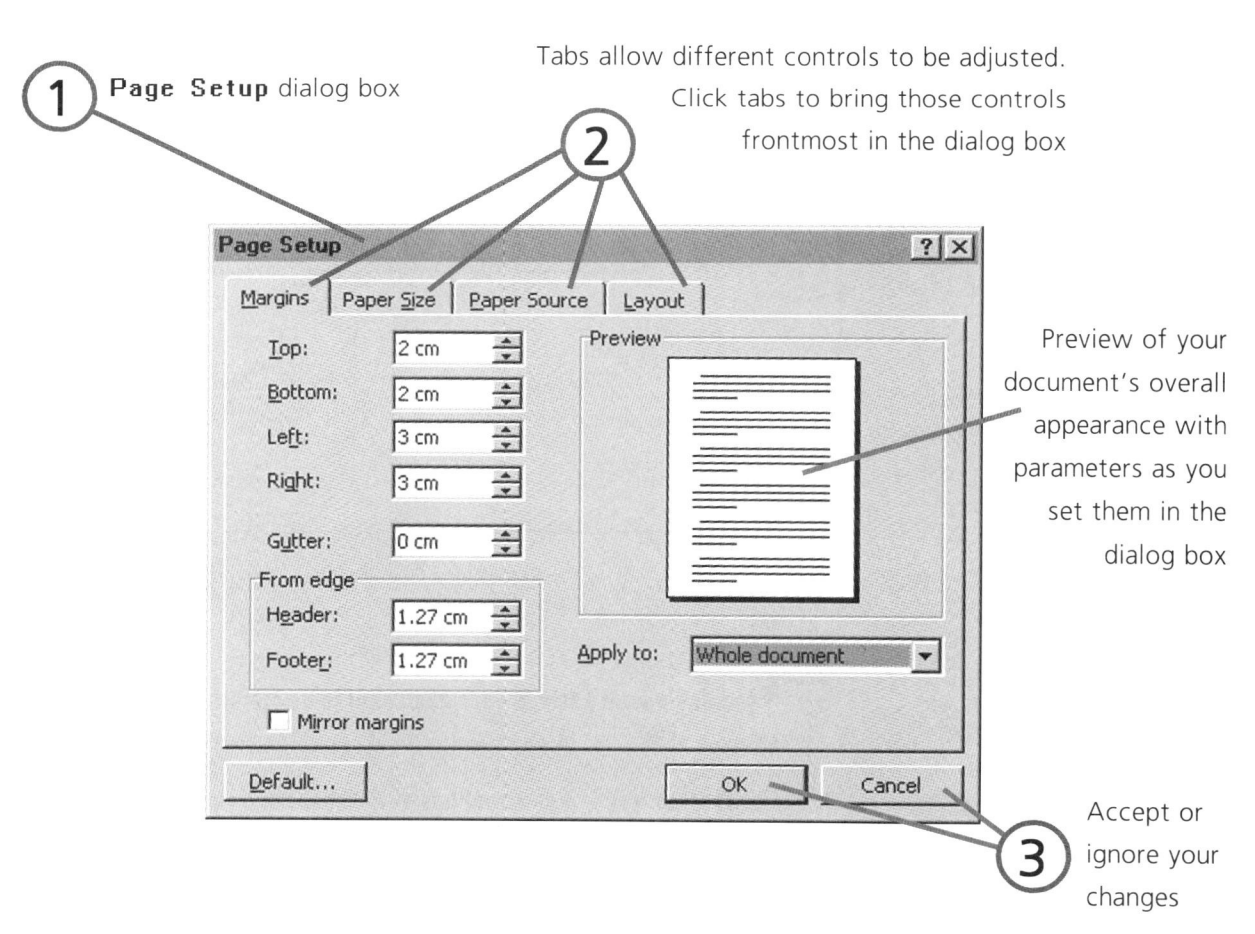

(1) **Page Setup** dialog box

Tabs allow different controls to be adjusted. Click tabs to bring those controls frontmost in the dialog box (2)

Preview of your document's overall appearance with parameters as you set them in the dialog box

(3) Accept or ignore your changes

Margins

Margins are imaginary guides on a document page, outside of which text isn't normally situated. By default, Word creates margins for any new document — usually of 1 inch (2.54 cm) from top and bottom of the page, and 1.25 inches (3.17 cm) from left and right page edge.

You can change margins, either for a whole document or for a section, from the **Page Setup** dialog box.

Basic steps:

1. Choose **File→Page Setup**, or type `Alt`+`F` then `U`, to call up the **Page Setup** dialog box
2. Click the **Margins** tab if it's not already frontmost (see opposite)
3. Adjust margin dimensions to suit

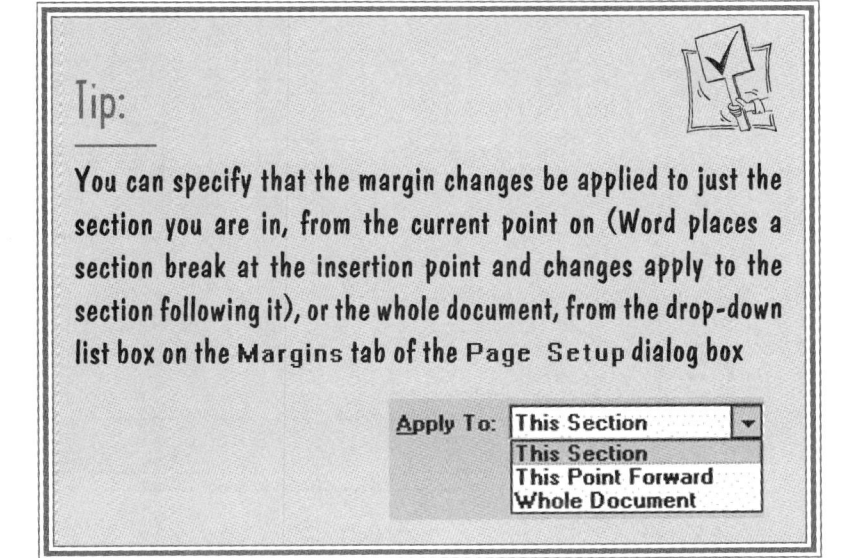

Tip:

In many of these tabs (and in many other dialog boxes, for that matter) adjustments can be made to some controls by increasing or decreasing in preset steps by clicking on the up or down arrows to the right of the entry boxes. Alternatively, you can click on the entry box you want to change then enter the exact value you want

Tip:

You can specify that the margin changes be applied to just the section you are in, from the current point on (Word places a section break at the insertion point and changes apply to the section following it), or the whole document, from the drop-down list box on the Margins tab of the Page Setup dialog box

Apply To: This Section
- This Section
- This Point Forward
- Whole Document

Margins (contd)

Some of the controls of the **Margins** tab of the **Page Setup** dialog box allow you to control how pages are printed for double-sided purposes (that is, for the likes of books and reports).

If **Mirror Margins** check box is checked, these entry boxes change to show **Inside** and **Outside** margin measurements

Preview always shows the effects of entries and controls

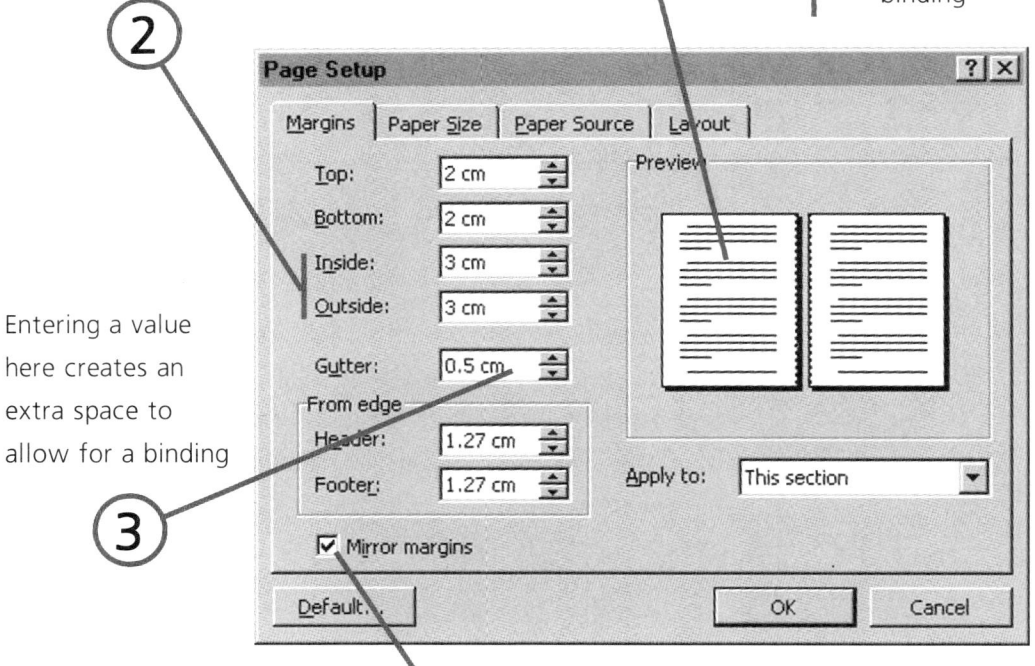

Entering a value here creates an extra space to allow for a binding

Basic steps:

1. If the document is to be double-sided, check the **Mirror Margins** check box

2. Change the **Inside** and **Outside** margins measurements to suit your requirements

3. If the you plan to bind your document with a ring or similar method, enter a value in the **Gutter** entry box — this gives extra space inside the inside margins to allow for the binding

Check here for margins which are equal on the insides, and equal on the outsides of each left and right hand page

Basic steps:

1 Choose **View→Page Layout**, or type `Alt`+`V` then `P`, or (best) click the Page Layout button 📄 to view your document in page layout view

2 Drag your margins to suit

As an alternative to using the **Page Setup** dialog box, you can adjust margins by dragging margin boundaries in page layout view (or print preview — see page 140). This is probably faster, though you have little accuracy, you can't specify how much of the document you want to apply changes to (current section, current point forward, or the whole document — dragging from the ruler applies changes to just the current section, or whole document if no section break exists), and mirror margin and gutter margin controls aren't available.

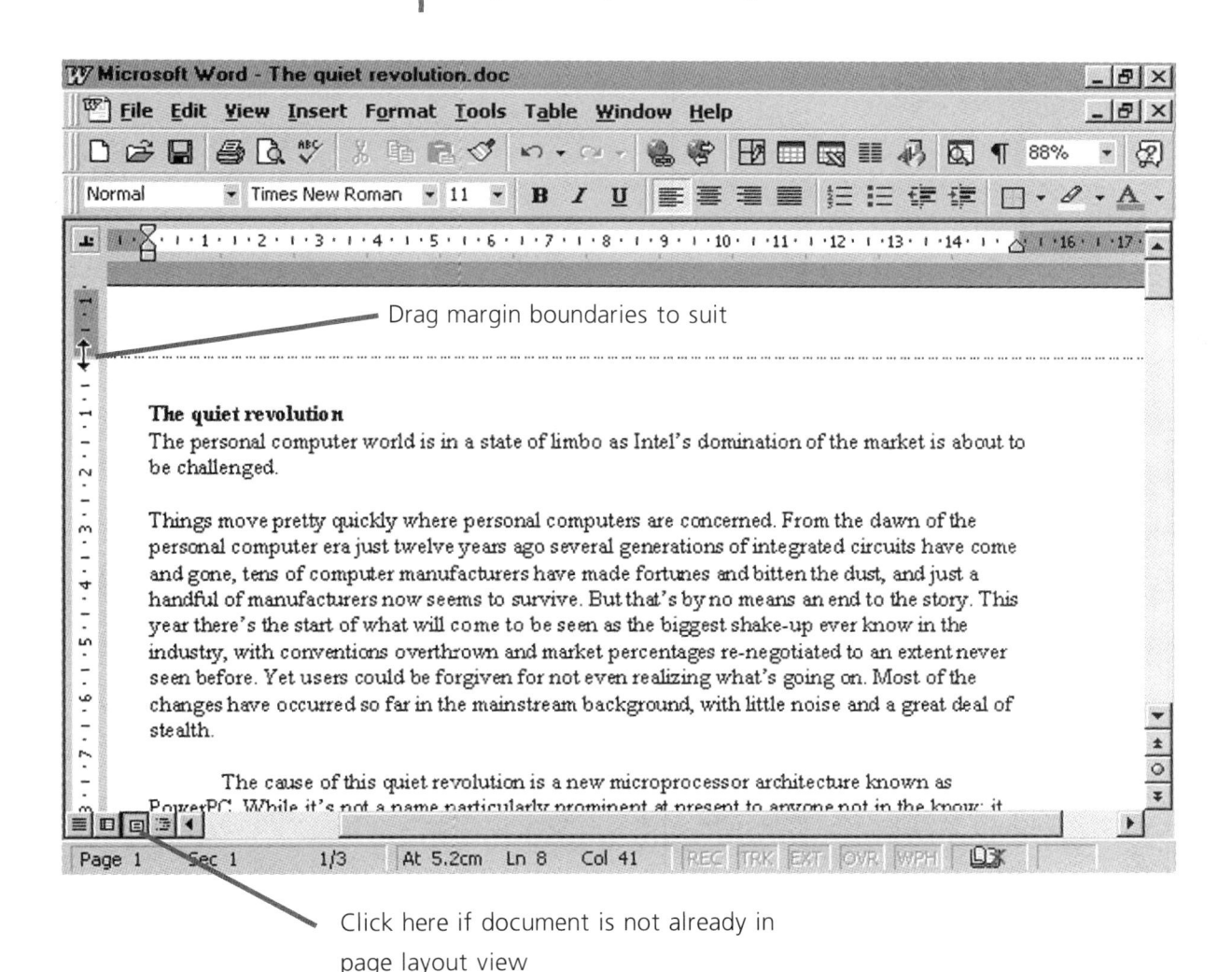

Drag margin boundaries to suit

Click here if document is not already in page layout view

79

Headers and footers

A header is a heading (often called a running head) which appears at the top of each page in a document or section of a document. A footer is at the bottom of each page. You can put text or graphical items in either and you can format them in the usual ways.

Basic steps:

1 To create either a header or a footer choose **View→Header and Footer**, or type [Alt]+[V] then [H]. The document changes to page layout view and displays the header entry box and the Header and Footer toolbar

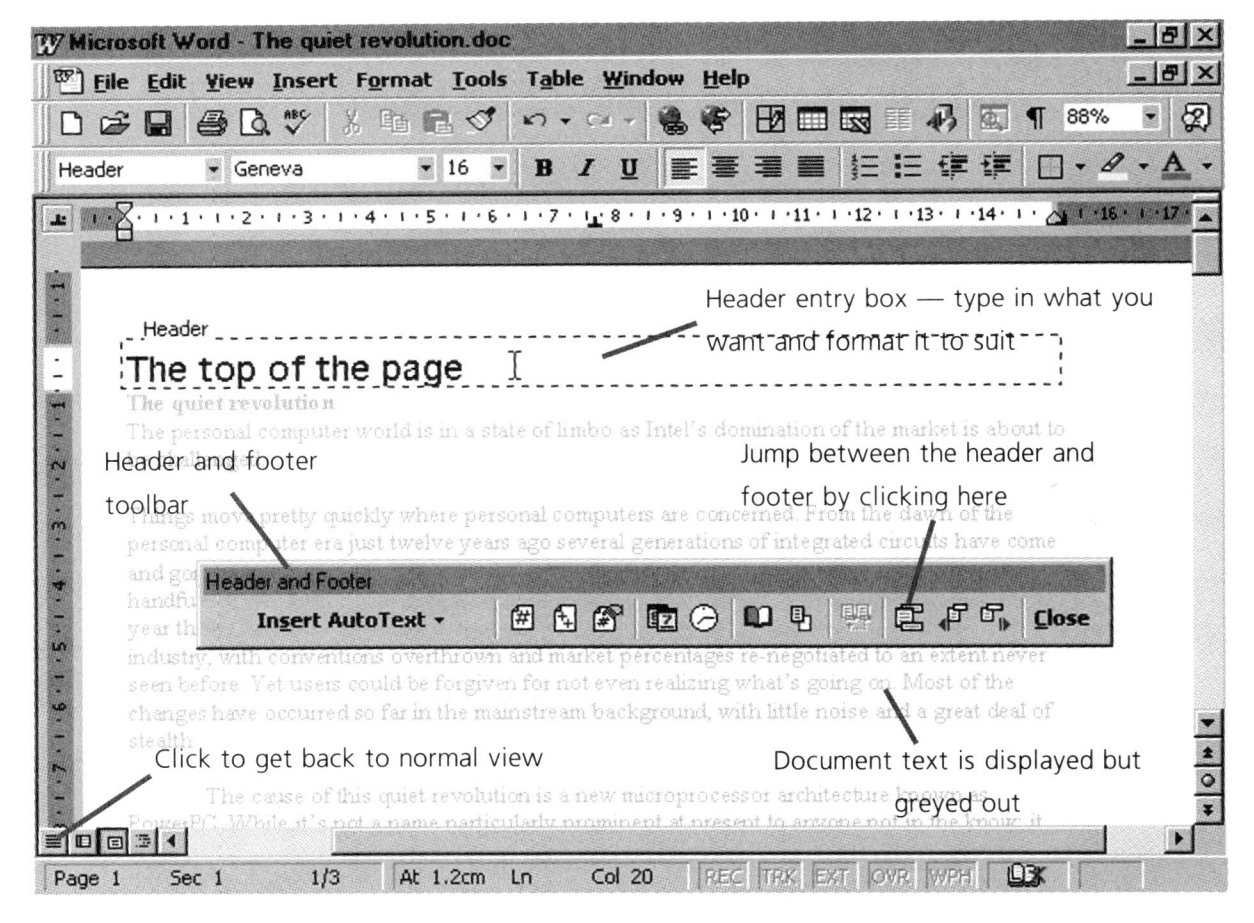

Header entry box — type in what you want and format it to suit

Header and footer toolbar

Jump between the header and footer by clicking here

Click to get back to normal view

Document text is displayed but greyed out

80

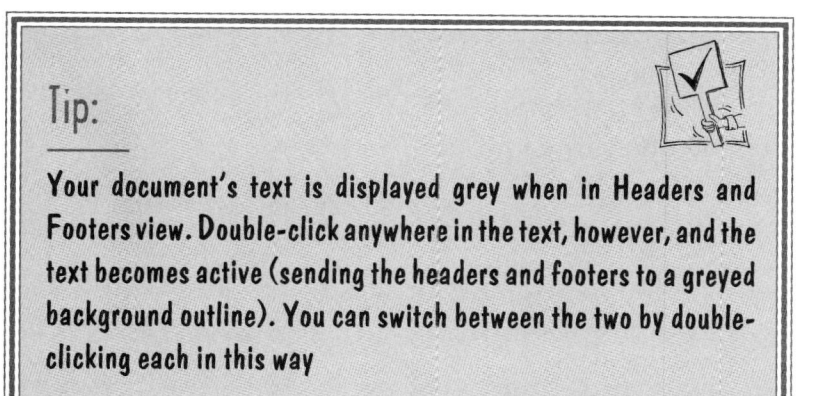

> **Tip:**
>
> Your document's text is displayed grey when in Headers and Footers view. Double-click anywhere in the text, however, and the text becomes active (sending the headers and footers to a greyed background outline). You can switch between the two by double-clicking each in this way

> **Tip:**
>
> Headers and footers apply to individual sections – in other words, you can have different headers and footers for each section if you want

Double-click a greyed header to make it active

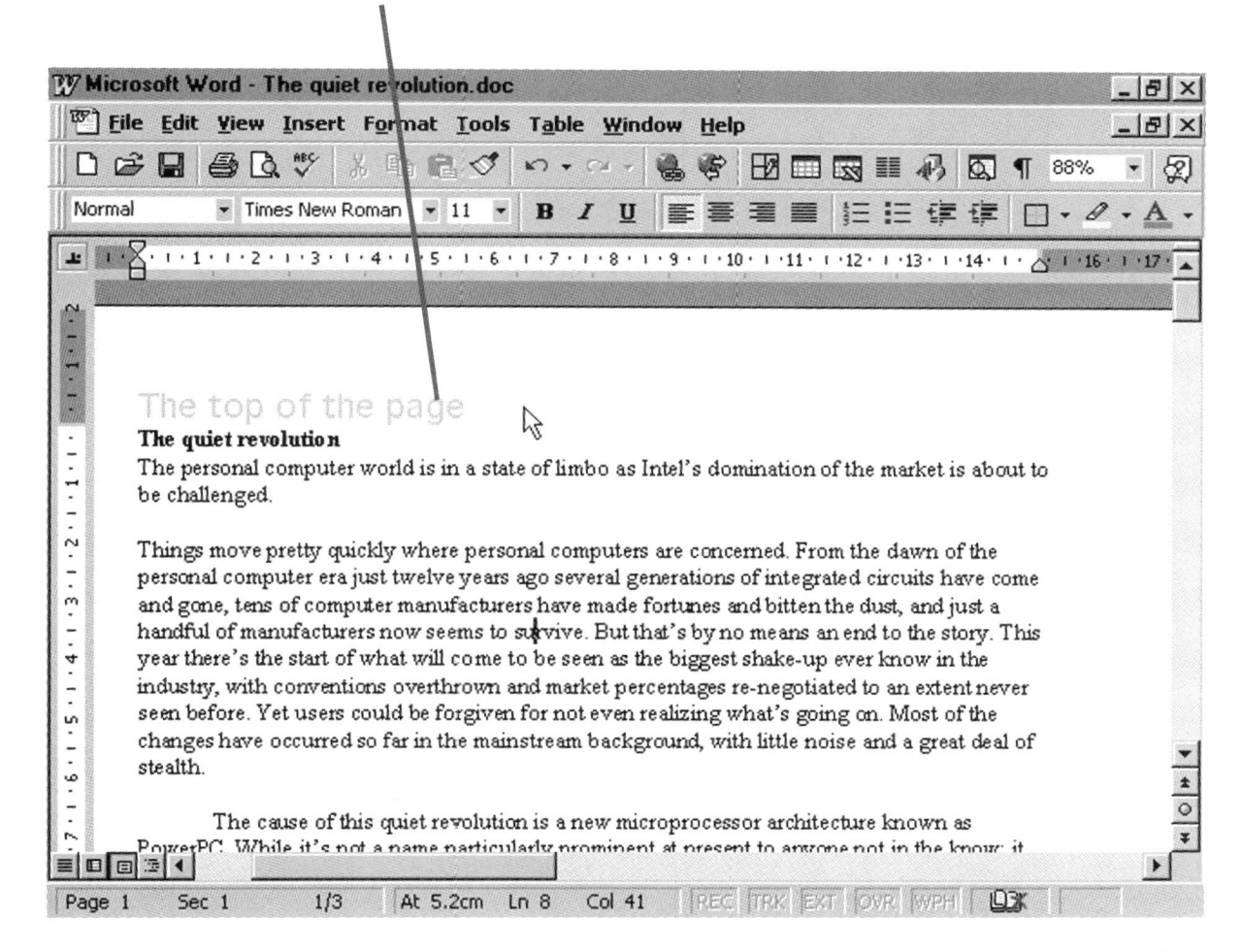

Headers & footers (contd)

The Headers and Footers toolbar has a number of buttons. Use these to access various features and entries you can make into a header or footer.

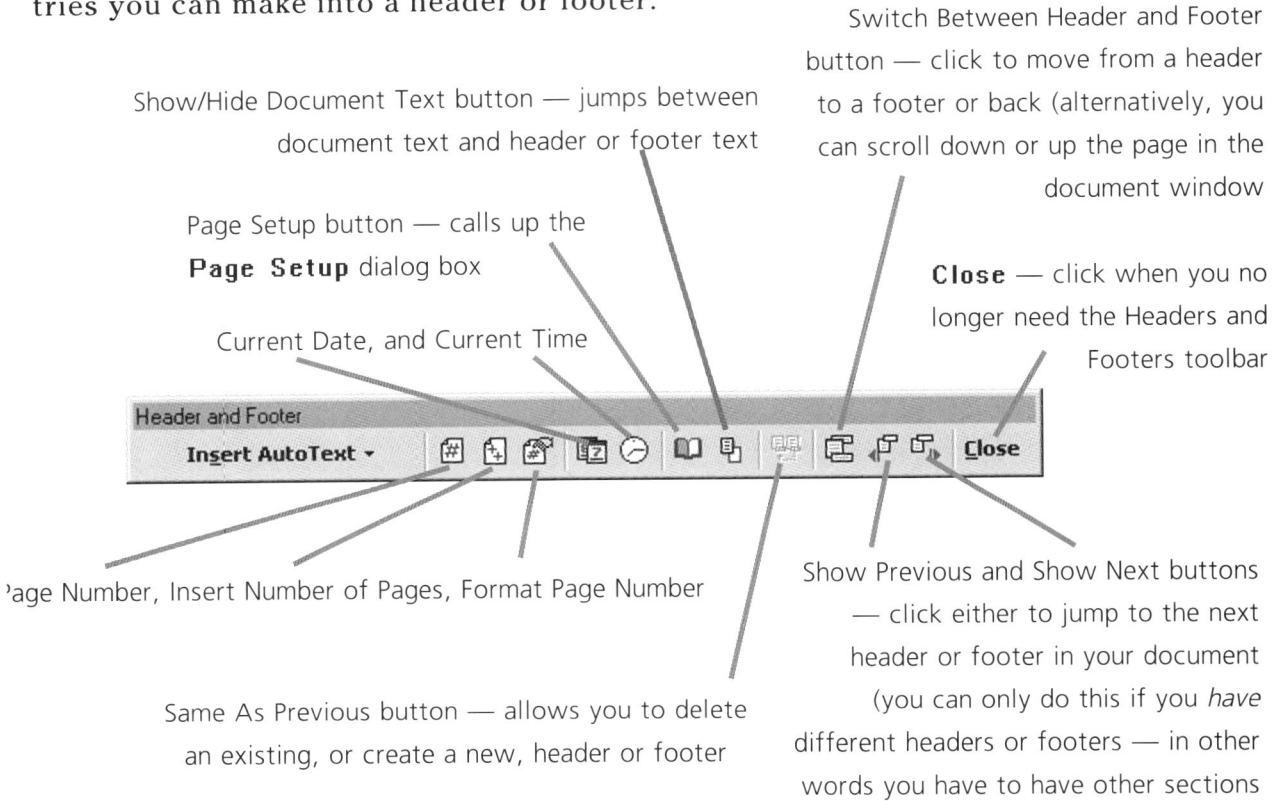

Show/Hide Document Text button — jumps between document text and header or footer text

Page Setup button — calls up the **Page Setup** dialog box

Current Date, and Current Time

Switch Between Header and Footer button — click to move from a header to a footer or back (alternatively, you can scroll down or up the page in the document window

Close — click when you no longer need the Headers and Footers toolbar

Page Number, Insert Number of Pages, Format Page Number

Same As Previous button — allows you to delete an existing, or create a new, header or footer

Show Previous and Show Next buttons — click either to jump to the next header or footer in your document (you can only do this if you *have* different headers or footers — in other words you have to have other sections with other headers or footers set up)

Tip:

Remember you can format a header or a footer in exactly the same way you format ordinary document text. You can embolden, italicise, underline and so on. You can make it centrally aligned or right aligned if you want. You are not restricted to just one line of text. You can also use a graphical item.

Also remember that each section you create can have its own header and footer – use this feature to set up a header for each chapter of a large document, for example

Basic steps:

1 Choose **View ↪ Page Layout**, or type [Alt]+[V] then [P], or (best) click the Page Layout button 📄 to view your document in page layout view

2 Drag margin and header (or footer) boundaries to suit

You can adjust the distance from a page edge taken up by a header at the top of your document page (or the footer at the bottom) from the **Page Setup** dialog box (the **From Edge** entries). You can also change margins from here (allowing you to adjust the distance between the header or footer and the document text.

An easier way, however, is to switch to page layout view and drag the various boundaries to suit what you want.

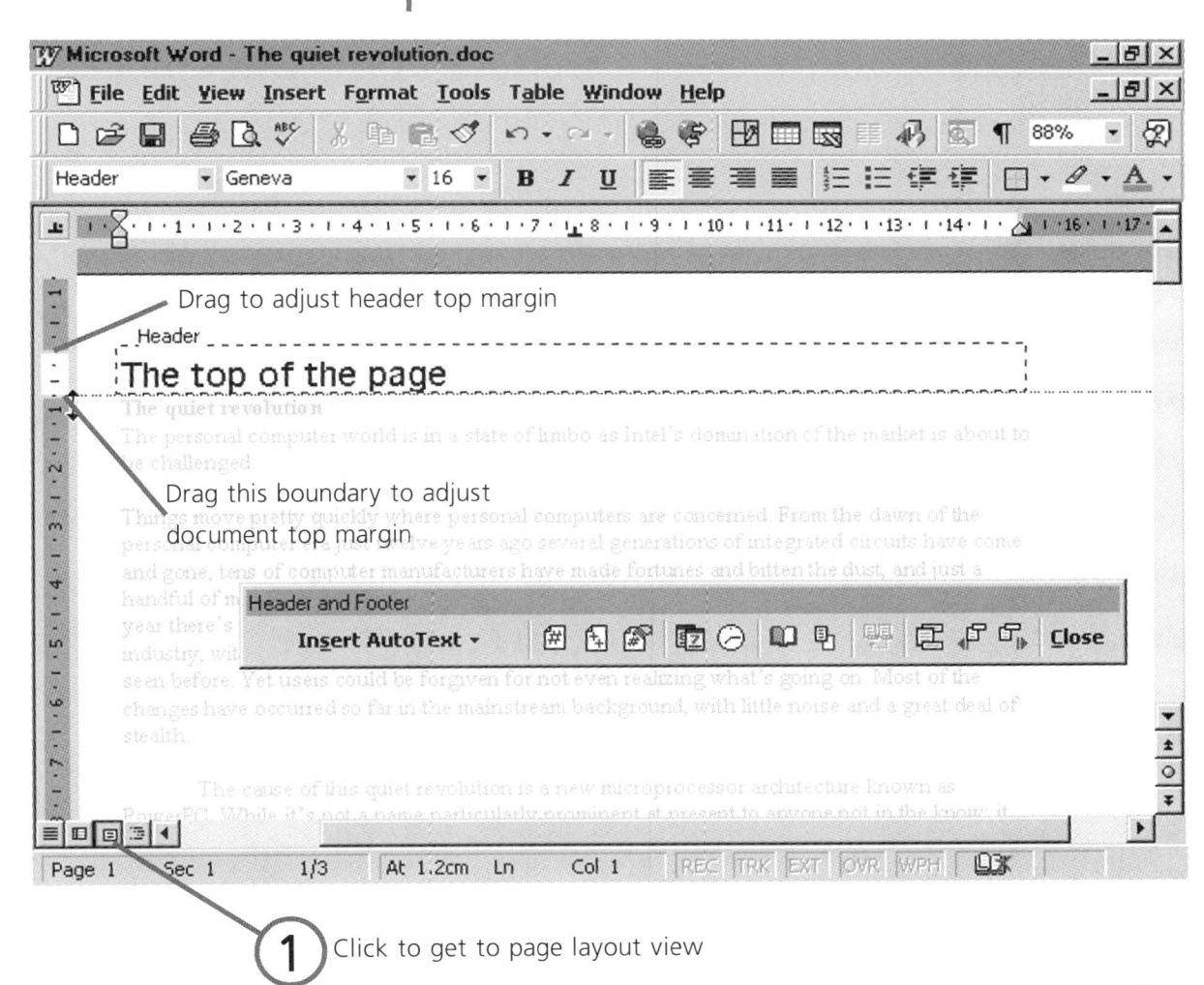

Drag to adjust header top margin

Drag this boundary to adjust document top margin

① Click to get to page layout view

83

Line numbers

Word can display and print line numbers alongside text. This can be useful in technical documentation, and even required in legal literature.

Line numbers are:

- printed in the left margin
- numbered excluding lines in tables, headers, footers and some other parts of a document
- only visible on-screen in page layout view (or print preview — see page 140).

Basic steps:

1. Choose **File→Page Setup**, or type `Alt`+`F` then `U` to call up the **Page Setup** dialog box. Click the **Layout** tab if it's not already frontmost. Next click the **Line Numbers** button to call up the **Line Numbers** dialog box

2. Check the **Add Line Numbering** check box to create line numbers

3. Adjust controls to suit and click **OK** to accept and view line numbers

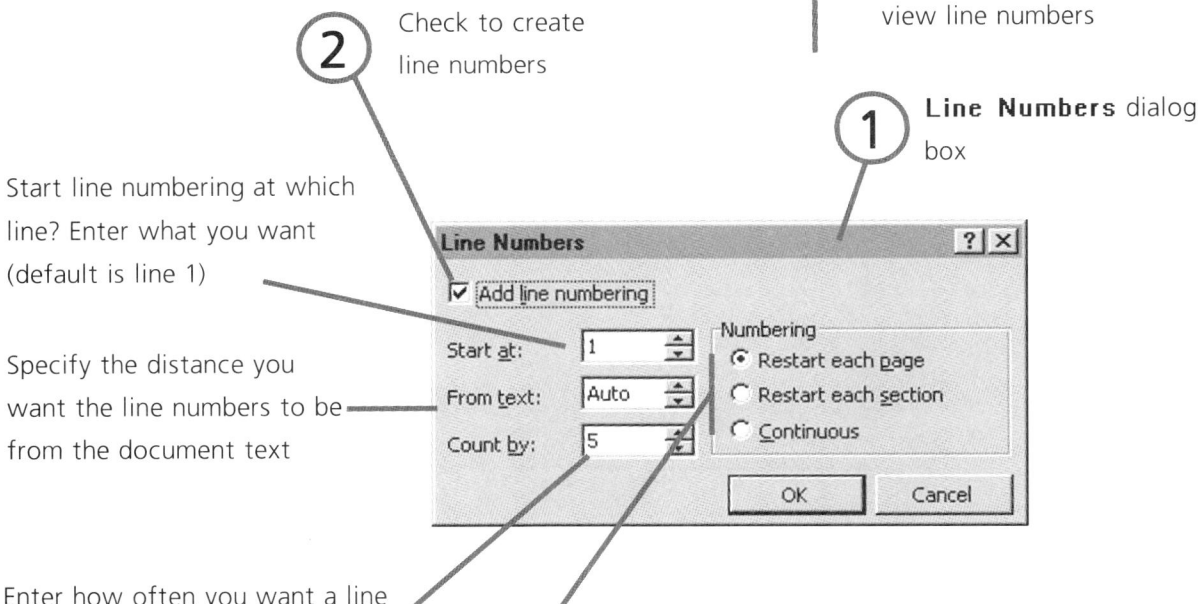

(2) Check to create line numbers

(1) **Line Numbers** dialog box

Start line numbering at which line? Enter what you want (default is line 1)

Specify the distance you want the line numbers to be from the document text

Enter how often you want a line number to occur — for example, if you only want a line number every 10 lines — 10, 20, 30 and so on — enter 10

Click a button to specify whether the line numbers restart at the top of each page; restart at the beginning of each section in the document; or are continuous throughout

③ Line numbers are visible in page layout (or print preview) views only

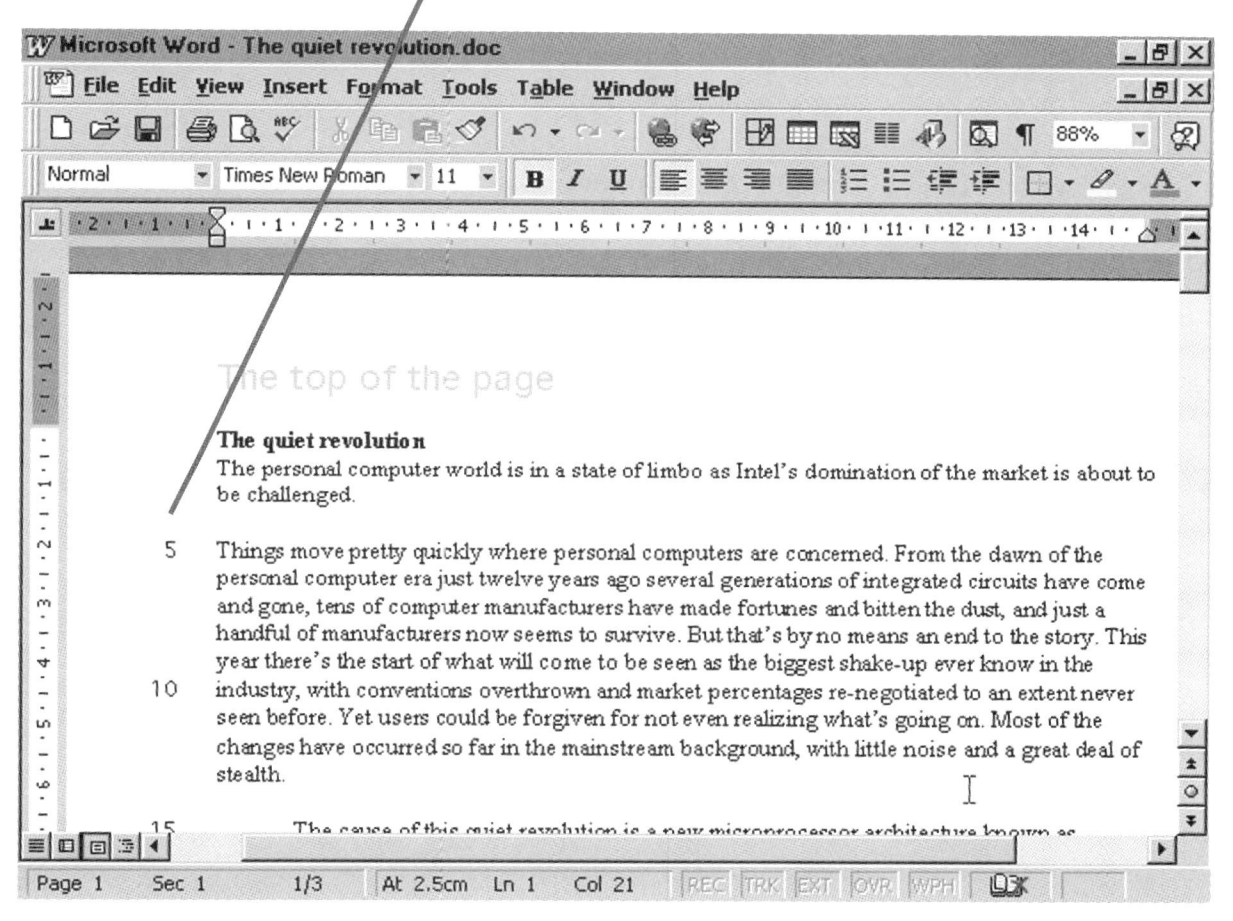

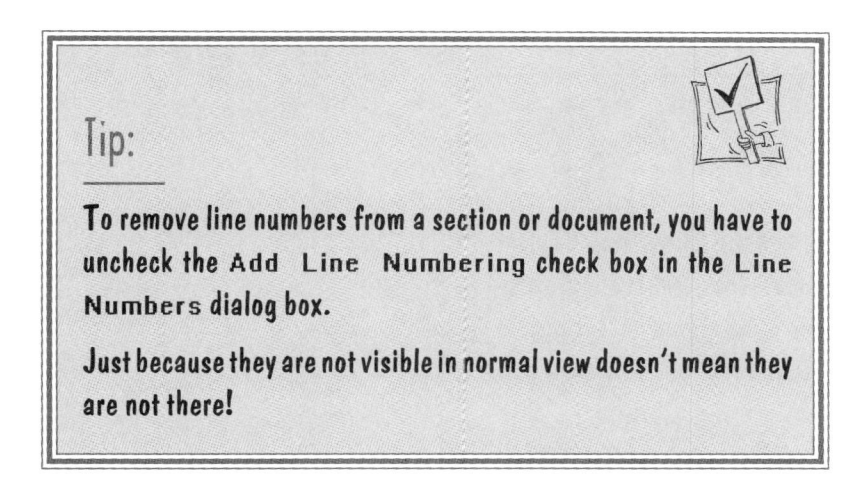

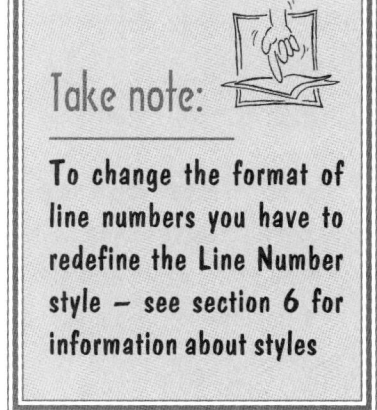

Tip:

To remove line numbers from a section or document, you have to uncheck the Add Line Numbering check box in the Line Numbers dialog box.

Just because they are not visible in normal view doesn't mean they are not there!

Take note:

To change the format of line numbers you have to redefine the Line Number style – see section 6 for information about styles

Columns

Generally, text in a Word document is in a single column — that is, a single vertical division down the page. You can, however, create two or more columns of text quite simply, where columns are unattached or where a story flows from the bottom of one column to the top of the next. Columns can be used to create newspaper-style or newsletter-style documents, or indeed books such as this one.

You can create columns in your document from either:

- a button on the Standard toolbar; or
- the **Columns** dialog box.

Basic steps:

USING THE STANDARD TOOLBAR

1 Select the text you want to be formatted into columns, then click the Columns button on the Standard toolbar

2 Drag across the drop-down window to select the number of columns you want

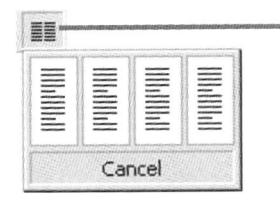

Click the Columns button to display this drop-down window

Drag across to select the number of columns you want — let go the mouse button to accept

3 Columns

Take note:

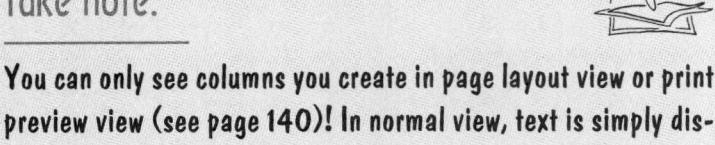

You can only see columns you create in page layout view or print preview view (see page 140)! In normal view, text is simply displayed at the width of a *single* column — so if your text is across two columns on the page, normally viewed text will only be a half page wide

Basic steps:

FROM THE COLUMNS DIALOG BOX

1. Select the text you want to be formatted into columns, then choose **Format▸Columns** to call up the **Columns** dialog box
2. Choose the number of columns you want
3. Change column widths and other controls to suit your requirements

> **Tip:**
>
> If you select text then format it into columns, Word automatically inserts section breaks before and after the text. This way you can have different numbers of columns in different parts of the document — columns are section parameters, remember
>
> If you simply position the insertion point in your document before formatting into columns (that is, you *don't* select any text), the whole section (the whole *document* if no section breaks are present in the document) is formatted

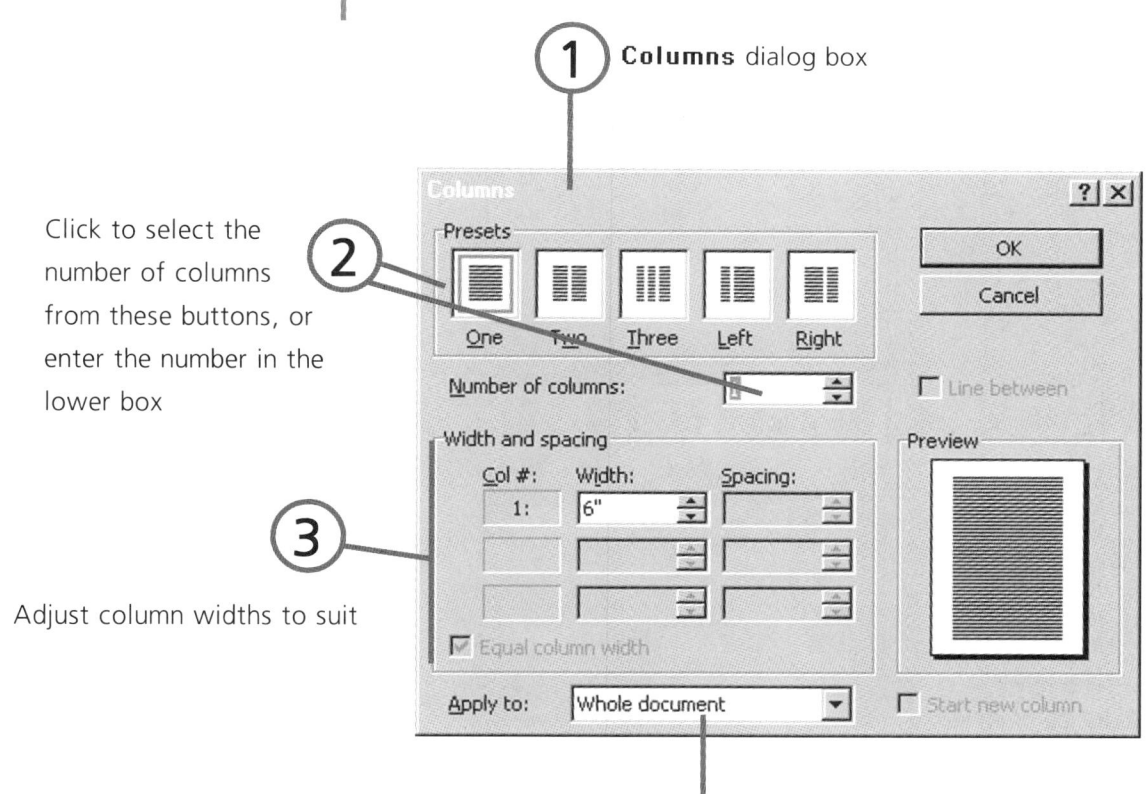

① **Columns** dialog box

Click to select the number of columns from these buttons, or enter the number in the lower box ②

Adjust column widths to suit ③

Specify which part of document to apply columns to (whole document, current section, or from this point on)

87

Columns (contd)

If you want to format your section or document into even-width columns, the quickest method is with the Columns button ▦ on the Standard toolbar.

On the other hand, if you want *uneven* columns you have to use the **Columns** dialog box. The **Columns** dialog box also gives some other controls unavailable with the Columns button:

- the spacing between columns
- whether a line between columns is displayed
- whether the columns apply to the whole document, the current section, or from the current point on.

> **Tip:**
>
> If you want multi-column text underneath single column text first enter text without any column formatting. Next, select the text to be multi-column formatted and format it. Word automatically creates section breaks before and after the multi-column formatted section

Click here to give two columns of unequal width — measurements in the width entry boxes are automatically adjusted to suit

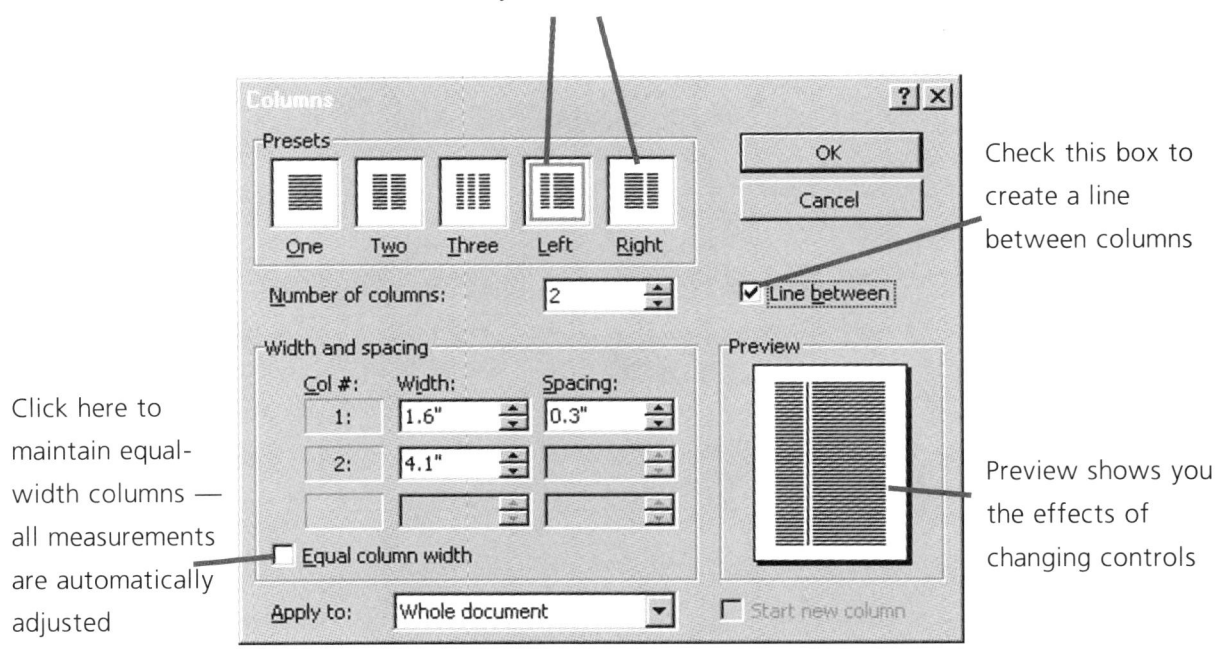

Check this box to create a line between columns

Click here to maintain equal-width columns — all measurements are automatically adjusted

Preview shows you the effects of changing controls

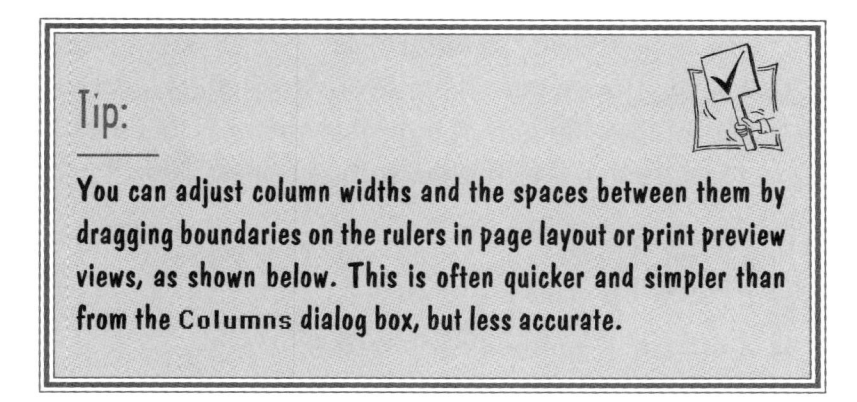

Tip:

You can adjust column widths and the spaces between them by dragging boundaries on the rulers in page layout or print preview views, as shown below. This is often quicker and simpler than from the Columns dialog box, but less accurate.

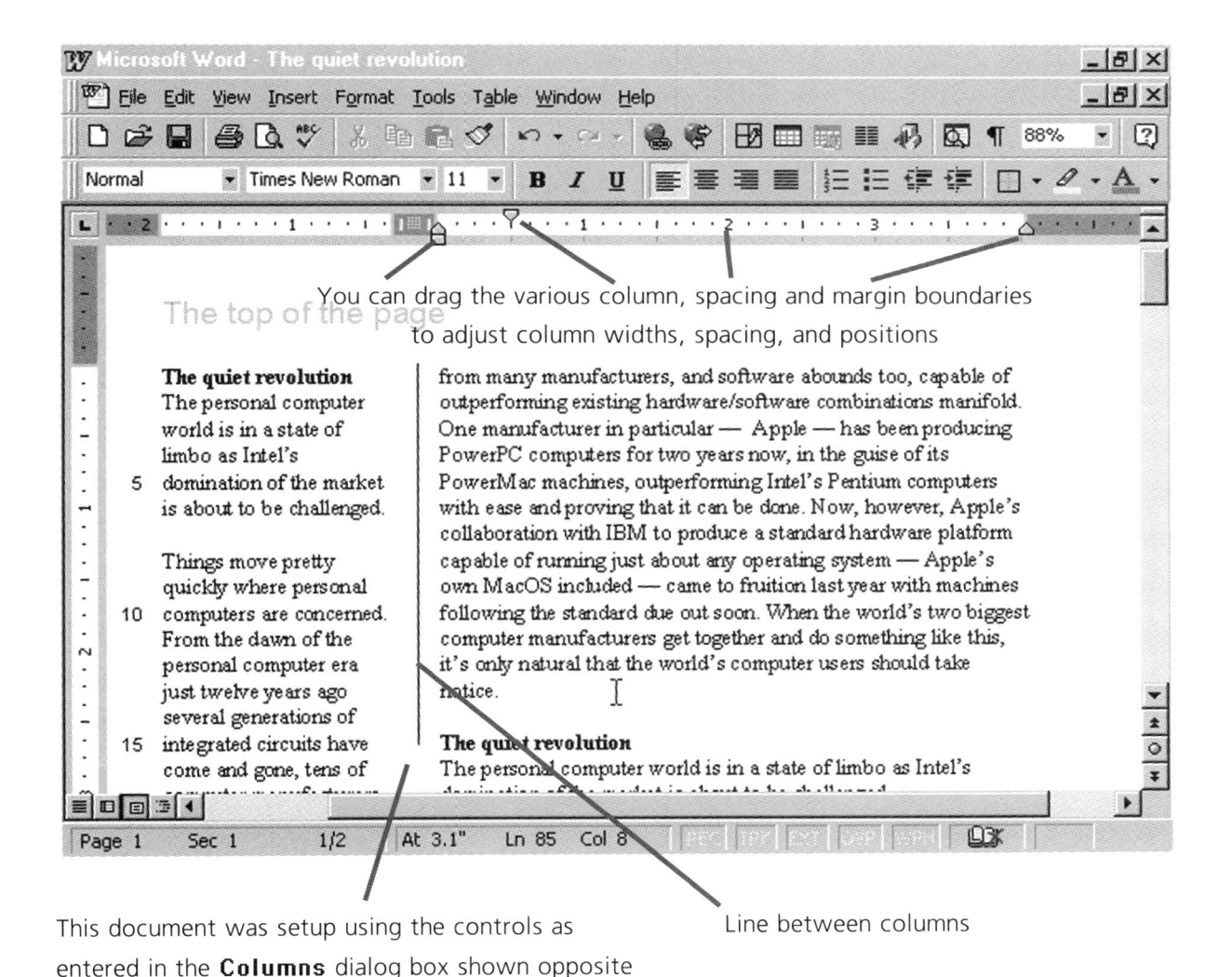

You can drag the various column, spacing and margin boundaries to adjust column widths, spacing, and positions

The top of the page

This document was setup using the controls as entered in the **Columns** dialog box shown opposite

Line between columns

89

Summary for Section 4

- Use a section where you need to change certain parameters for only *part* of your document. The parameters for which a section has to be created include:
    - a different page size
    - different margins
    - a different number of columns
    - a different header or footer
    - different line numberings.

- If you change any of these parameters for *the whole document*, don't use a section.

- Create margins, headers and footers, and columns from dialog boxes (as this is most exact), but remember you can adjust them and their spacings by dragging boundaries in page layout (or print preview) view.

5 Text control

Finding text 92

Replacing 94

Spelling 96

AutoCorrect 100

AutoText 102

Outlining 104

Tables 108

Table conversions 111

Table formatting 112

Counting your words 113

Graphics 114

Summary for Section 5 118

Finding text

Although it probably sounds odd, one of the main jobs a word processor is asked to do in everyday life is to find text. You'd think a word processor had enough coping with all it's asked to do with text without having to actually find the stuff for you too, wouldn't you?

Problem is, in long documents it's not always easy for us to locate specific instances of small pieces of text. Let's say you have worked for weeks and weeks on your latest novel, and you decide that little bit around half way through about your heroine's need for money needs expanding somewhat. What do you do? You could scroll through the book, screen-by-screen, trying to find where it is, but that could take hours — you wrote it weeks ago remember — and you haven't a real idea exactly where it is.

Let Word do the job for you.

Basic steps:

1 Choose **Edit→Find**, or type [Alt]+[E] then [F], or type [Ctrl]+[F]. This calls up the **Find and Replace** dialog box

2 In the **Find What** entry box, type in the text you want to locate

3 If your text contains formats, special characters or other controls, click the **More** button to extend the dialog box

4 Specify the controls you want to control the search

5 Click the **Find Next** button to start the search

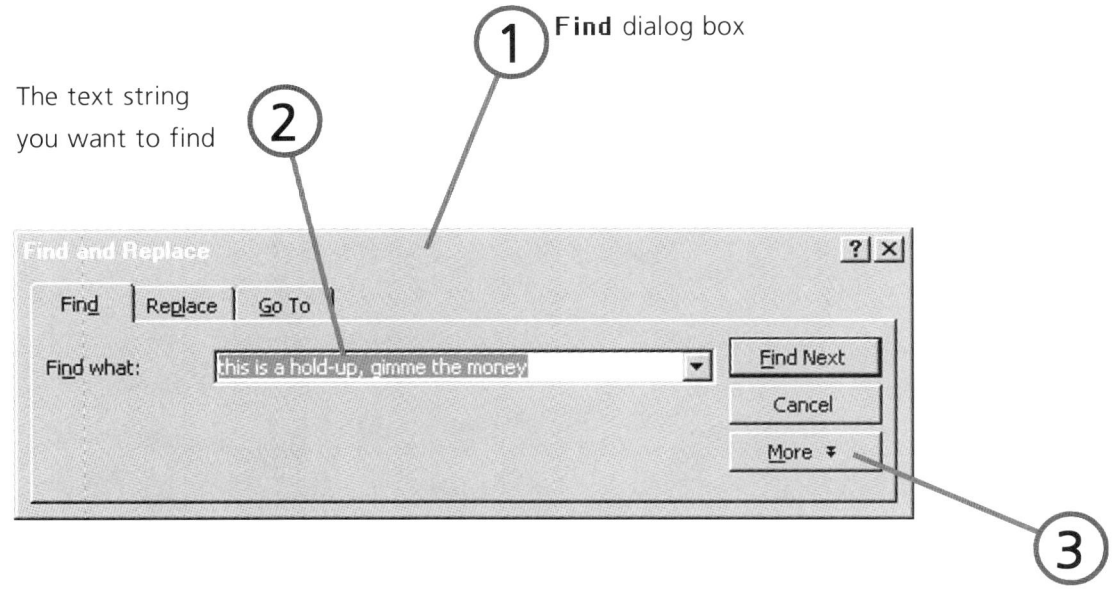

① **Find** dialog box

② The text string you want to find

③ Click if things other than just text can be specified

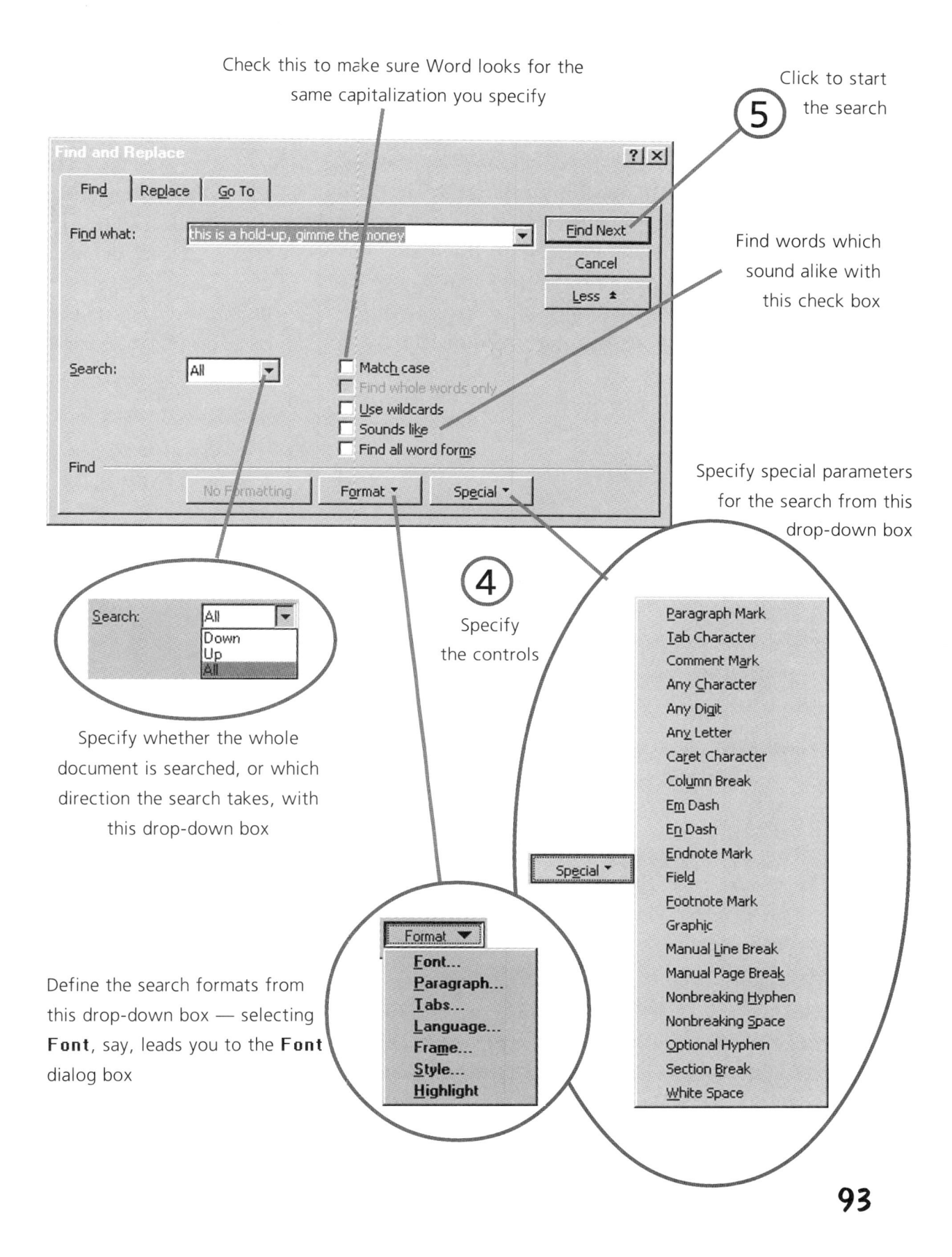

Check this to make sure Word looks for the same capitalization you specify

(5) Click to start the search

Find and Replace ? X

Find | Replace | Go To

Find what: this is a hold-up, gimme the money

- Find Next
- Cancel
- Less ±

Find words which sound alike with this check box

Search: All

- [ ] Match case
- [ ] Find whole words only
- [ ] Use wildcards
- [ ] Sounds like
- [ ] Find all word forms

Find

No Formatting | Format ▼ | Special ▼

Specify special parameters for the search from this drop-down box

(4) Specify the controls

Search: All / Down / Up / All

Specify whether the whole document is searched, or which direction the search takes, with this drop-down box

Special ▼
- Paragraph Mark
- Tab Character
- Comment Mark
- Any Character
- Any Digit
- Any Letter
- Caret Character
- Column Break
- Em Dash
- En Dash
- Endnote Mark
- Field
- Footnote Mark
- Graphic
- Manual Line Break
- Manual Page Break
- Nonbreaking Hyphen
- Nonbreaking Space
- Optional Hyphen
- Section Break
- White Space

Format ▼
- Font...
- Paragraph...
- Tabs...
- Language...
- Frame...
- Style...
- Highlight

Define the search formats from this drop-down box — selecting **Font**, say, leads you to the **Font** dialog box

93

Replacing

In the **Find and Replace** dialog box you may have noticed a tab marked **Replace**. Clicking this leads you to the **Replace** dialog box (or you can call up the dialog box directly). This lets you find text in the same way we've seen, then replaces the instances of text with a different text string. Say, your heroine's request for cash doesn't sound too cool, and you want to change it to something with a bit more class. Easy — get Word to replace it.

Take note:

As you specify a format in either the Find dialog box or the Replace dialog box, the format is shown in the Format fields directly below the Find What and Replace With entry boxes (see opposite for example)

Tip:

While Word will happily find and replace text strings for you (formatted or unformatted) it is equally at home finding and replacing just formats (without any text string associated with them).

So, for example, you can find instances of text which are underlined (<u>a typical typists' method of emphasising text</u>) and replace them all with italicised text (*the usual typographers' emphasis method*) by specifying the formats to suit. Remember not to enter any text in either of the Find What or Replace With entry boxes

Basic steps:

1. Choose **Edit→Replace**, or type [Alt]+[E] then [E], or type [Ctrl]+[H], or (as we've seen) click the **Replace** tab in the **Find** dialog box. This calls up the **Replace** dialog box
2. Enter the text string to look for
3. Type in the text string to replace it
4. Click the **More** button if you want to specify controls
5. Specify the controls (see page 93 for details)
6. Click the **Find Next** button to find the next occurrence of the string, or:
7. Begin the replacements using other buttons

② The text string to be found — leave blank if you're just looking for formats

① **Replace** dialog box

④ Click for more controls

③ Text string to replace found text — leave blank if you're just wanting to replace formats

Click to clear formats from the active entry box

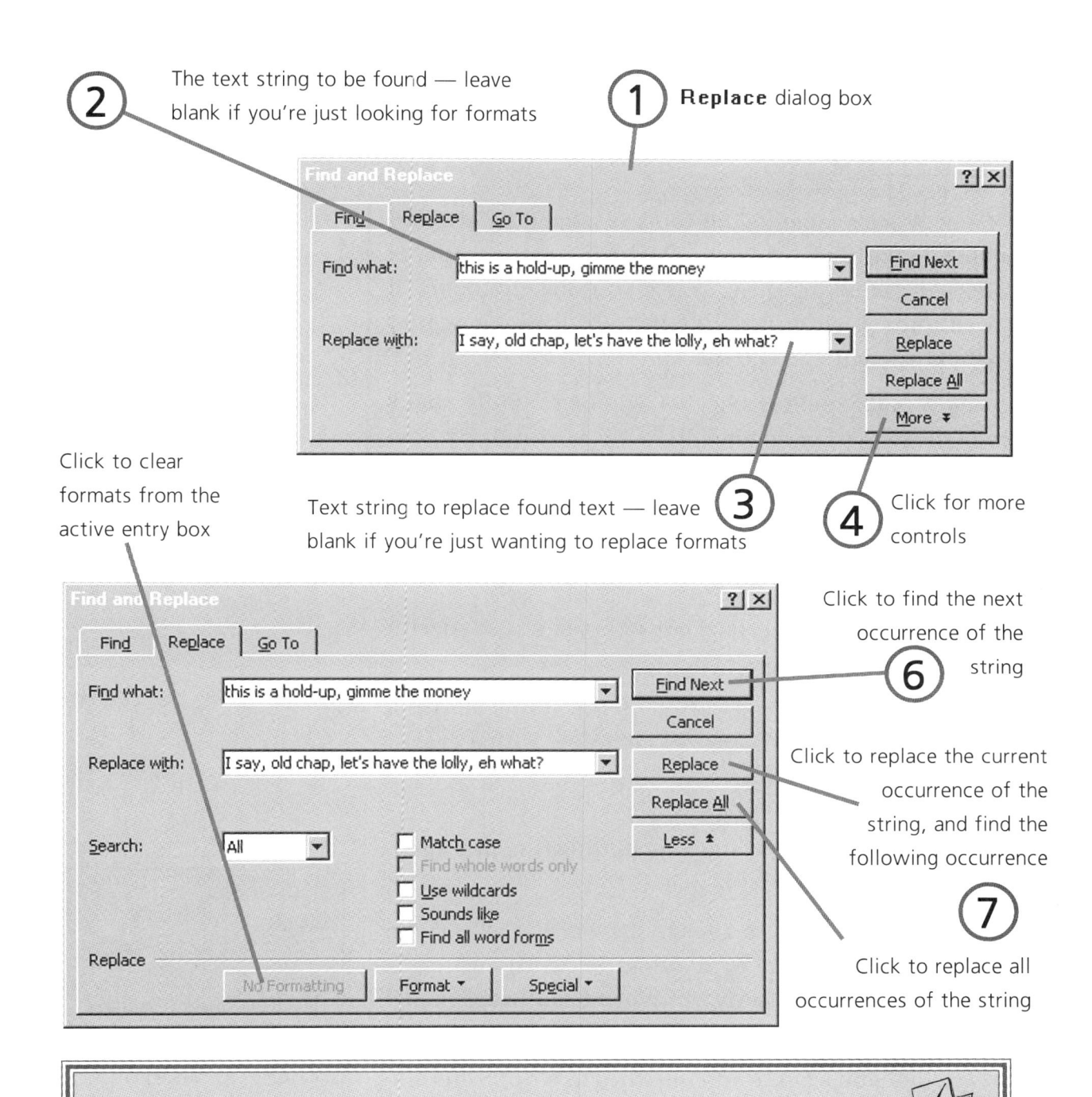

⑥ Click to find the next occurrence of the string

Click to replace the current occurrence of the string, and find the following occurrence

⑦ Click to replace all occurrences of the string

Tip:

In either the Find or the Replace dialog boxes you can specify formats using the format drop-down box, or you can — much more easily — just click on a toolbar button representing the format. If you want to find bold text, say, just click the Bold button **B** in the Formatting toolbar while the insertion point is in the Find What entry box

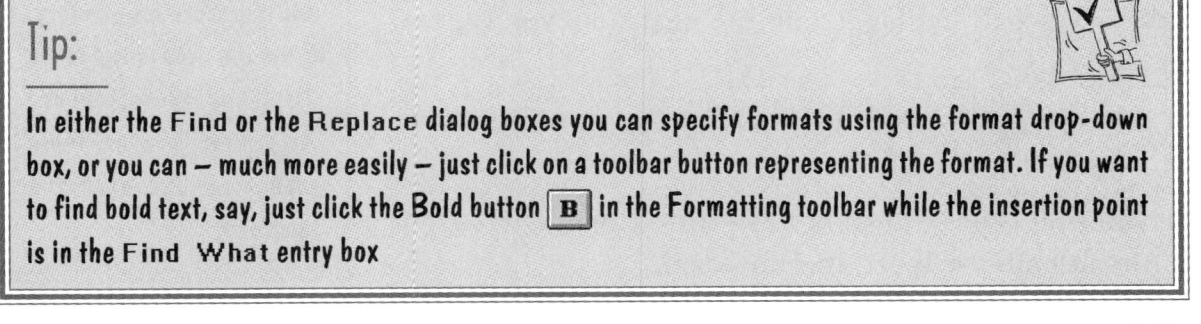

Spelling

One of Word's most useful tools is a spelling checker which looks through your document and compares each word with the words in an electronic dictionary. If Word finds a word in the dictionary, it assumes that word is spelled correctly.

Using Word's spelling checker you can rapidly check even the longest of documents — far more quickly than you could *read* through the document, at least.

Under default conditions the spelling checker works automatically, telling you of your spelling mistakes in two ways:

● highlighting the words it considers mis-spelled with a wavy red underline

● changing the spelling button on the status bar from its normal 📖 to 📖 — complete with a cross.

MAKING USE OF WORD'S SPELLING CHECKER

Your course of action following notification of a spelling depends on

● whether you want to change the word at all (maybe it's a person's name, or a scientific word) which is actually spelled correctly but Word hasn't recognized it

● whether you want to add the word to Word's dictionary, so it won't be flagged up the next time you type it in

● whether you want to correct the spelling of a mis-spelled word

● whether you want to have the word corrected automatically by Word from now on.

Basic steps:

IF THE WORD IS CORRECT

1 Click the underlined word with your right mouse button

2 Choose **Ignore All** from the drop-down menu — the underlined highlighting is removed from the word (and any other entries of the word)

Tip:

If you type a word regularly which Word incorrectly assumes is mis-spelled, add it to Word's dictionary. From the drop-down menu displayed above, choose Add. From now on, Word recognizes the word and ignores it

① Click a correctly spelled word, that is underline highlighted, with your right mouse button

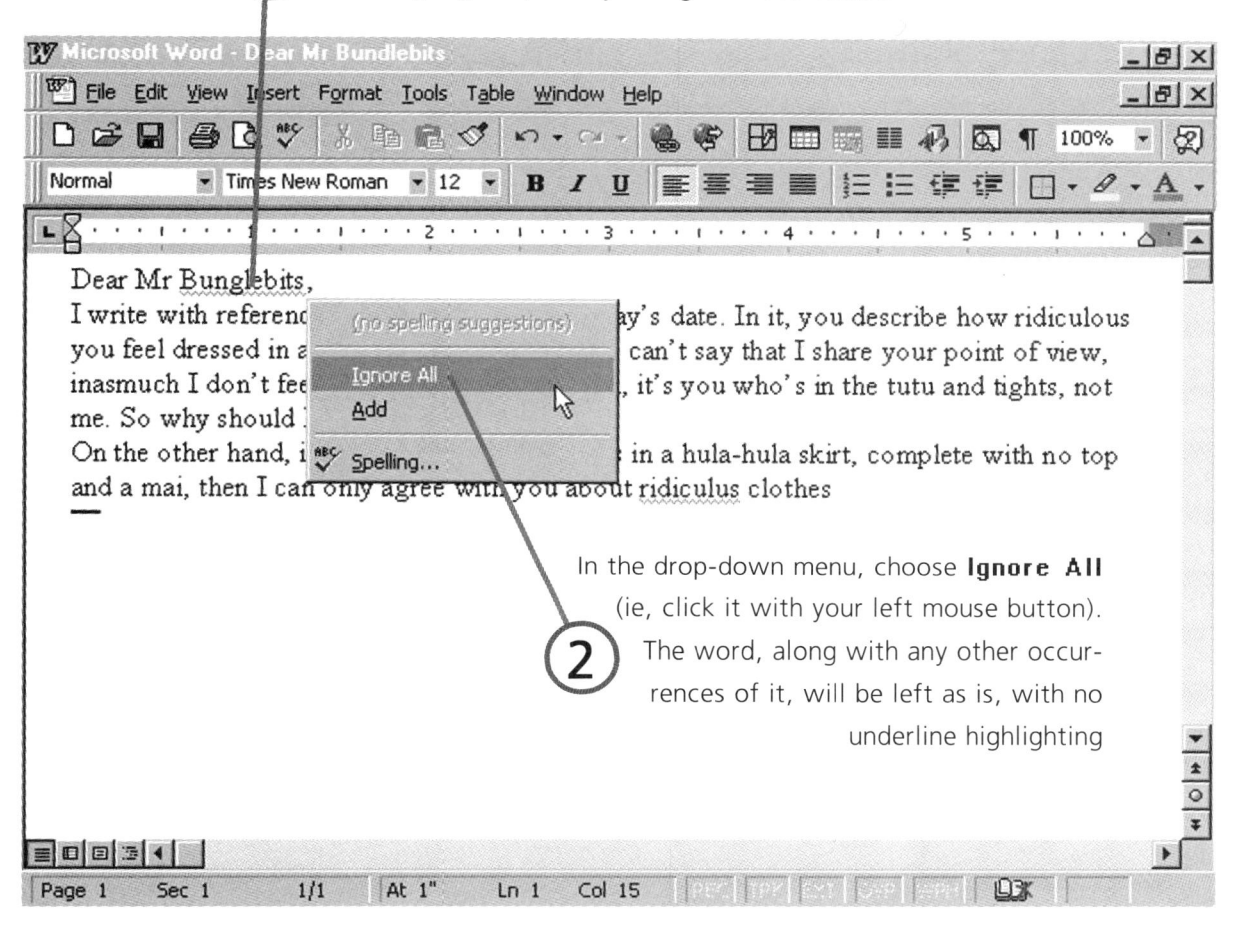

② In the drop-down menu, choose **Ignore All** (ie, click it with your left mouse button). The word, along with any other occurrences of it, will be left as is, with no underline highlighting

Take note:

While Word's spelling checker is an extremely useful tool, you must remember that it only compares words in your document with the words in an electronic list called a dictionary. If the words in your document are mis-spelled in-context but in fact make properly spelled words out-of-context, Word *still* assumes they are spelled correctly. Thus, Word thinks *with complements* (instead of *with compliments*) is OK. Remember the anonymous ode:

> I have a spelling checker – it came with my pea see
> It plainly marques four my revue mistakes eye cannot sea
> I've run this poem threw it, I'm shore your pleased too no
> Its let a perfect inn it's weigh – my checquer told me sew

Spelling (contd)

Basic steps:

IF THE WORD IS INCORRECT

1 Click the underlined word with your right mouse button

2 Choose the correct spelling of the word from the drop-down menu

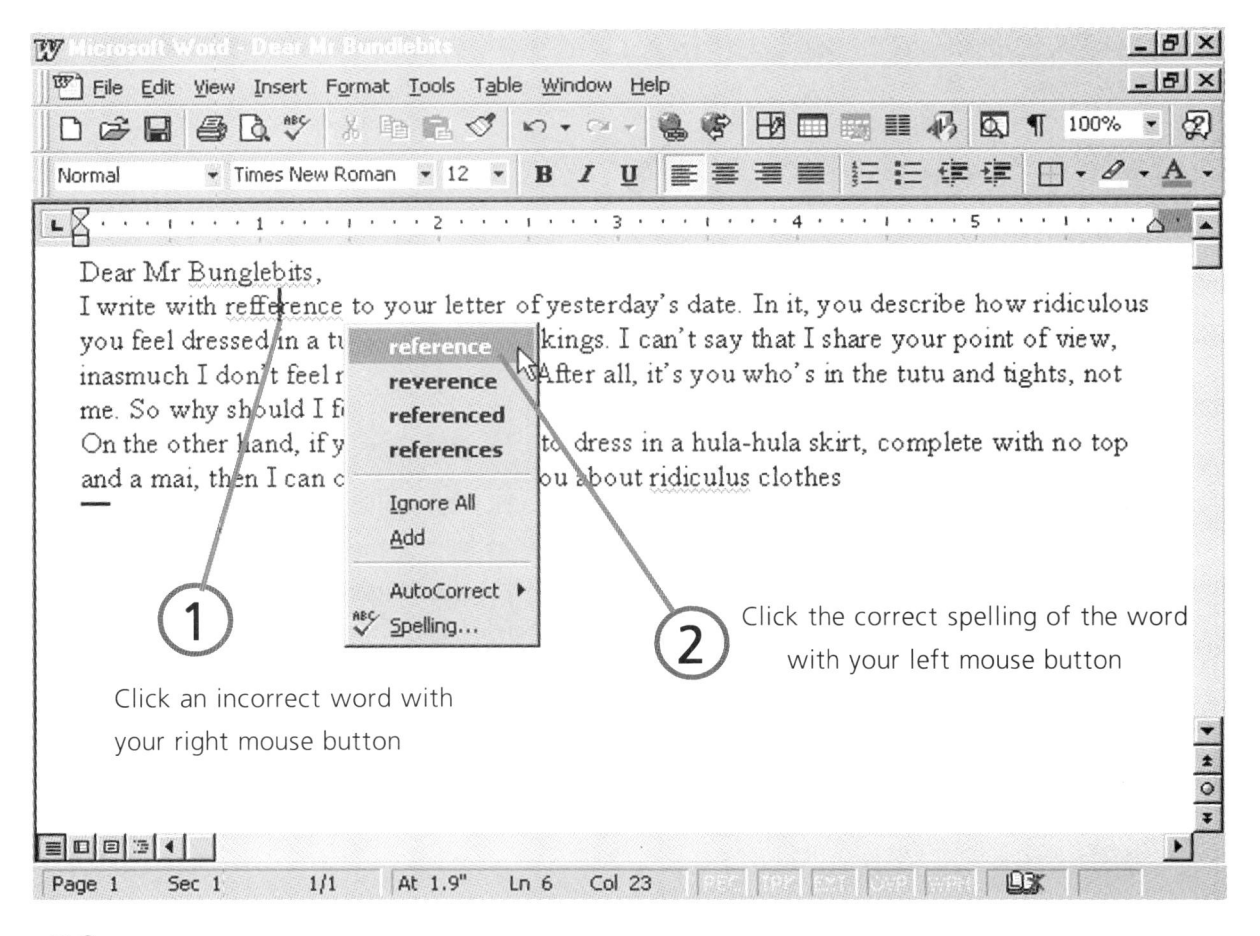

Tip:

You can have Word correct your bad spelling on-the-fly with AutoCorrect. If there's a word in particular you regularly misspell, click on it with your right mouse button and choose Spelling from the drop-down menu. In the resultant dialog box type or choose the correct spelling and click AutoCorrect. From now on Word will correct it for you immediately as you type it incorrectly

① Click an incorrect word with your right mouse button

② Click the correct spelling of the word with your left mouse button

CHANGING SPELLING OPTIONS

1 Choose **Tools→Options** to call up the **Options** dialog box

2 Click the **Spelling and Grammar** tab

3 Change options to suit, then click **OK**

Word gives you several options to change how it monitors and controls your spelling.

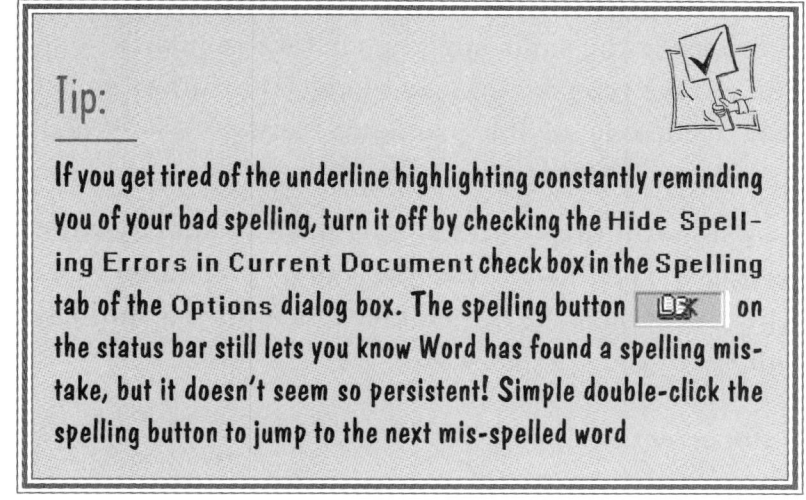

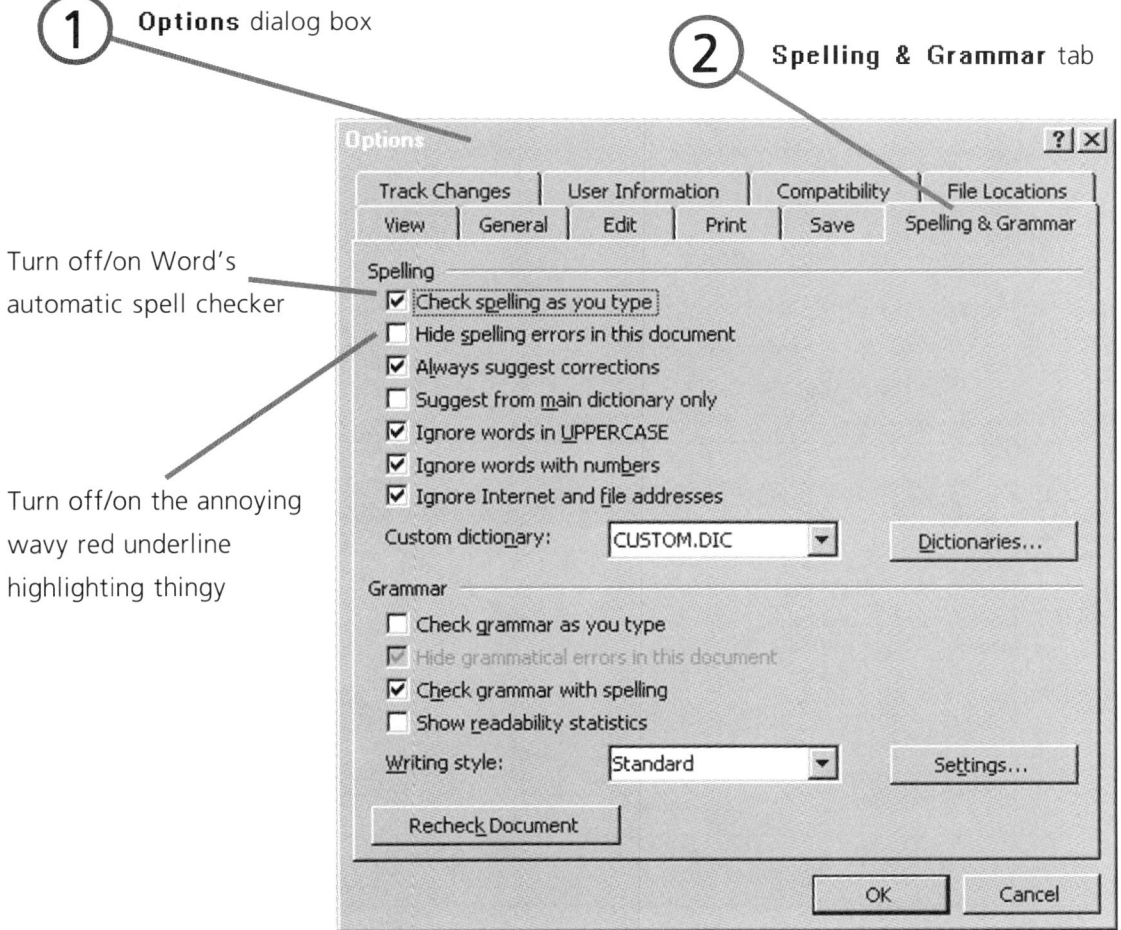

> **Tip:**
>
> If you get tired of the underline highlighting constantly reminding you of your bad spelling, turn it off by checking the Hide Spelling Errors in Current Document check box in the Spelling tab of the Options dialog box. The spelling button on the status bar still lets you know Word has found a spelling mistake, but it doesn't seem so persistent! Simple double-click the spelling button to jump to the next mis-spelled word

(1) **Options** dialog box

(2) **Spelling & Grammar** tab

Turn off/on Word's automatic spell checker

Turn off/on the annoying wavy red underline highlighting thingy

99

AutoCorrect

If you make the same spelling mistake regularly — say you always type *anf* instead of *and* (the author's problem; well, one of his problems, anyway) — Word's AutoCorrect feature is a boon.

To use AutoCorrect you simply have to specify which mistakes you make, and the correct spelling. Then whenever you make the mistake it is replaced automatically with the correct word.

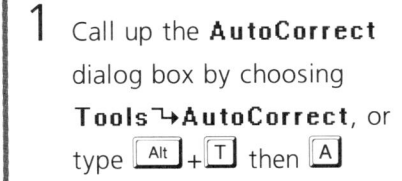

AutoCorrect dialog box

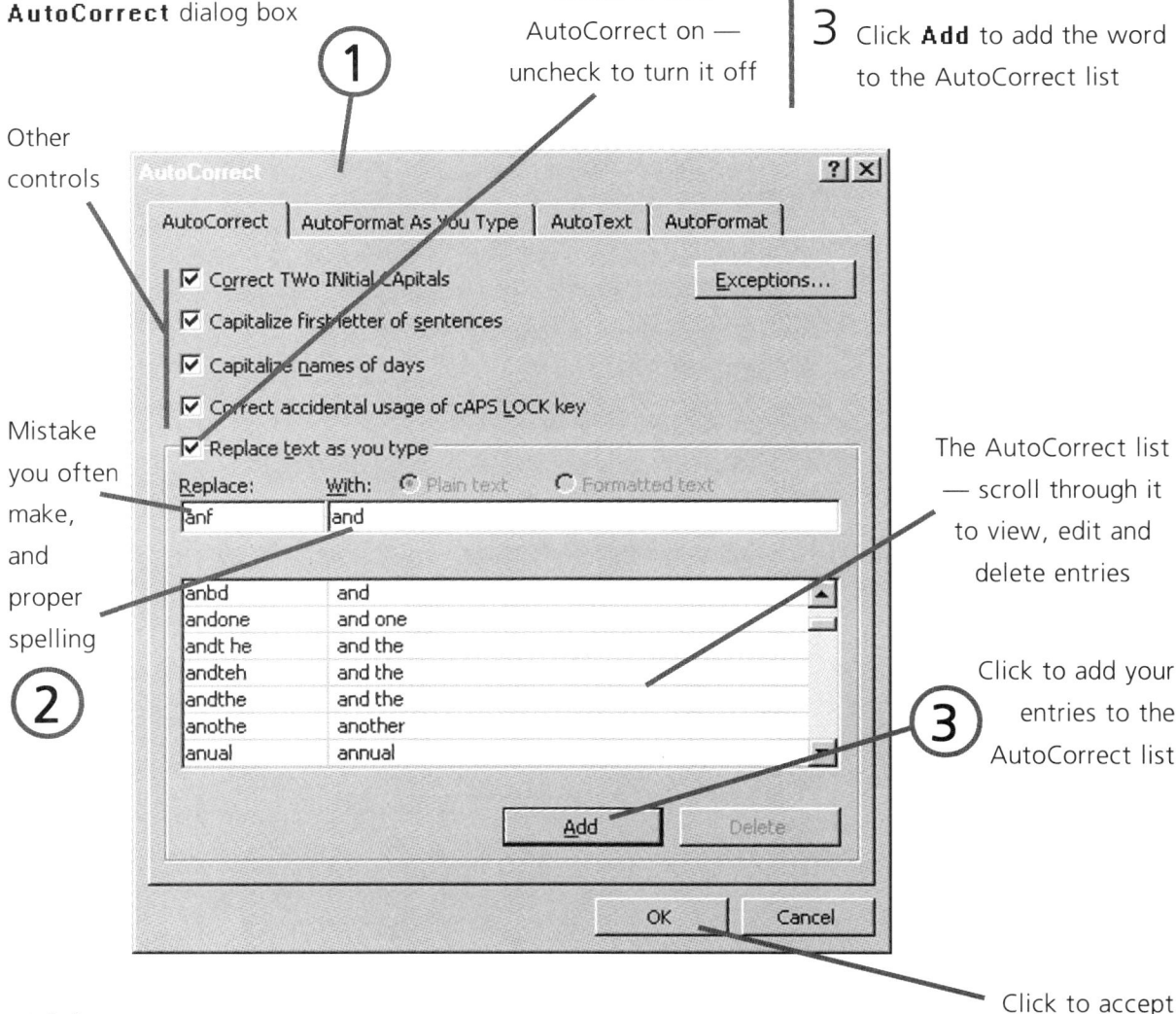

Basic steps:

1. Call up the **AutoCorrect** dialog box by choosing **Tools⇝AutoCorrect**, or type [Alt]+[T] then [A]
2. Type in the spelling mistake you often make into the **Replace** entry box, and the proper spelling in the **With** entry box
3. Click **Add** to add the word to the AutoCorrect list

Check to turn AutoCorrect on — uncheck to turn it off

Other controls

Mistake you often make, and proper spelling

The AutoCorrect list — scroll through it to view, edit and delete entries

Click to add your entries to the AutoCorrect list

Click to accept

100

Tip:

Remember that you can create an AutoCorrect entry direct from the drop-down menu as you click an underline highlighted word with your right mouse button..

If you find that Word is finding the same spelling error repeatedly, follow the tip on page 98 to enter it automatically into the AutoCorrect list

Tip:

AutoCorrect can be used to insert chunks of text into a document when you type a simple keyword. For example, a phrase like *Yours sincerely,* at the end of a letter can have a keyword such as *ys*. As you type *ys* and hit the Enter or ↵ key, Word automatically replaces it with the longer phrase.

Phrases upto 255 characters (including spaces and punctuation) are possible, so a considerable amount of *boilerplate text* (as it's known in the computer business) can be accessed using AutoCorrect. For longer boilerplate text, and items you access less frequently, use Word's AutoText feature instead of AutoCorrect (see over)

Take note:

Word detects when you have finished a word — hence knows when to replace it, if it has an AutoCorrect entry — when an end-of-word specifier (usually a space) occurs.

So if the spelling error is followed by another letter, Word doesn't recognise the mistake and cannot correct it with AutoCorrect

Tip:

Not only text can be replaced by AutoCorrect entries. Graphics can be included; as can all formatting such as emboldening, sections, borders and shades and so on.

Put your company letterhead into an AutoCorrect entry, and make light work of typing letters

AutoText

Word has the ability to greatly speed-up the entering of text you regularly use in the guise of AutoText.

AutoCorrect, of course (see previous pages), allows you to do this as an automatic — on-the-fly as-you-type — feature. If you don't want it to occur automatically but instead want manual control over automatic insertion of entries, use AutoText.

To use an AutoText entry in your documents, you first have to create it.

Basic steps:

CREATING AN ENTRY

1 Type the text, select it, then choose **Insert ↳ AutoText ↳ New**, or type `Alt` + `F3` This calls up the **AutoText** dialog box

2 Enter a new name for the entry (if the default name isn't suitable)

3 Click **OK** to accept the new entry

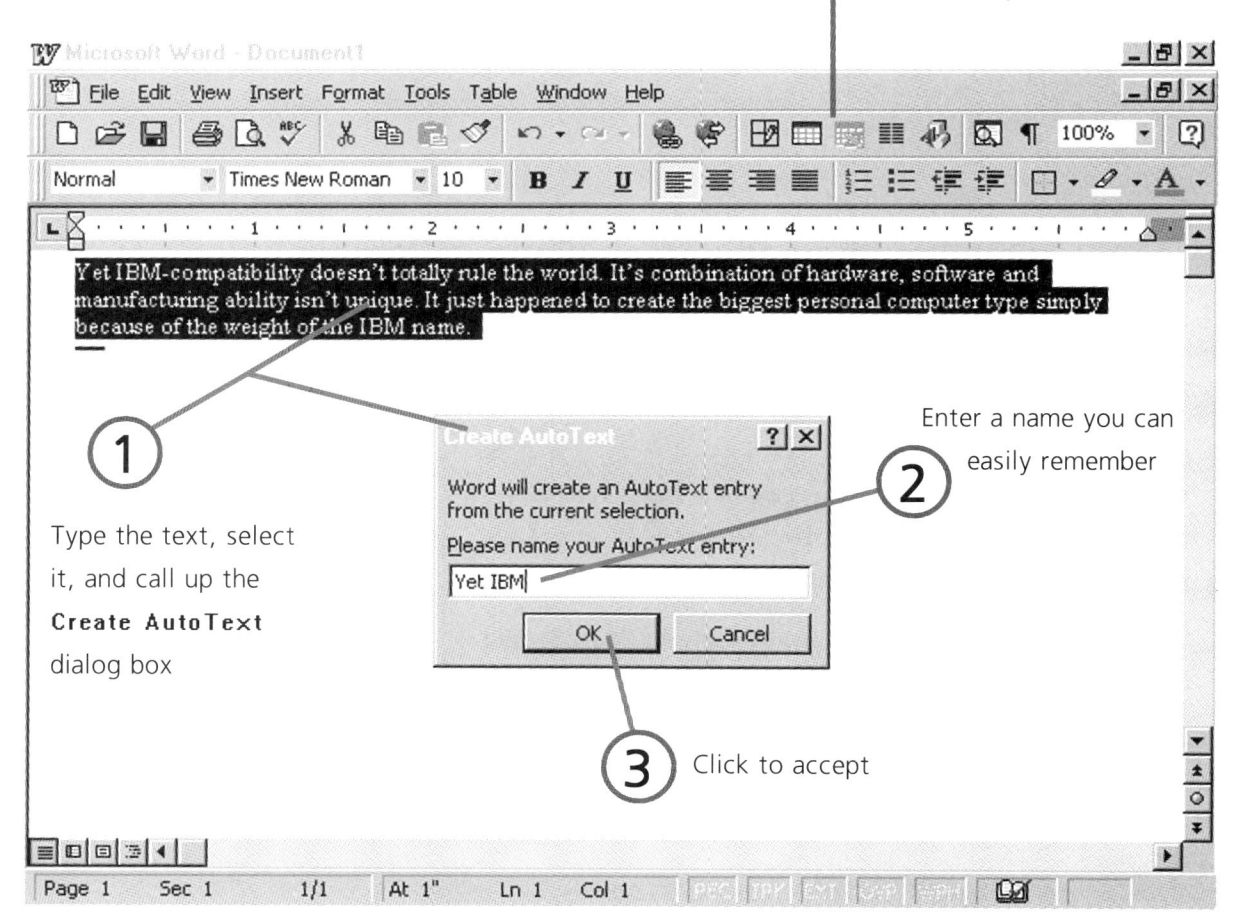

① Type the text, select it, and call up the **Create AutoText** dialog box

② Enter a name you can easily remember

③ Click to accept

USING AN ENTRY

1 When you want to insert an AutoText entry into your document, type in the entry name you previously allocated — as you do a screentip is displayed which shows the first few words of the AutoText entry associated with the name

2 Hit `F3`. The entry is inserted into the document

...then press `F3`

Once your entry is created, you can use it wherever and whenever you want in your documents.

When you want to insert an AutoText entry, simply type in the entry name...

ScreenTip shows you the AutoText entry associated with the name

Tip:

As with AutoCorrect, the entries you create for AutoText can include graphical items and text formatting. Like AutoCorrect entries, too, you can use AutoText to insert boilerplate text into your documents.

In fact, the only *real* difference between AutoText and AutoCorrect as far as the ordinary user — you — is concerned, is how the entries are inserted into your documents.

AutoCorrect entries are inserted automatically, as soon as the entry name is typed.

AutoText entries are inserted semi-automatically — *you* have to specify that the entry name be replaced with the entry.

They each have their uses

Outlining

We saw an outline view back on page 17. Outlining is another way of looking at your Word documents and, what's more important, is the best way of controlling how the various text parts within a document are organized and arranged.

Easiest way to see how outlining works is with an example. Let's say you've been working long and hard at a chapter of your book. It's a long chapter and technically quite involved — so involved that you're sure there's a problem somewhere, but you're not exactly sure *where*.

Basic steps:

1 Choose **View→Outline**, or type `Alt`+`V` then `O`, or (best) click the Outline button at the lower-left corner of the document window. Your document is displayed in outline view

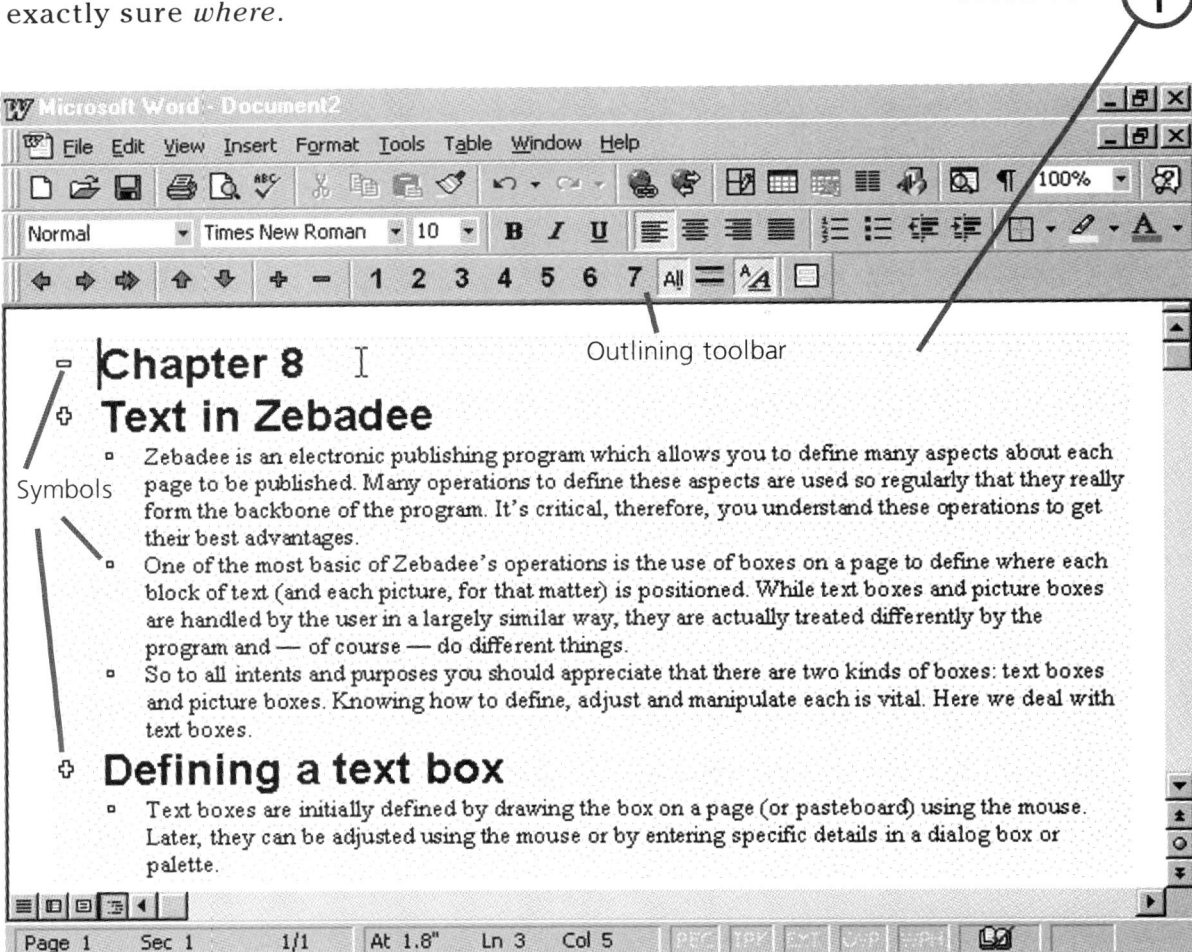

A document in outline view

Outlining toolbar

Symbols

Chapter 8
Text in Zebadee

- Zebadee is an electronic publishing program which allows you to define many aspects about each page to be published. Many operations to define these aspects are used so regularly that they really form the backbone of the program. It's critical, therefore, you understand these operations to get their best advantages.
- One of the most basic of Zebadee's operations is the use of boxes on a page to define where each block of text (and each picture, for that matter) is positioned. While text boxes and picture boxes are handled by the user in a largely similar way, they are actually treated differently by the program and — of course — do different things.
- So to all intents and purposes you should appreciate that there are two kinds of boxes: text boxes and picture boxes. Knowing how to define, adjust and manipulate each is vital. Here we deal with text boxes.

Defining a text box

- Text boxes are initially defined by drawing the box on a page (or pasteboard) using the mouse. Later, they can be adjusted using the mouse or by entering specific details in a dialog box or palette.

Outline symbols

In outline view, your document is displayed with its headings and body text displayed with various symbols to their left. The symbols indicate what is associated with the various parts of a document.

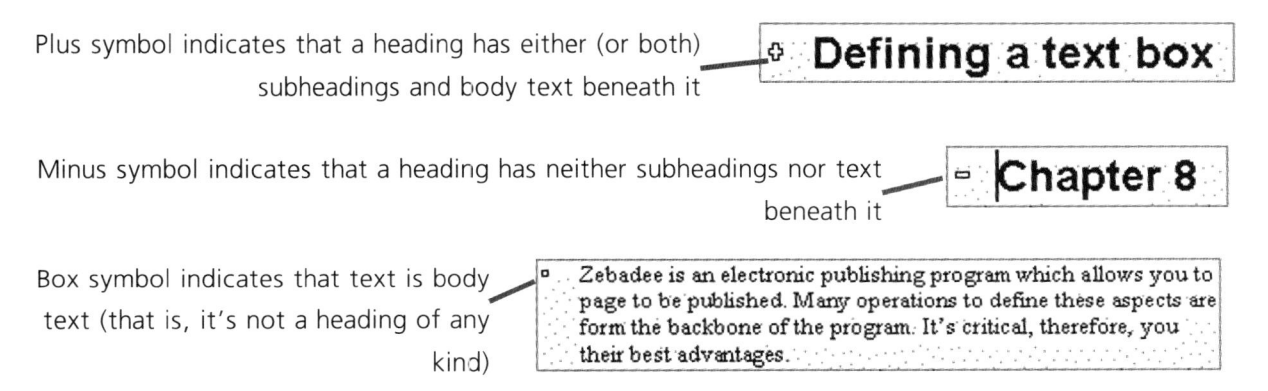

Plus symbol indicates that a heading has either (or both) subheadings and body text beneath it — ✣ **Defining a text box**

Minus symbol indicates that a heading has neither subheadings nor text beneath it — ▫ **Chapter 8**

Box symbol indicates that text is body text (that is, it's not a heading of any kind) — ▫ Zebadee is an electronic publishing program which allows you to page to be published. Many operations to define these aspects are form the backbone of the program. It's critical, therefore, you their best advantages.

Outlining toolbar

Along with outline view comes the Outlining toolbar, with its new buttons

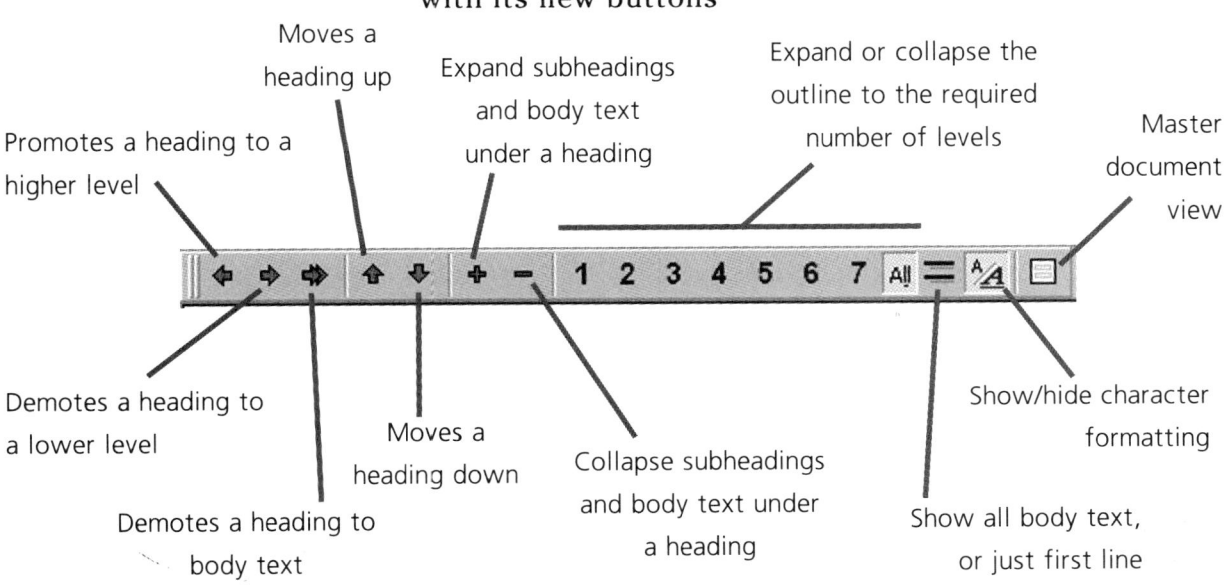

- Promotes a heading to a higher level
- Moves a heading up
- Expand subheadings and body text under a heading
- Expand or collapse the outline to the required number of levels
- Master document view
- Demotes a heading to a lower level
- Moves a heading down
- Collapse subheadings and body text under a heading
- Show/hide character formatting
- Demotes a heading to body text
- Show all body text, or just first line

Outlining (contd)

In essence, outlining allows you to:

- get an overall view of your document — to various degrees of complexity

- easily move headings around (while their associated subheadings and body text parts move automatically with them).

Another example can show you.

Document with character formatting hidden and levels collapsed to level 1

Basic steps:

1 Click the Show/hide character formatting button and the Expand/collapse to level 1 button on the Outlining toolbar.

   Now all character formatting has gone, and only the first level headings are displayed

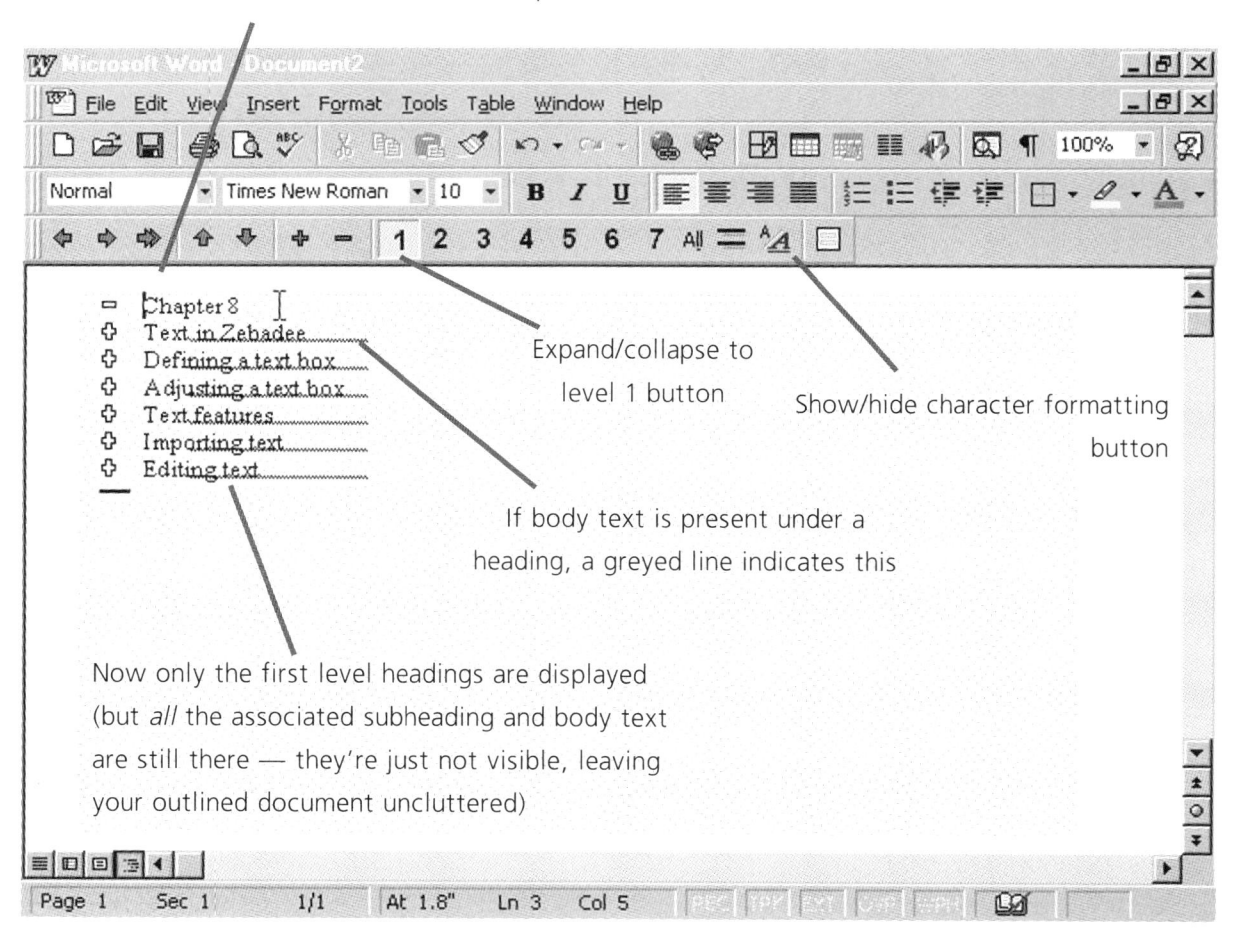

Expand/collapse to level 1 button

Show/hide character formatting button

If body text is present under a heading, a greyed line indicates this

Now only the first level headings are displayed (but *all* the associated subheading and body text are still there — they're just not visible, leaving your outlined document uncluttered)

2. Select the headings *Defining a text box*, and *Adjusting a text box*. Now click the Demote heading button ⇨ on the Outlining toolbar

3. Select the heading *Editing text*, then click the Move heading up button ⇧

From this position, let's now say you realise that:

● the level 1 headings *Defining a text box*, and *Adjusting a text box* really *should* be level 2 headings

● the heading *Editing text* should be before the heading *Importing text*.

With outlining, that's easily done.

Headings demoted to next level down

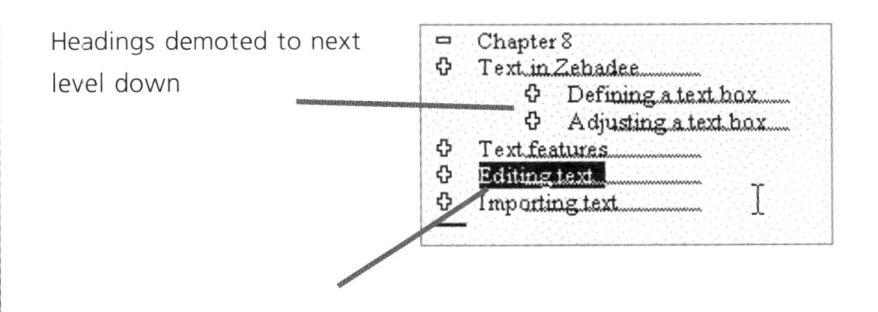

- Chapter 8
- ✛ Text in Zebadee
  - ✛ Defining a text box
  - ✛ Adjusting a text box
- ✛ Text features
- ✛ Editing text
- ✛ Importing text

Heading moved up

Take note:

Remember that in outline view it may *look* as though your text has disappeared but it hasn't — if you expand the outline again your text will come back (phew!)

Tip:

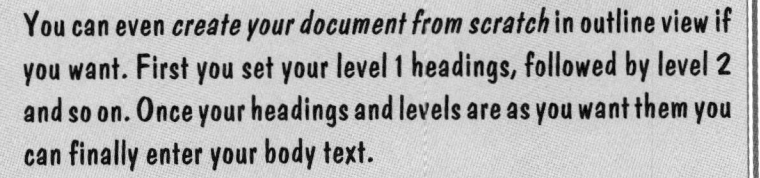

You can even *create your document from scratch* in outline view if you want. First you set your level 1 headings, followed by level 2 and so on. Once your headings and levels are as you want them you can finally enter your body text.

Writing a document in this manner means your document can be logically structured

Tip:

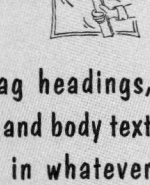

You can drag headings, subheadings and body text around too, in whatever state of expansion or collapse they are — just like drag-and-drop editing, except more powerful. Much more powerful!

Tables

Earlier in the book we saw how to produce a simple table using tab stops. This is fine for just that — simple tables — but for anything more complex than just a couple of rows and columns things can be made much easier with Word's in-built table feature.

Tables are made up by a collection of *cells*, in rows and columns. Word displays a table in *gridlines* (dotted lines around all the cells of a table) which are not printed and are merely provided on-screen for guidance.

You can add text or graphical elements to cells of a Word table, and you can format text in any character or paragraph format as usual.

You create a table in one of two ways:

- from the **Insert Table** dialog box
- with the Table button on the Standard toolbar.

Basic steps:

INSERT TABLE DIALOG BOX

1 Position the insertion point where you want to create a table, then choose **Table↪Insert Table**, or type [Alt]+[A] then [I]. This calls up the **Insert Table** dialog box

2 Enter the numbers of columns and rows you want

3 Click **OK** to create the table — Word displays the empty table as dotted gridlines

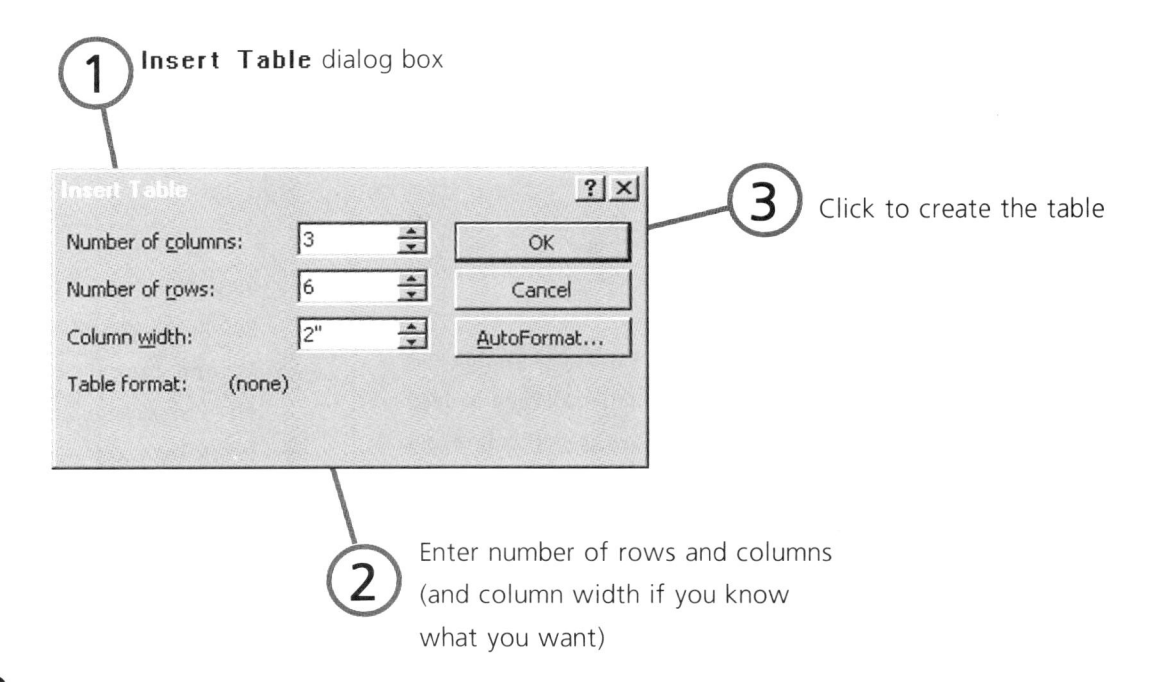

1. **Insert Table** dialog box

3. Click to create the table

2. Enter number of rows and columns (and column width if you know what you want)

INSERT TABLE BUTTON

1 Position the insertion point where you want to create a table, then click the Insert Table button 🏛 on the Standard toolbar

2 Drag across the drop-down grid to select the number of columns and rows you want, then let go the mouse button

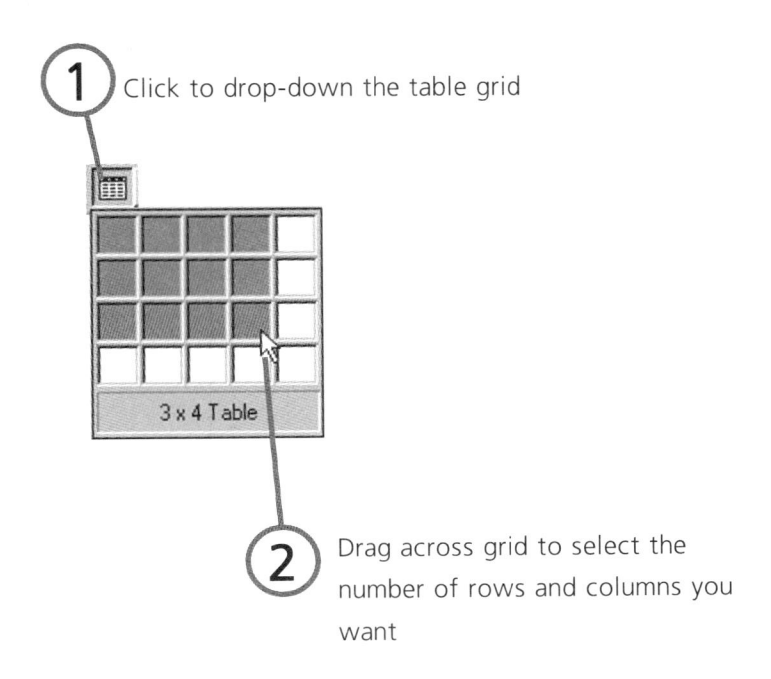

(1) Click to drop-down the table grid

3 x 4 Table

(2) Drag across grid to select the number of rows and columns you want

The insertion point is positioned at the top-left cell in the table ready for you to enter text. You move around in a table by clicking the mouse in another cell, tabbing with the `Tab` key, or pressing the ↑↓←→ keys in the direction you want to move.

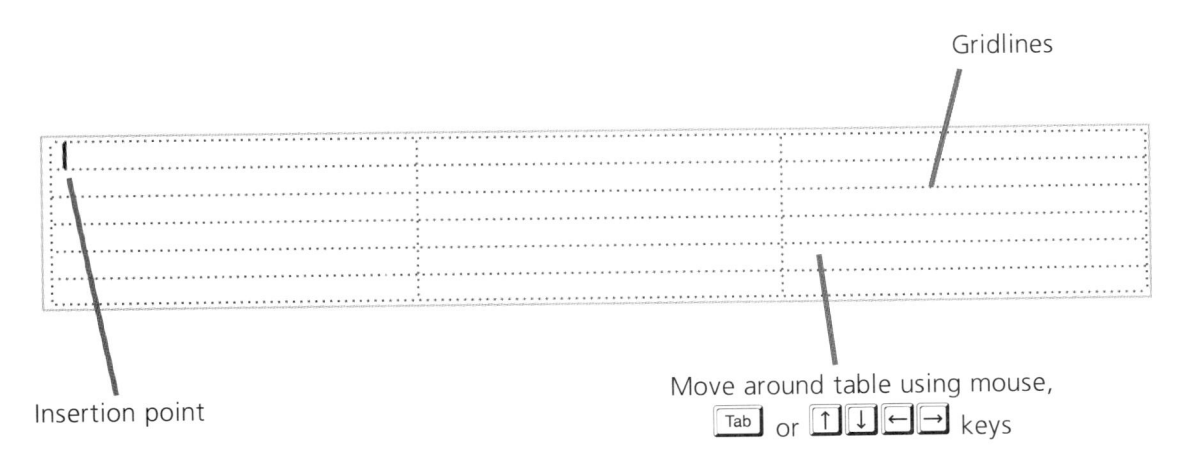

Gridlines

Insertion point

Move around table using mouse, `Tab` or ↑↓←→ keys

109

Tables (contd)

Once you've created a table you can change it to suit. You can drag column widths and indents from the document ruler (bottom) and you can drag a column gridline left or right to suit directly from the table.

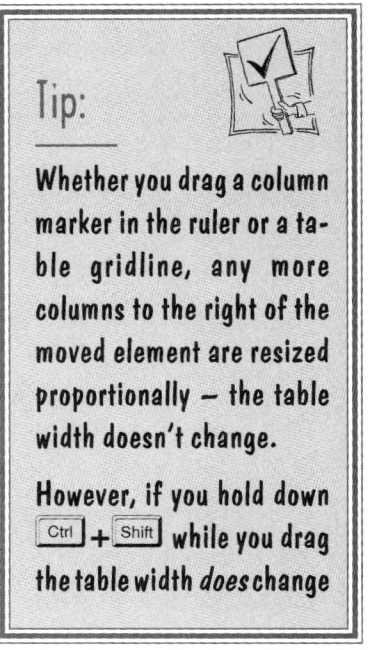

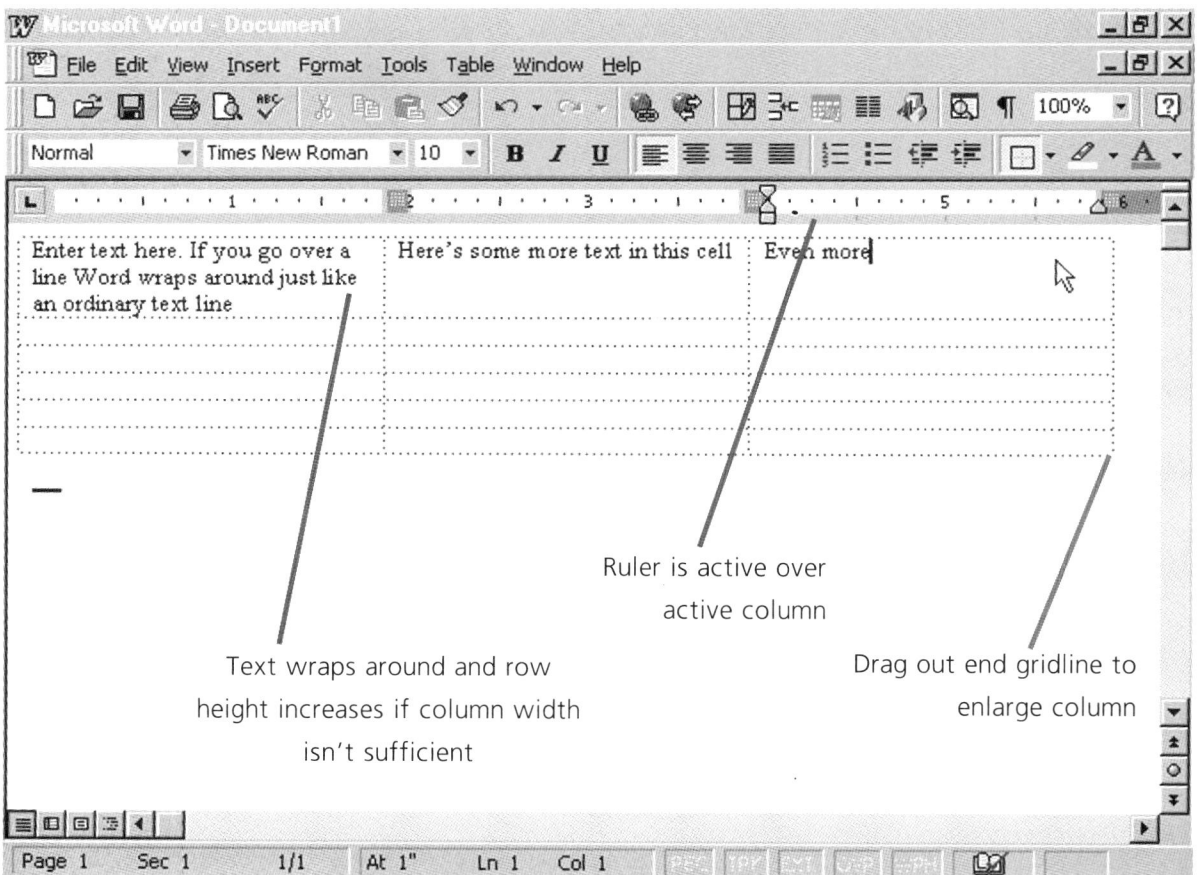

> **Tip:**
>
> Whether you drag a column marker in the ruler or a table gridline, any more columns to the right of the moved element are resized proportionally — the table width doesn't change.
>
> However, if you hold down Ctrl + Shift while you drag the table width *does* change

Text wraps around and row height increases if column width isn't sufficient

Ruler is active over active column

Drag out end gridline to enlarge column

Table conversions

Even if you've already entered text you can still convert it into a Word table. Simply make sure there are separators which Word recognises — commas or tabs between the items of text you want in each cell, and paragraph marks between each row — in the text.

Select the text you want to convert into a table — make sure it has adequate separators (1)

Capital spending	The Students are Revolting	The Food is Too	Cost (£)
Way too much	Henry	Spaghetti	99.99
Way, way too much	John	Eggs and bacon	4.50
Way, way, way too much	Wilhelmina	Stew	1.38

(2) Converted into a table

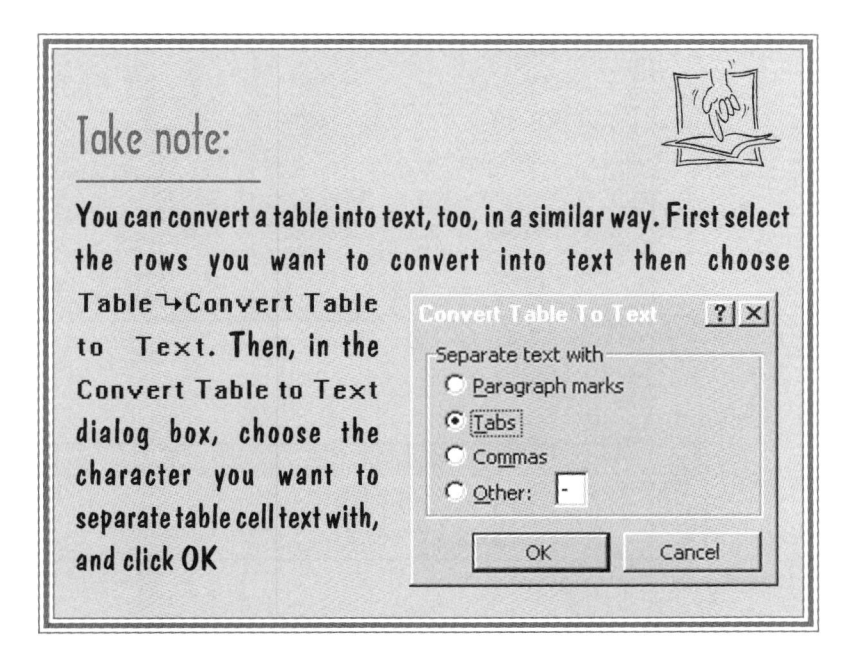

Basic steps:

1 Select the text you want to convert to a table

2 Click the Insert Table button on the Standard toolbar — that text is converted into a table

Take note:

You can convert a table into text, too, in a similar way. First select the rows you want to convert into text then choose Table→Convert Table to Text. Then, in the Convert Table to Text dialog box, choose the character you want to separate table cell text with, and click OK

Convert Table To Text
Separate text with:
○ Paragraph marks
● Tabs
○ Commas
○ Other: -

Table formatting

Once you've created a table, you can format it in all the usual ways. However, Word gives you several suggested options to format it automatically, which are both faster and (probably) better than doing it manually.

Basic steps:

1. Select the table and choose **Table → Table AutoFormat**, or type `Alt`+`A` then `F`, to call up the **Table AutoFormat** dialog box
2. From the list of formats select one you want
3. Click **OK** to accept this format onto your table

(1) **Table AutoFormat** dialog box

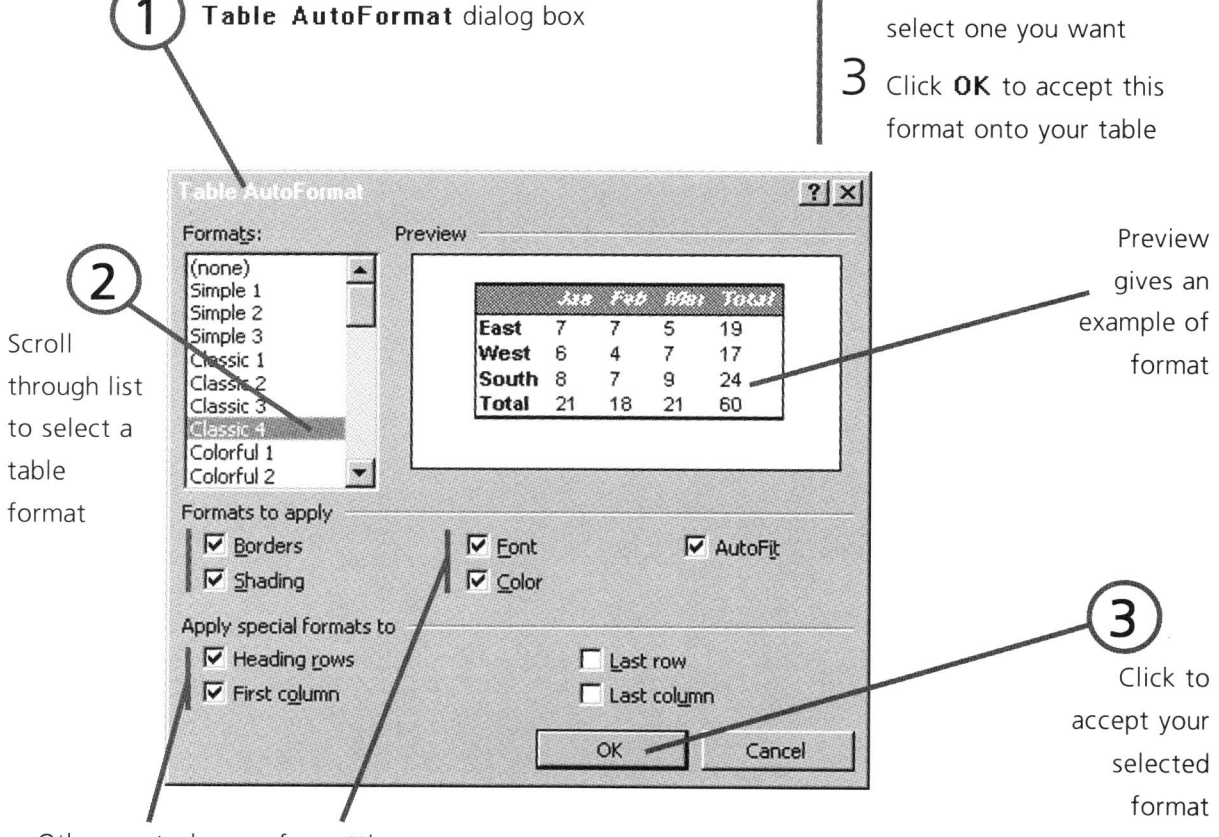

(2) Scroll through list to select a table format

Other controls over formatting

Preview gives an example of format

(3) Click to accept your selected format

The table on the previous page, formatted with the Classic 4 format above

112

Counting your words

When all your text has been entered into a document, it's often necessary to count the total number of words in it. Most publishers need a word count, for example, to give some idea of how long a document is, therefore a rough estimate of how many pages it'll fill in the finished publication.

Word can do much more than just count the words in a document, however.

Basic steps:

1. Choose **Tools→Word Count**, or type `Alt`+`T` then `W`, to call up the **Word Count** dialog box

Word Count dialog box

Document statistics

Click to close when you've finished reviewing your document's vital statistics

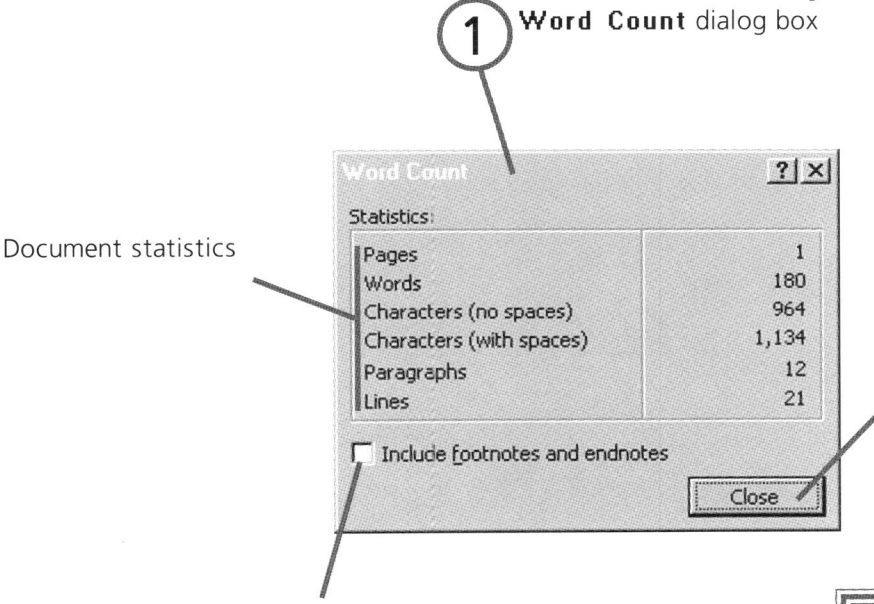

Check to include any footnotes and endnotes in the word count

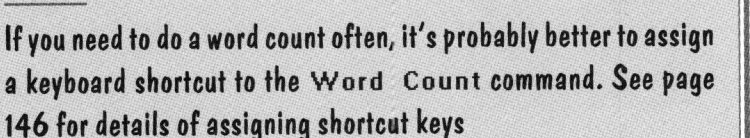

Tip:

If you need to do a word count often, it's probably better to assign a keyboard shortcut to the Word Count command. See page 146 for details of assigning shortcut keys

Tip:

If you select text prior to calling up the Word Count dialog box, only the selected text (pages, words, characters, paragraphs and lines) is included

113

Graphics

You can import a graphic created in another application into a Word document. There are several kinds of graphic files you may want to import, but the principle is the same, whatever the kind. Also, once imported, any graphic can be edited in several ways.

Basic steps:

IMPORTING A GRAPHIC

1 Position the insertion point where you want the graphic to be placed. Choose **Insert → Picture → From File**, or type `Alt` + `I` then `P`, then `F`

2 Locate the graphic you want in the **Insert Picture** dialog box and click **OK**. The graphic is imported to your document

Insert Picture dialog box

①

Locate graphic file you want to import

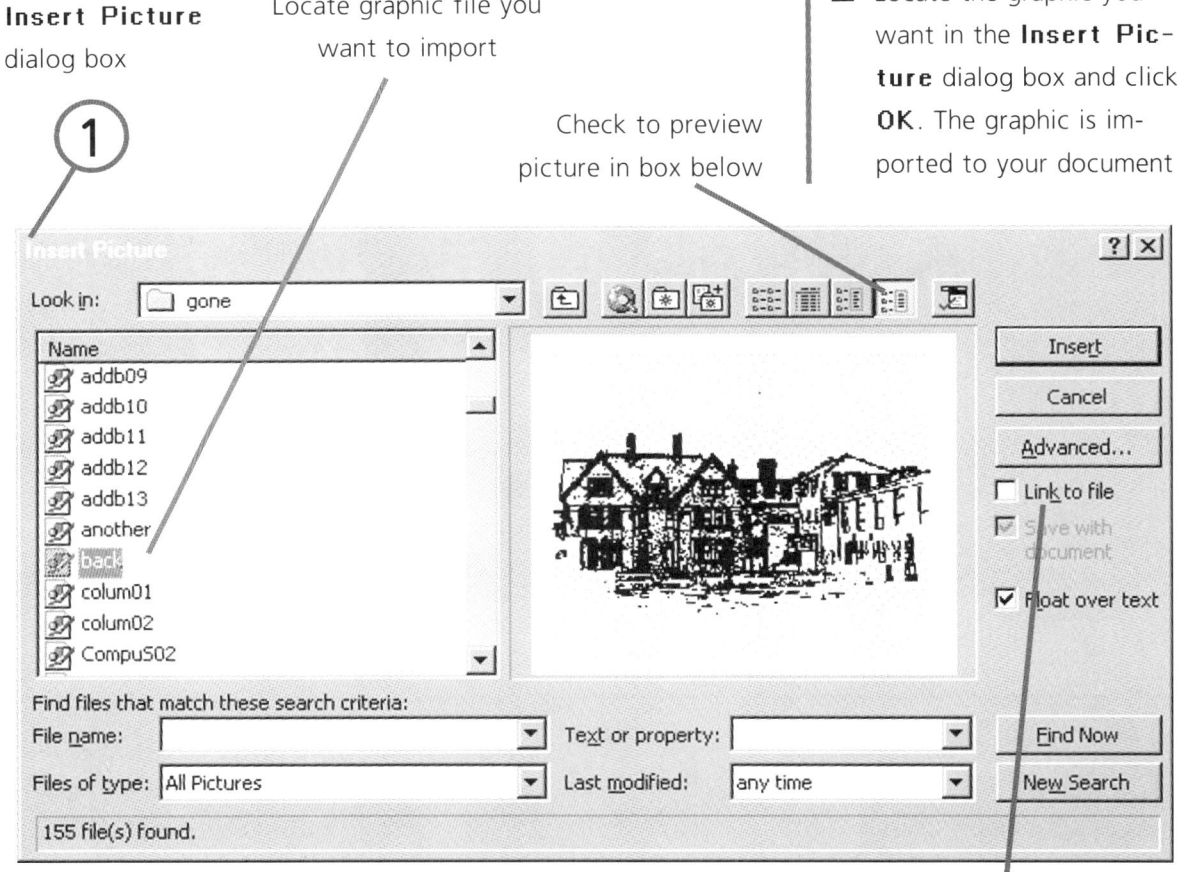

Check to preview picture in box below

You can create a link to a graphic file by checking here, such that the file itself is not imported (only its screen representation and details of the link). This keeps your Word document file size down, while Word refers to the link as it prints the document

114

Resizing a graphic

Once a graphic file has been imported into a Word document, editing is simple — the most basic form of editing (and the one most commonly undertaken) is resizing to suit the document

EDITING A GRAPHIC

1. Click a graphic in a Word document
2. Drag any of the box handles to adjust the size or shape

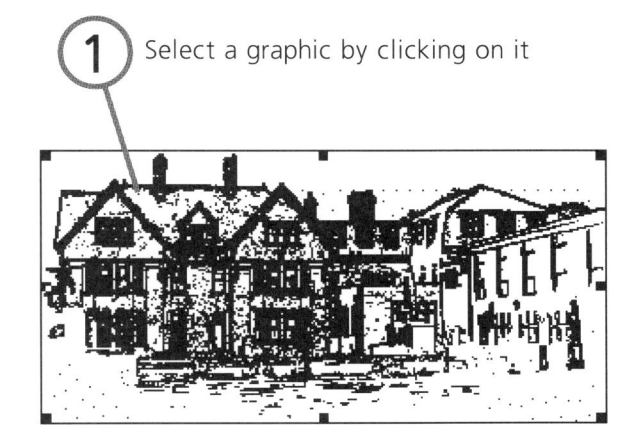

① Select a graphic by clicking on it

As you let go the mouse button, the graphic resizes itself

Drag a box handle to resize a graphic. Dragging a corner handle resizes the graphic proportionally. Dragging a middle handle resizes it disproportionately

Take note:

Word uses special files called graphics filters to let it import graphics files. While Windows bitmaps (with the extension .bmp), Windows metafiles (.wmf) and tag image file format files (.tif) are imported directly, you need filters (available from Microsoft) to import any other graphics file formats

Graphics (contd)

On install, Word has many clip art files that you can make use of, in the same way that you use your purpose-created graphics files.

Tip:

Look on your original CD-ROM installer for Word – there are many more clip art files on it

Basic steps:

1 Position the insertion point where you want the graphic to be placed. Choose **Insert↪Picture↪Clip Art**, or type **Alt**+**I** then **P**, then **C**

2 Locate the clip art you want in the **Microsoft Clip Gallery** dialog box and click **Insert**. The clip art is imported to your document

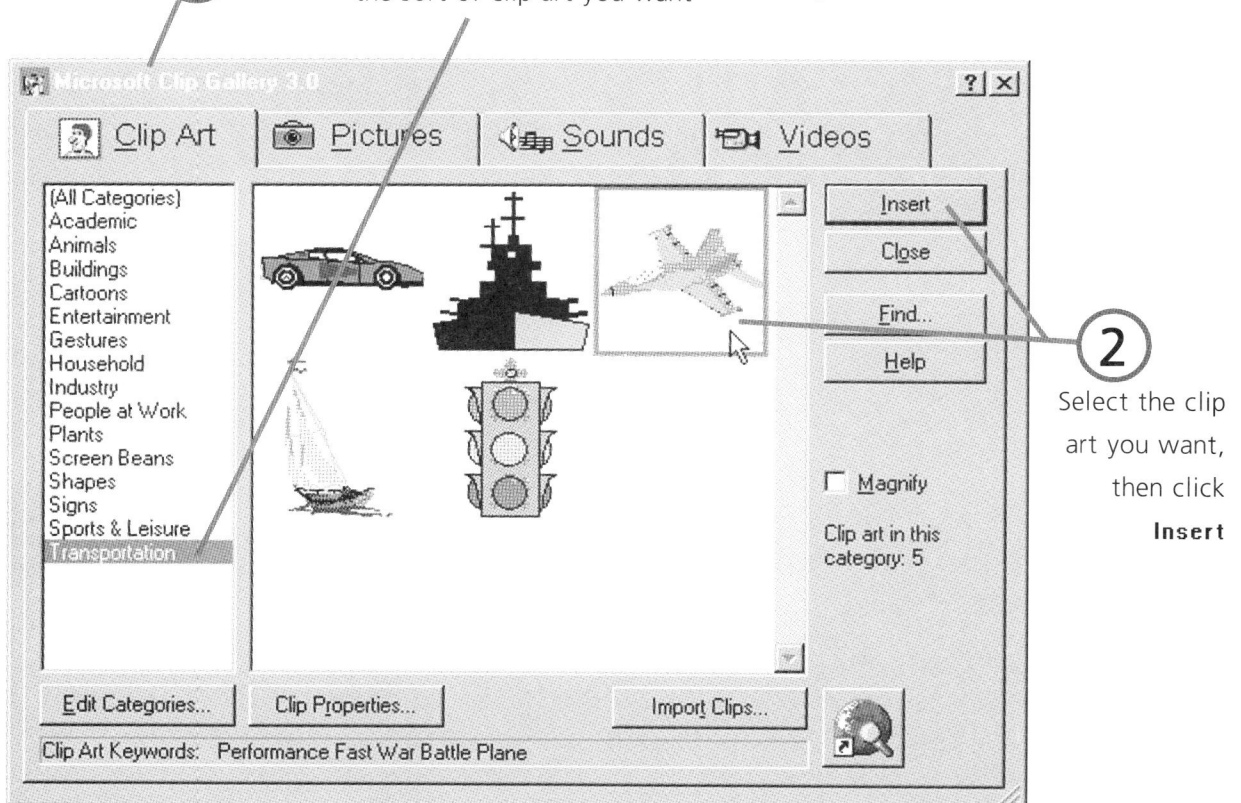

Microsoft Clip Gallery dialog box

Clip art is devided into categories — click the category corresponding to the sort of clip art you want

Select the clip art you want, then click **Insert**

Editing with the Picture toolbar

You can make use of the Picture toolbar in Word to edit graphics you have imported into a document

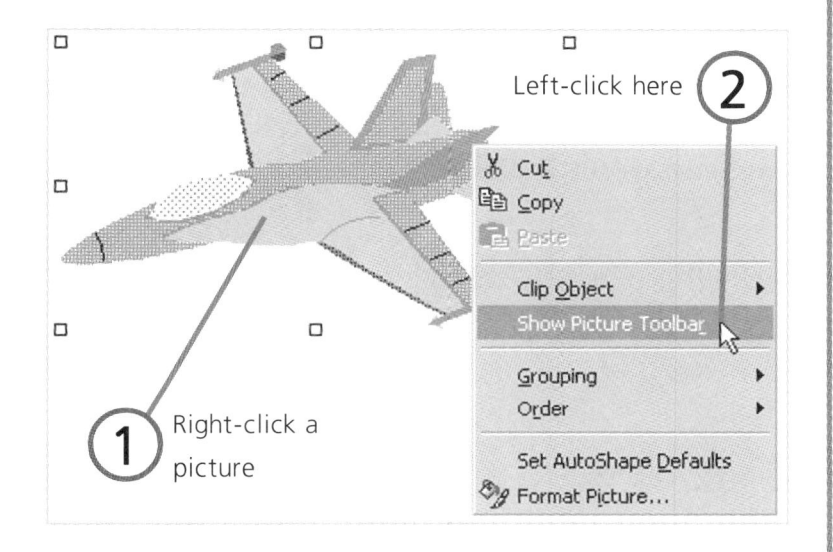

Left-click here ②

① Right-click a picture

Picture toolbar ③

Insert picture

Image control

More and less contrast

More and less brightness

Crop

Line style

Text wrapping

Format picture

Set transparent colour

Reset picture

Basic steps:

You can call up the Picture toolbar in one of two main ways:

1 Right-click the picture. In the resultant menu, choose **Show Picture Toolbar**

or:

2 Right-click any toolbar and check the Picture toolbar button (as on page 11)

then:

3 In the Picture toolbar, choose your weapons… err, no, tools, that's it

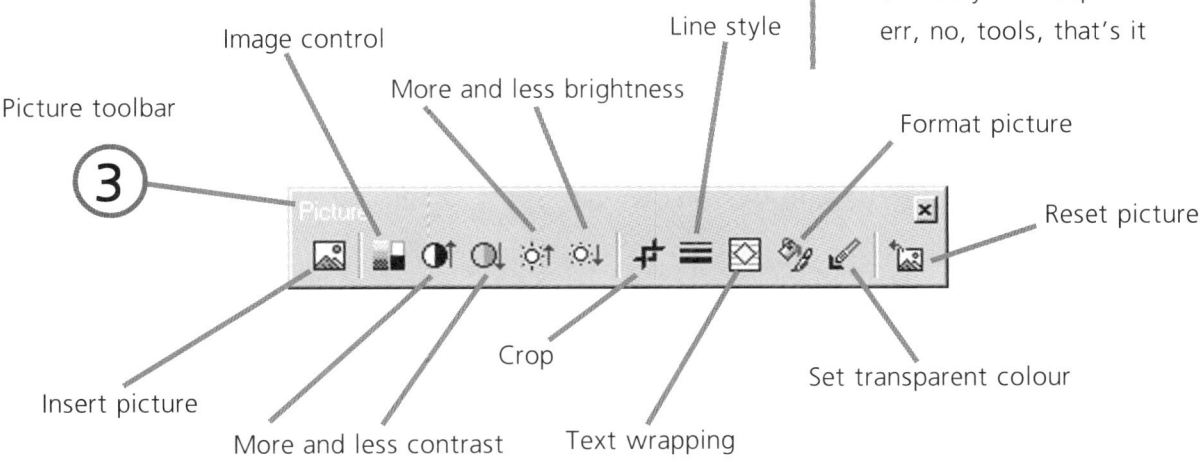

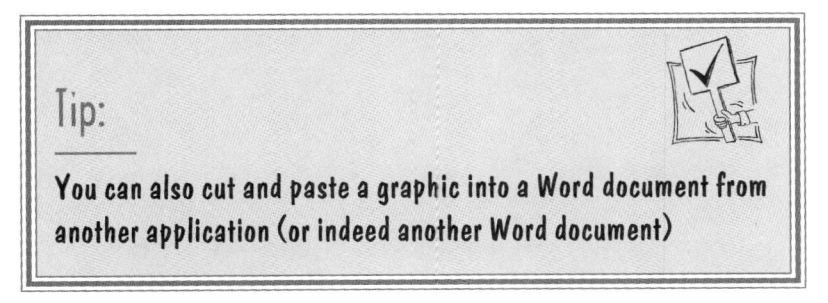

Tip:

You can also cut and paste a graphic into a Word document from another application (or indeed another Word document)

Summary for Section 5

- Use Word's powerful find and replace commands to search for and change text or even just formatting within your documents.

- Word's spelling checker can locate instances of mis-spelled words, but remember that a word mis-spelt in-context may still make a word spelled correctly out-of-context.

- Use AutoCorrect to correct spelling mistakes you regularly make, and automatically insert phrases at your abbreviated prompt.

- Use AutoText to insert phrases at your manual prompt.

- Remember that outlining helps you to organise your documents logically, and can be a boon when writing too.

- Tables in Word can be most effectively created with the **Table** command.

- You can import certain graphics files into your Word documents, then edit them in various ways.

6 Automatic formatting

Styles 120

Character and paragraph styles 123

Creating styles 124

More about styles 130

About templates 134

Creating a template 136

Summary for Section 6 138

Styles

Styles are the first method of automatic formatting. They are *extremely* important, because:

● their use makes it easy to define the formats which any particular paragraph has applied to it

● styles are groups of formats gathered together under one label (all the formats considered in Section 3 — and some others — can be gathered together and given just a single style name)

● if you apply a style to selected text *all* that text has the same formats applied to it simultaneously

● all you need to do to apply a style to selected text is choose that style from a drop-down list — the text is formatted with all the individual formats just by this one action

● you can use styles instantly, because any Word document has default styles already built in.

Basic steps:

1. Enter some text into a new Word document. Don't bother applying any character or paragraph formats yet. Make sure you type in a few paragraphs and make the top paragraph and some others single line ones — say headings or subheadings

2. Select the top heading of the document (you can simply click anywhere in the first paragraph) then click the Style drop-down list box of the Formatting toolbar

   Select the top paragraph of the entered text — you don't need to select the *whole* paragraph, you only need to click *in* it

```
Report into the oxidation of ferrous materials under load conditions
Oxidation defined
Under most circumstances, ferrous materials have iron in them. Iron is a substance which
combines with oxygen under certain conditions, forming a chemical compound called an
oxide.
Oxides are often of no concern — aluminum oxide for example is actually of some
benefit in aluminum substances because it creates a hard barrier against physical damage
to the rest of the material.
Ferrous oxide, on the other hand, is of concern. Ferrous oxide, aka iron oxide, aka rust is
of particular importance because:
it is unsightly
it is weaker than its non-oxidised counterpart.
Load conditions
Under certain conditions ferrous oxidation occurs more rapidly than under other
conditions. There are two critical conditions which, when applied together to ferrous
materials, make the likelihood of oxidation much greater. These two conditions are:
application of moisture in the form of water or water vapour
application of oxygen in the form of gas.
It is reasonably safe to say that if either of these conditions can be prevented then ferrous
oxidation does not occur.|
```

1. Enter unformatted text into your document

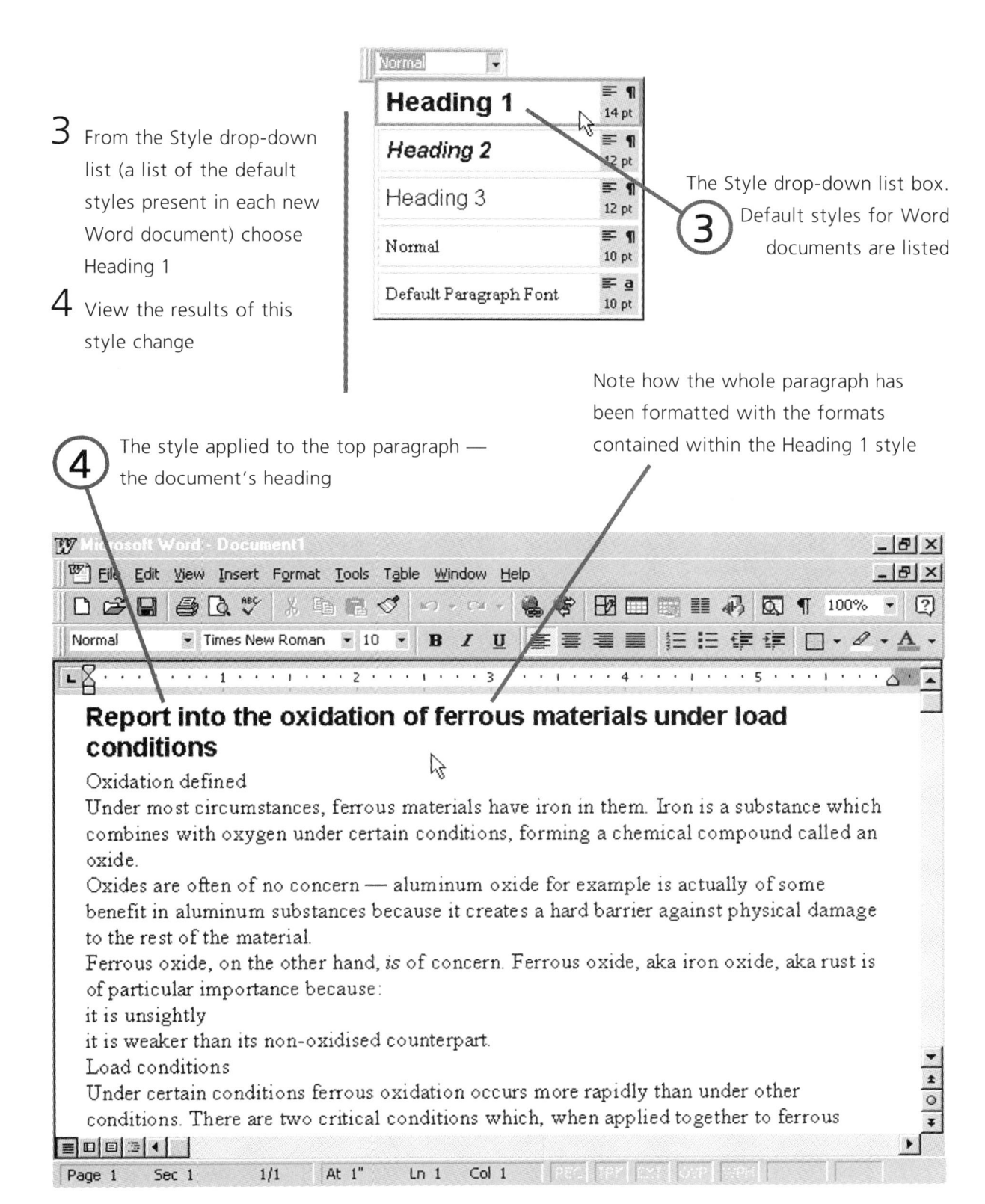

3 From the Style drop-down list (a list of the default styles present in each new Word document) choose Heading 1

4 View the results of this style change

The Style drop-down list box. Default styles for Word documents are listed

Note how the whole paragraph has been formatted with the formats contained within the Heading 1 style

The style applied to the top paragraph — the document's heading

Report into the oxidation of ferrous materials under load conditions

Oxidation defined

Under most circumstances, ferrous materials have iron in them. Iron is a substance which combines with oxygen under certain conditions, forming a chemical compound called an oxide.

Oxides are often of no concern — aluminum oxide for example is actually of some benefit in aluminum substances because it creates a hard barrier against physical damage to the rest of the material.

Ferrous oxide, on the other hand, *is* of concern. Ferrous oxide, aka iron oxide, aka rust is of particular importance because:

it is unsightly

it is weaker than its non-oxidised counterpart.

Load conditions

Under certain conditions ferrous oxidation occurs more rapidly than under other conditions. There are two critical conditions which, when applied together to ferrous

Styles (contd)

Basic steps:

5 Continue applying styles in the same way, trying out the other heading styles available

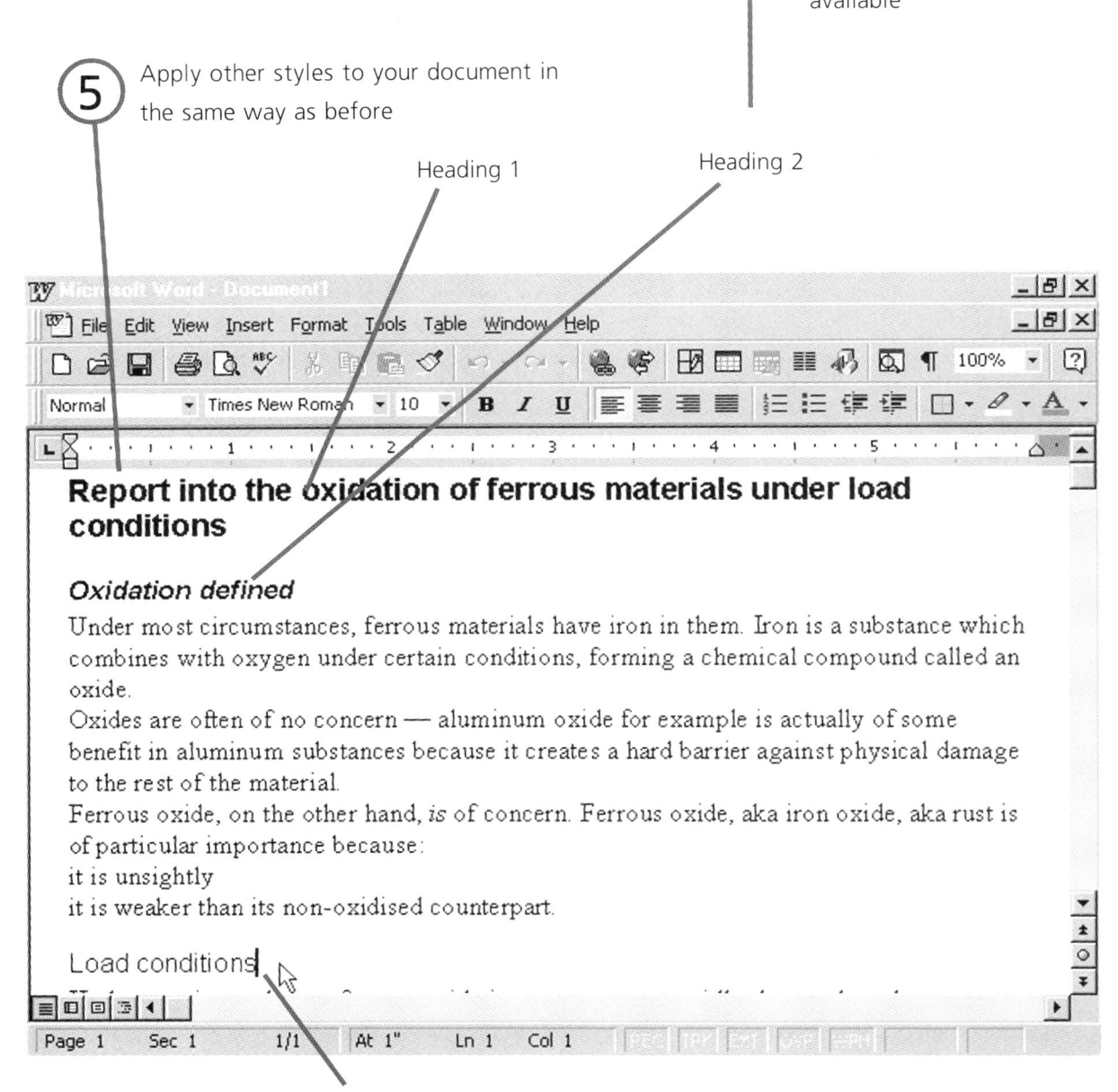

⑤ Apply other styles to your document in the same way as before

Heading 1

Heading 2

Report into the oxidation of ferrous materials under load conditions

Oxidation defined

Under most circumstances, ferrous materials have iron in them. Iron is a substance which combines with oxygen under certain conditions, forming a chemical compound called an oxide.

Oxides are often of no concern — aluminum oxide for example is actually of some benefit in aluminum substances because it creates a hard barrier against physical damage to the rest of the material.

Ferrous oxide, on the other hand, *is* of concern. Ferrous oxide, aka iron oxide, aka rust is of particular importance because:

it is unsightly

it is weaker than its non-oxidised counterpart.

Load conditions

Heading 3

Character and paragraph styles

There are two types of styles:

- character styles
- paragraph styles.

They are identified by their appearance in the Styles drop-down list of the Formatting toolbar. They work in essentially the same way (that is, you select the text to be stylised, then select the style) but what they do to the selected text differs.

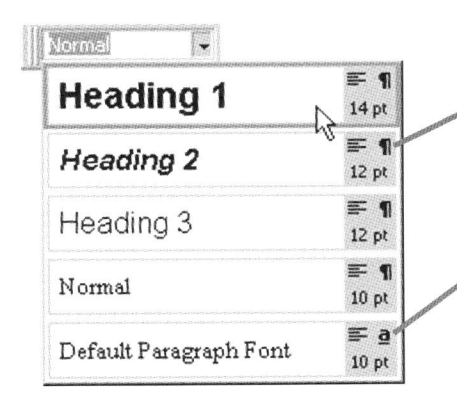

Paragraph styles are displayed with a paragraph symbol after them. When you apply a paragraph font to selected text, the *whole* paragraph has the formats applied

Character styles are displayed with a character symbol after them. When you apply a character style to text, only *selected* text (that is, *not* the whole paragraph — unless the whole paragraph is selected!) has the formats applied

Take note:

Styles are important for at least two reasons:

- because they speed up the way you can format a document. Rather than formatting each selection of text with individual character and paragraph formats (which can take some time if you have quite a few formats to apply) you can apply *all* the formats in one operation

- because the formats you apply as a style are always the same, there is no chance that you have forgotten any particular formats — if you apply each format individually you will probably forget some of them — all text with a particular style applied is identical in formats

Creating styles

There are three main ways you can create your own paragraph style:

- apply formats to your own sample text, until it is the way you want it, then create the style from those formats (for most people, this is ideal)
- adapt another style to suit
- copy styles from other documents to your own.

Basic steps:

1. To create a style from your own sample text, apply formats to your text until it is the way you want it (look again at Section 3 if you're a bit hazy about formatting)

2. Select the text you want to make a style of

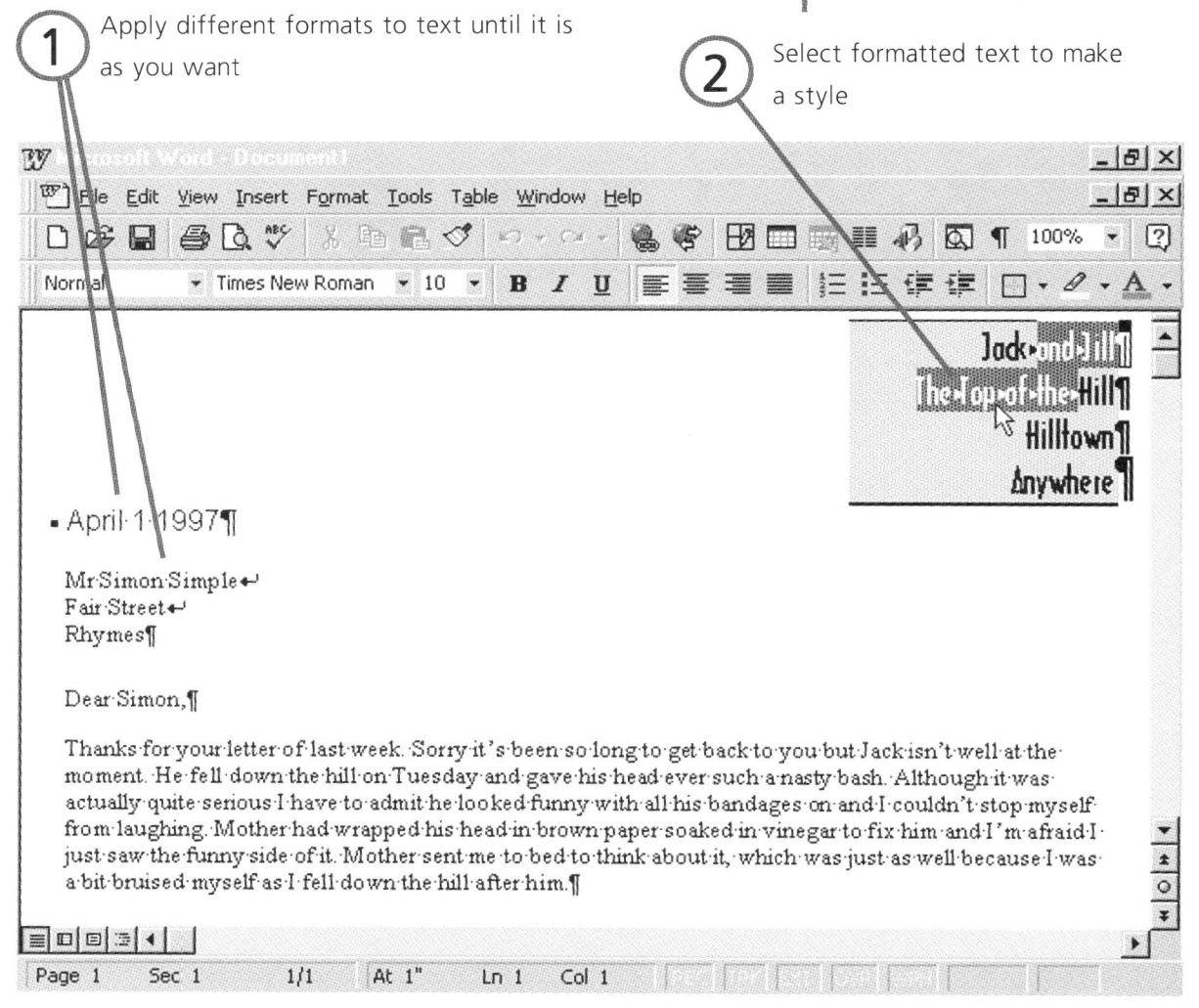

① Apply different formats to text until it is as you want

② Select formatted text to make a style

3 Choose **Format→Style**, or type **Alt**+**O**] then **S**, to call up the **Style** dialog box. Click **New** to call up the **New Style** dialog box

4 Enter a name for your style

5 Check the **Add to Template** check box, then click **OK**, then click **Close** in the **Style** dialog box

If you repeat this procedure for all the different styles within your document, when you have finished you will end up with a number of styles which have been added to Word (in the Normal template, actually), and which will be present whenever you open a new document following that template.

Next time you want to produce a similar looking document the styles are already there to use. Simply enter your text in the new document, select the text to be formatted with any particular style, then apply the style from the Formatting toolbar's Style button drop-down list. The text is formatted as you defined.

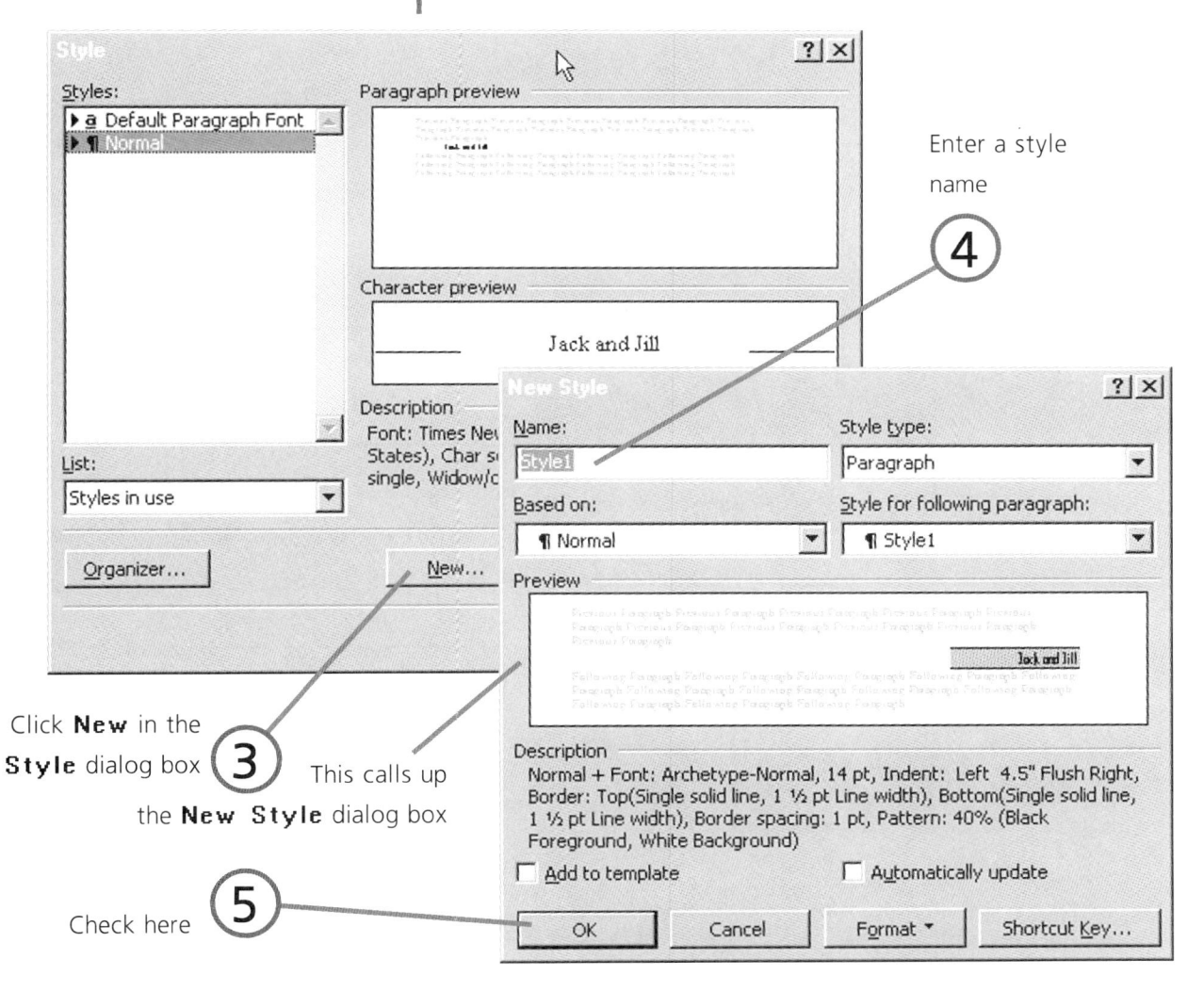

Enter a style name

④

Click **New** in the **Style** dialog box ③ This calls up the **New Style** dialog box

Check here ⑤

125

Creating styles (contd)

One of the beauties of styles is their ability to be modified. What's more, if you modify a style *all* text in a document which has been formatted with that style is modified too. This is extremely useful when you're formatting a document to appear how you want it, but also it's a useful method of creating your own styles.

Basic steps:

1 To modify a style choose **Format→Style**, or type [Alt]+[O] then [S], to call up the **Style** dialog box

2 Select the style you want to modify in the **Styles** entry list, then click **Modify** to call up the **Modify** dialog box

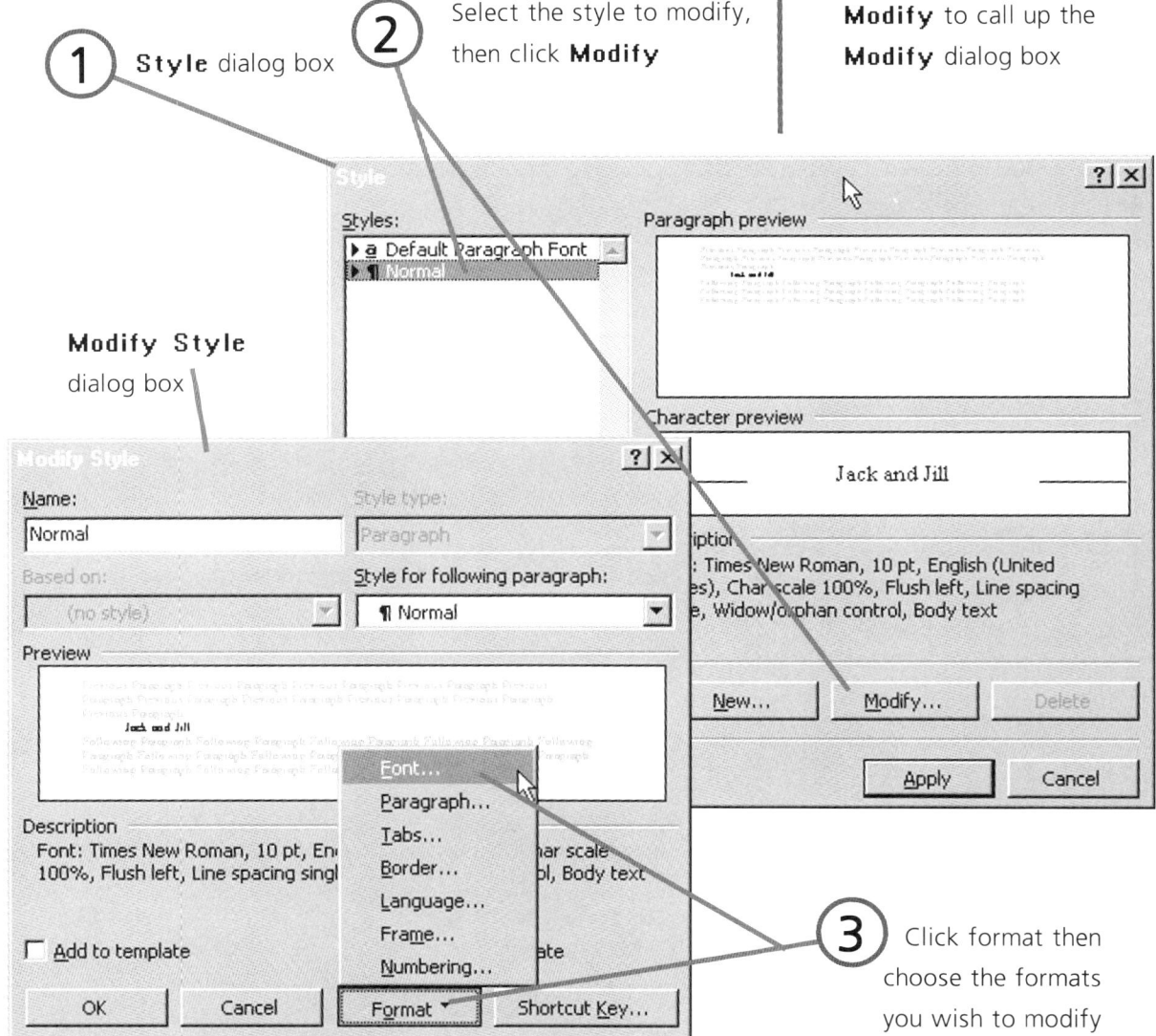

1 **Style** dialog box

2 Select the style to modify, then click **Modify**

Modify Style dialog box

3 Click format then choose the formats you wish to modify

3 Click the **Format** button to drop-down a list of formats which you can modify, select the format you want and in the resultant dialog box adjust formats to suit. Repeat this if you want to modify more than one format type

Take note:

When you click the Format button at step 3, you can modify any of the formats we've seen already (along with some new ones). All the formats available in the drop-down list are assigned to the style — then, when you have finished, all text which is formatted with that style is modified too. In other words, you can make some immense changes to the appearance of your document quite simply just by modifying a style

Tip:

You can assign keyboard shortcuts to any style — simply modify the style as suggested here, and in the Modify Style dialog box click Shortcut Key, to call up the Customize dialog box with its Keyboard tab active. Enter the shortcut you want assigned to the style and if that shortcut isn't already used for some other function click Assign. Click Close, then OK in the Modify Style dialog box, followed by Close in the Style dialog box.

Now you can apply a style simply by selecting the text and pressing your keyboard shortcut

Creating styles (contd)

The last method of creating styles in a document is to copy styles from other documents which have the styles you want. It's the **Organizer** dialog box which allows you to do this, listing styles in two documents side-by-side, so that you can copy styles from one to the other.

The styles to be copied can be in a true Word document, or in a Word template. Word has many default templates which you can use for this purpose, and we'll use one to illustrate how you can do it.

Basic steps:

1. To copy one or more styles from one document to another, choose **Format→Style**, or type **Alt**+**O** then **S**, to call up the **Style** dialog box. Click the **Organizer** button to call up the **Organizer** dialog box

Organizer dialog box ①

② Click twice

③ Select a template

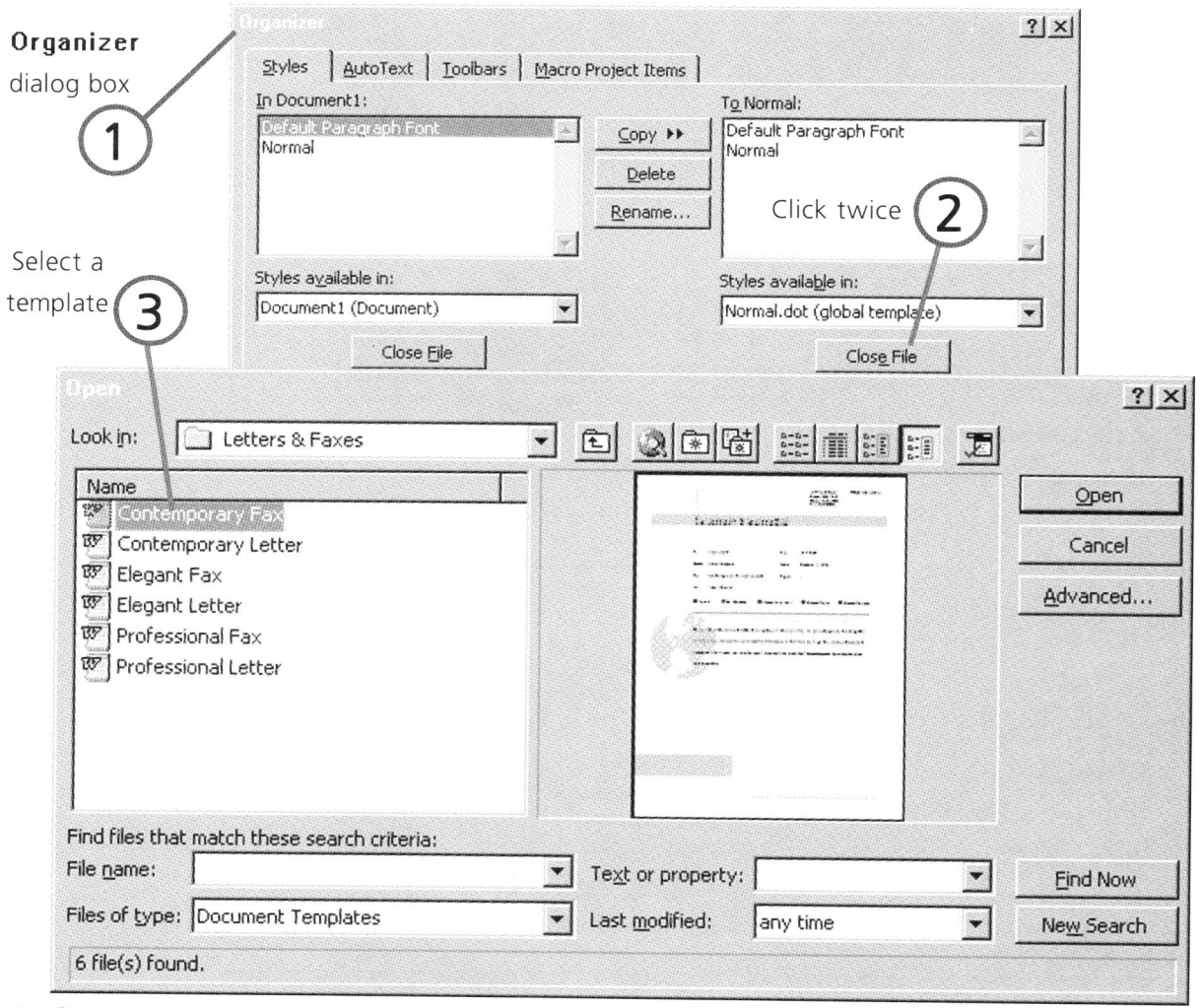

2 Click **Close File** on the right side of the dialog box (the button changes to **Open File**) then click **Open File**. This displays a list of available files which you can select. Locate the templates directory in the MSOffice directory on your hard disk and make sure you're listing files of document template *(*.dot)* types

3 Select a template in the list and click **Open**. Now the **Organizer** dialog box displays all the styles in the template in a scrollable list

4 You can select individual styles, or you can select multiple styles by Ctrl + clicking them

5 Copy them to your own document by clicking **Copy**

6 Click **Close** to close the **Organizer** dialog box, then try out your new styles in your own document

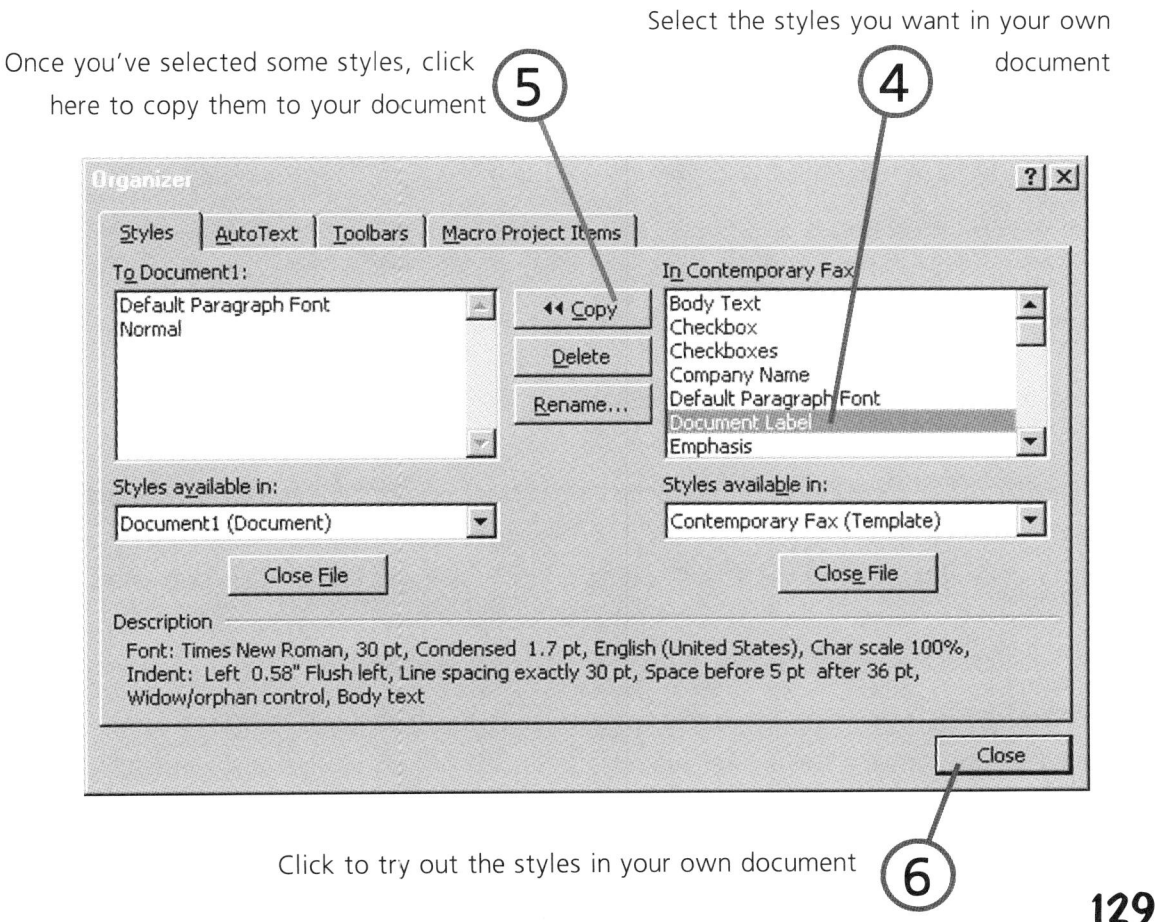

Once you've selected some styles, click here to copy them to your document ⑤

Select the styles you want in your own document ④

Click to try out the styles in your own document ⑥

129

More about styles

If you haven't already realized it, styles are very important to a word processor like Word. Styles form the key to producing professional documents with total consistency of formatting. Their use ensures efficient control over your documents.

However, there's a few additional things to know about styles which can make their use even more efficient. They are presented here as a collection of tips and notes — bear them in mind when you use Word.

> **Tip:**
> Format all text in a document with styles — that way if you want to change the document's appearance you only have to change a handful of styles, not the various text elements

> **Tip:**
> When you create a new document, base it on a template — templates are complete with their own styles which you can use immediately. If there's a particular style of document you want, design it then save it as a template. Each time you create a new document based on that template it'll be exactly as you want it. (Templates are covered later.)

> **Tip:**
> While we've said all along how you should enter all your text first, then apply styles to it there is a more elegant way which calls on Word styles' ability to change to another style when a paragraph ends. In either the New Style or the Modify Style dialog boxes there is a drop-down list box called Style for Following Paragraph. In here is a list of all available styles. Choose one. Then as your style which has a specified style to follow ends, the next style comes into force.
>
> This is useful, say, for headings and subheadings (which are nearly always of a single paragraph and are followed by, say, normal style). As you finish typing the heading text and press ⏎ or Enter, the next paragraph is automatically stylised with the next style

Tip:

You can arrange your document window to display which style is applied to a paragraph (see below) by adjusting the **Style Area Width** box in the **View** tab of the **Options** dialog box (choose **Tools→Options**, or type [Alt]+[T] then [O], then click **View** if it's not already at the front of the dialog box). Specify a width greater than 0 to display the style area in your document.

Take note:

If you delete a style (using, say, the **Delete** button on the **Style** dialog box) the Normal style is applied to all text which was formatted with the style

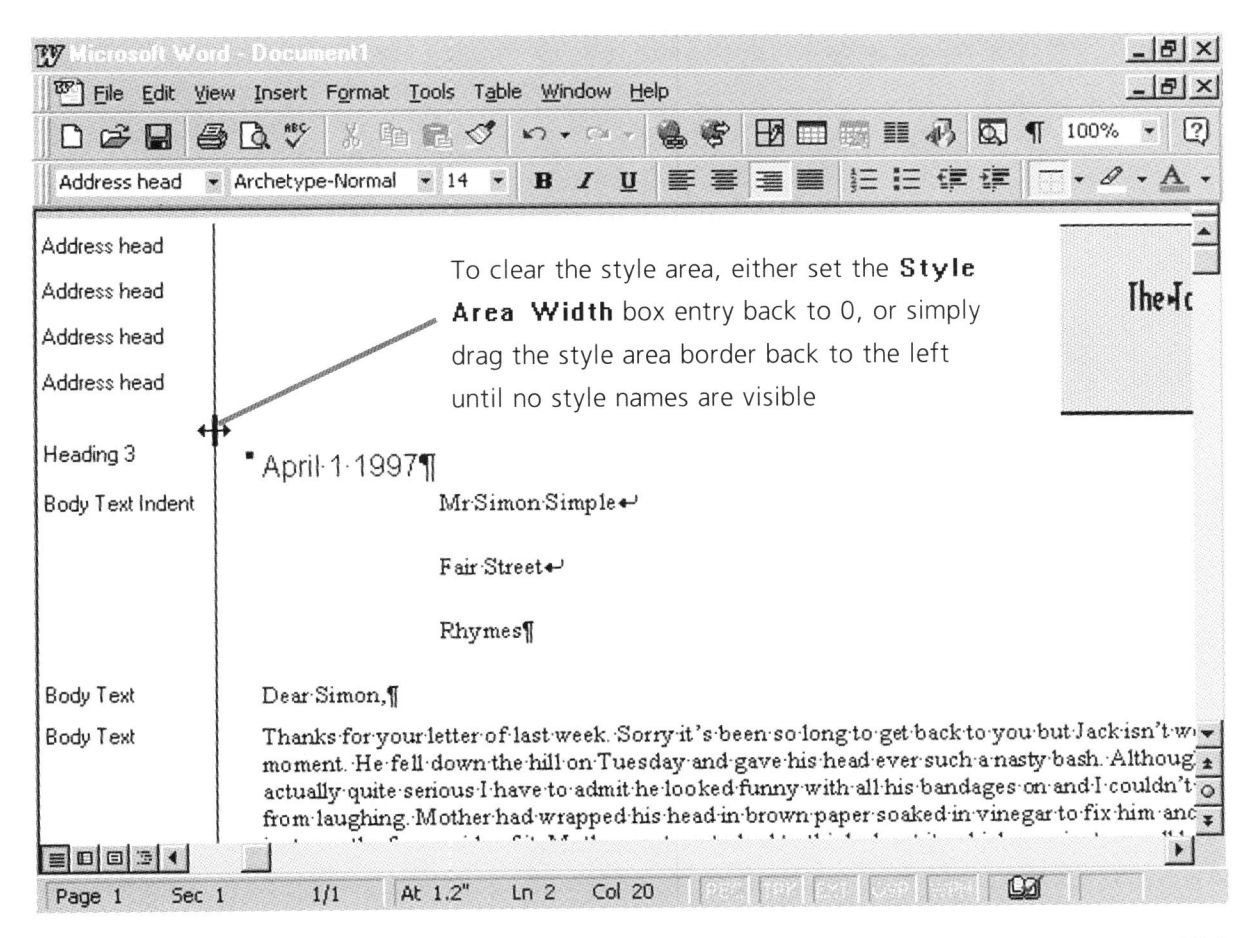

To clear the style area, either set the **Style Area Width** box entry back to 0, or simply drag the style area border back to the left until no style names are visible

More about styles (contd)

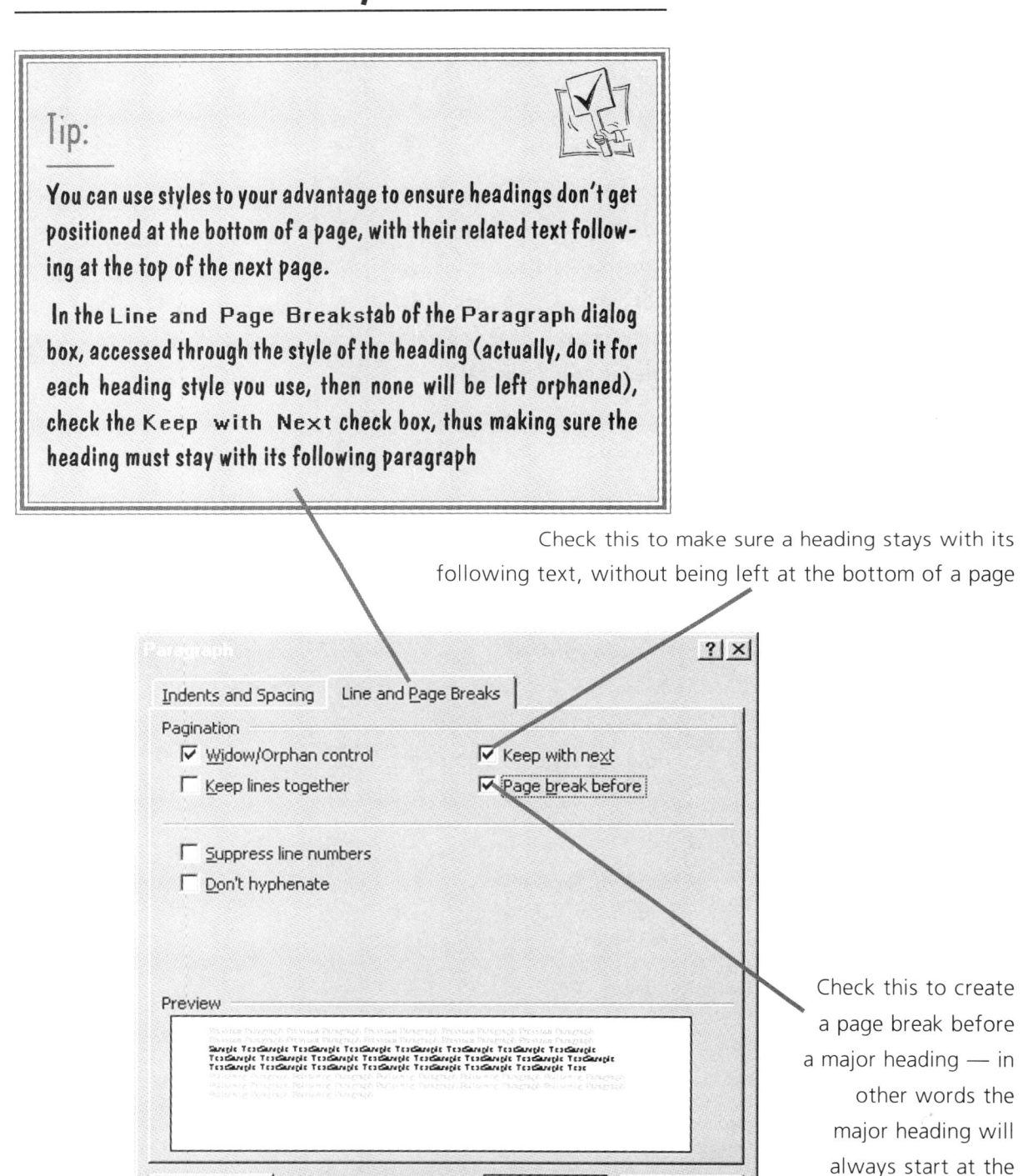

> **Tip:**
>
> You can use styles to your advantage to ensure headings don't get positioned at the bottom of a page, with their related text following at the top of the next page.
>
> In the Line and Page Breaks tab of the Paragraph dialog box, accessed through the style of the heading (actually, do it for each heading style you use, then none will be left orphaned), check the Keep with Next check box, thus making sure the heading must stay with its following paragraph

Check this to make sure a heading stays with its following text, without being left at the bottom of a page

Check this to create a page break before a major heading — in other words the major heading will always start at the top of a page

Take note:

If you change a font, or any other formatting parameter, in a style which another style is based on, the other style's font (or other parameter) changes too — unless you have already specified a different parameter in the second style

Tip:

You can use the above to advantage when you set up the styles in your document — to specify the style which will follow another style. For example, if you specify that a heading is followed by body text then, every time you type a heading and press Enter or ↵ (as long as Word knows that the heading *is* a heading — see next paragraph), the next paragraph will be in the body text style.

To enter styles as you go along, you *can* select the style from the style list box in the Formatting toolbar, but it's a lot easier to assign the style a keyboard shortcut which you can enter whenever you want to change style

Take note:

Styles are probably the most important feature of a word processor like Word. If you manage the styles in your documents properly, taking care in how they are formatted, how they are based, what text flow is associated with them and so on, your documents will be much better for it. Not only do they look *better*, but it is also much easier to make large formatting changes to suit the way you want your documents to look. For example, if all styles are based properly on each other in a hierarchical way a single change of font or size will change the whole document

Tip:

If you can't be bothered to arrange styles to best suit your documents, at least use Word's AutoFormat command. This does a largely similar job, automatically — properly defines styles are always better, on the other hand

About templates

In places throughout the book, the term *template* has been used, without any clear explanation. Now it's time to say exactly *what* a template is.

Effectively, a template is a skeleton document. It has all the bones of any document, in terms of document parameters — just not all the flesh in terms of text you enter.

Word uses templates to store all document parameters. Character and paragraph formats, tables, styles, sections, AutoText entries, graphical items and so on — and even text — can all be stored in a template.

Then, when you create a new document, you can base it on the chosen template and up pops a new document looking exactly as you want it — all you need to do is enter any final details and *hey, presto!*, a complete document. You could use a template, for example, when you create a letter. In the template might be a letterhead, complete with a company logo, and styles which specify fonts and formats for use in the letter. Another example could be a template setup for your monthly sales figures — the document is complete; you just add the figures. See over for details of creating your own template.

A default installation of Word includes a number of built-in templates as standard. When you first startup Word, the first document on-screen is even based on a template (the Normal template, actually). When you create a *new* document, on the other hand, you are given an option to choose which of the built-in templates you want to use for the document.

Basic steps:

1. Choose **File → New**, or type `Alt`+`F` then `N`, or type `Ctrl`+`N`. This calls up the **New** dialog box
2. Click a tab to see the templates associated with it
3. Click a template
4. Click **Template** if you want to create a new template based on the template chosen
5. Click **OK** to create the document based on that template

Tip:

You can bypass the New dialog box if you want to create a document speedily. Just click the New button on the Standard toolbar and a new document — based on the Normal template — is automatically created

(1) **New** dialog box

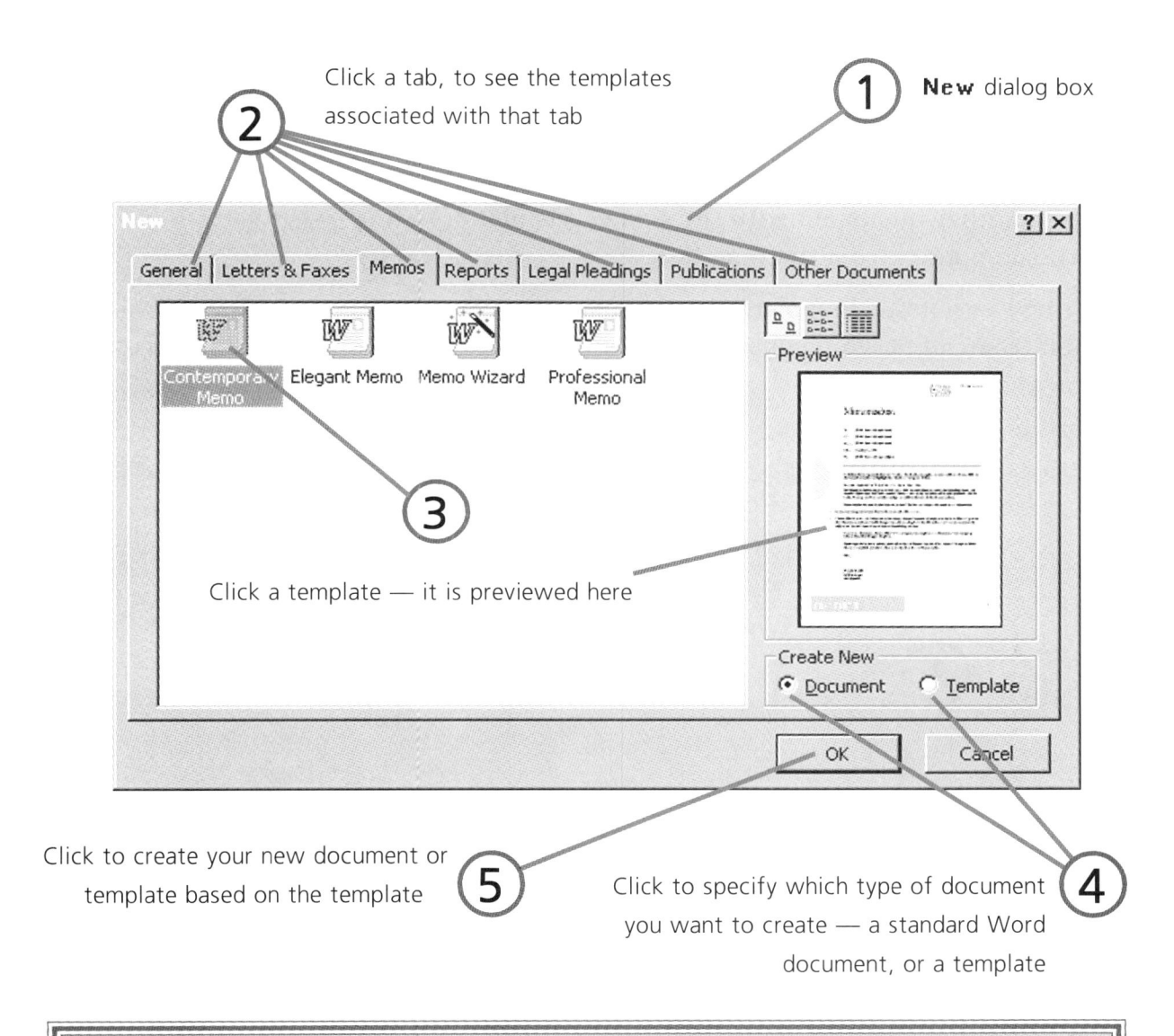

(2) Click a tab, to see the templates associated with that tab

(3) Click a template — it is previewed here

(4) Click to specify which type of document you want to create — a standard Word document, or a template

(5) Click to create your new document or template based on the template

Take note:

The Normal template is a special case template — it holds all the document parameters you use most in Word. All the toolbars, their buttons, their positions, the menus and shortcut keys, and everything else you have as default items, are stored in the Normal template. If you use another template to create other documents, on the other hand, all these features are still available in those other documents

Creating a template

It's easy to create your own template. If there's a document type you find you're using quite a lot, it's worth making a template of it, then whenever you want to create another document with the same style just create the document from the template.

Once you've got the document looking just the way you want it (remember, you only need the bare bones of it), follow the steps here.

Basic steps:

1. Choose **File→Save As**, or type **Alt**+**F** then **A**. This calls up the **Save As** dialog box
2. Click the **Save File as Type** drop-down list box to see the drop-down list of types you can save the document as
3. Select **Document Template**
4. Enter a name for your template — something easy to remember
5. Click **Save**

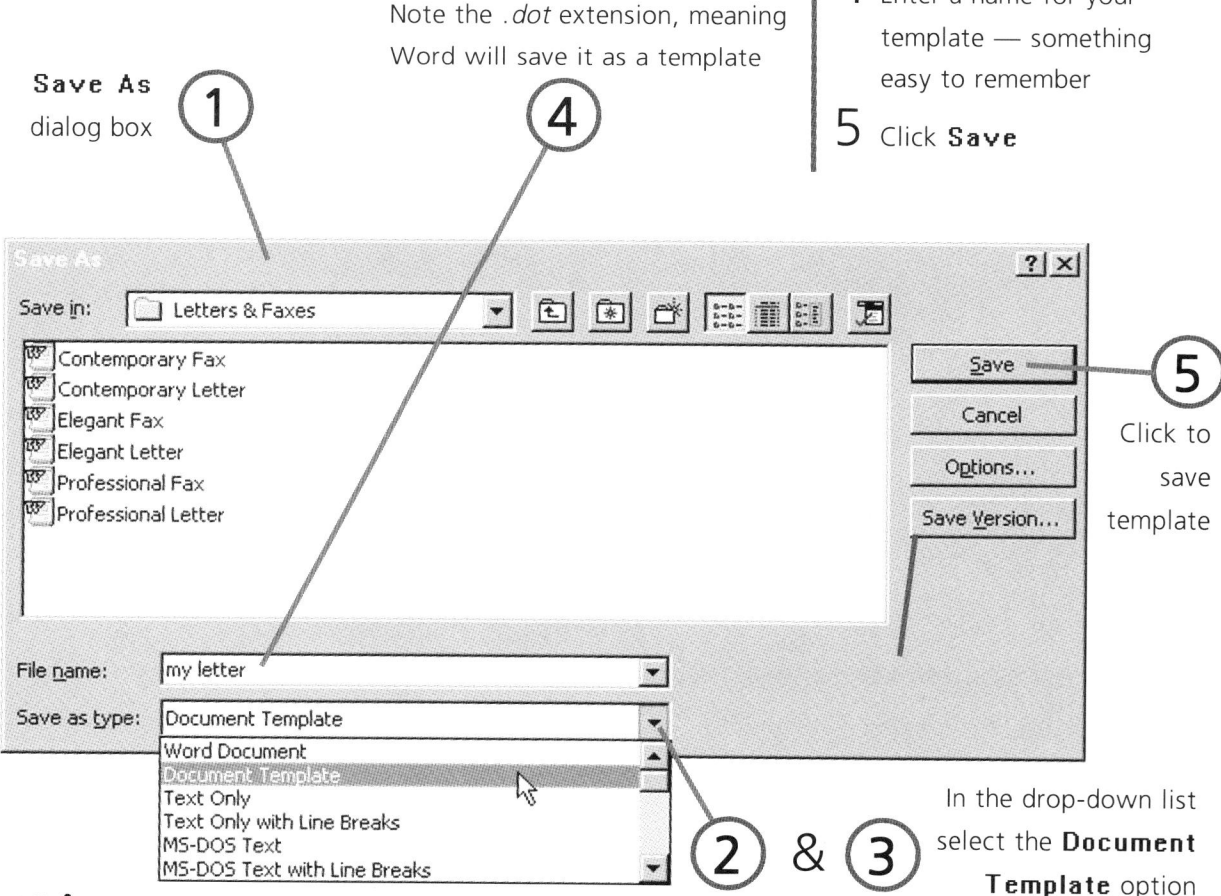

Save As dialog box ①

Enter a name you'll remember. Note the *.dot* extension, meaning Word will save it as a template ④

⑤ Click to save template

② & ③ In the drop-down list select the **Document Template** option

136

Here's an example of a template for a letterhead. It combines a heading with a border (the underlining) and a simple graphic

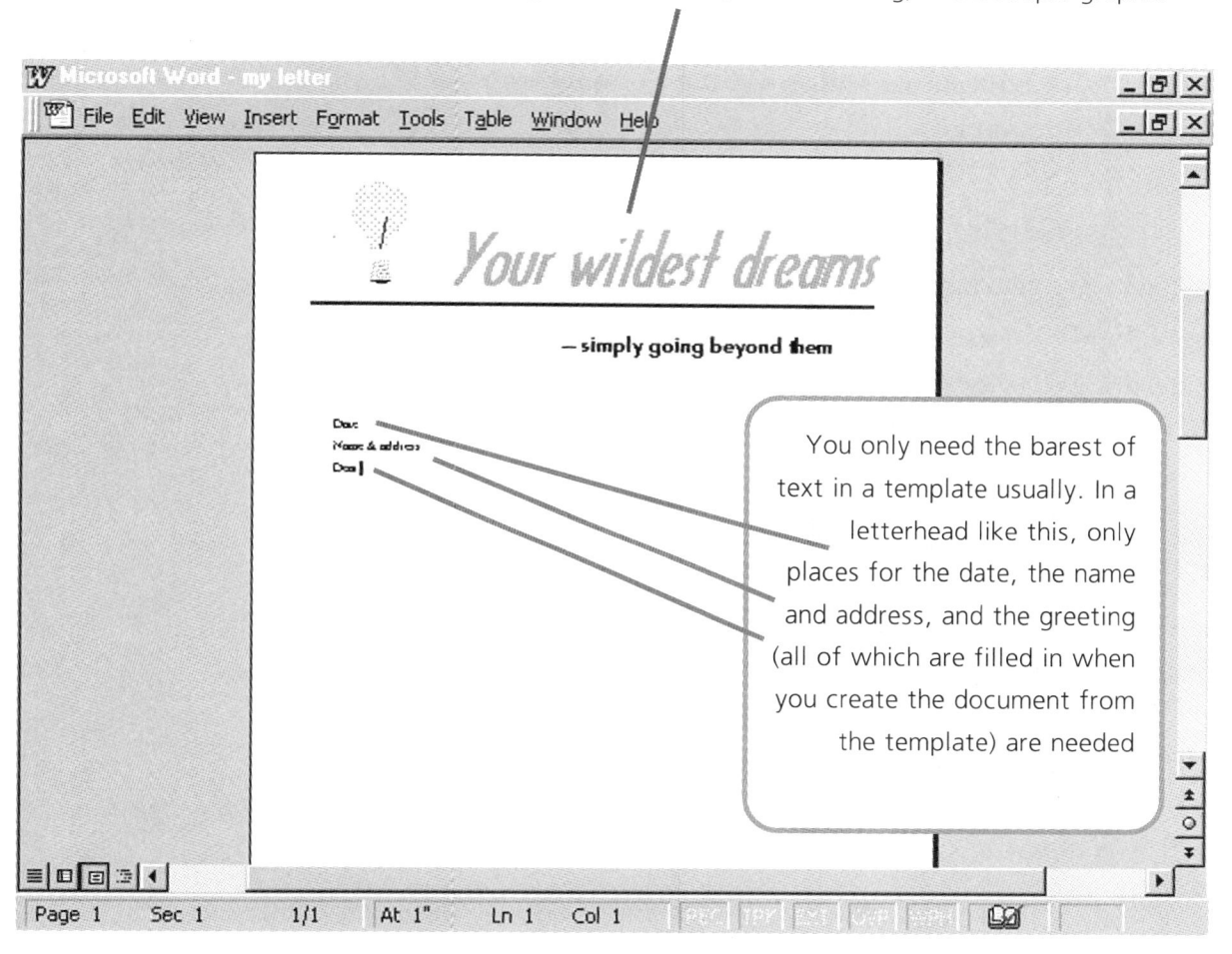

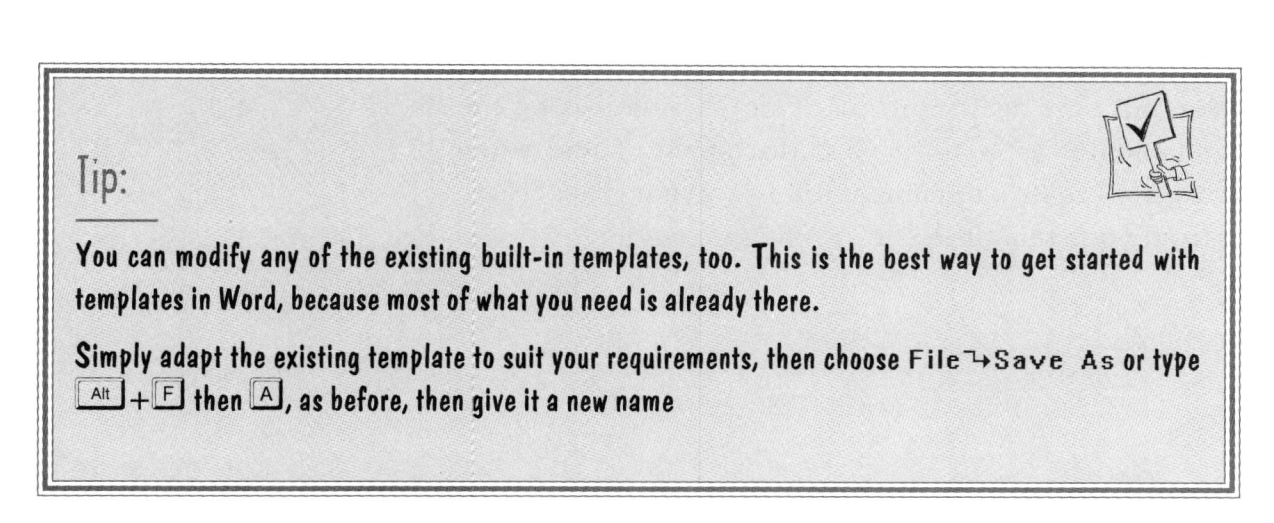

You only need the barest of text in a template usually. In a letterhead like this, only places for the date, the name and address, and the greeting (all of which are filled in when you create the document from the template) are needed

Tip:

You can modify any of the existing built-in templates, too. This is the best way to get started with templates in Word, because most of what you need is already there.

Simply adapt the existing template to suit your requirements, then choose File→Save As or type Alt + F then A, as before, then give it a new name

137

Summary for Section 6

- Use styles containing all formatting parameters you need in a document.

- Setup styles which are based on other styles. Use a hierarchy of styles to create your document.

- There are two kinds of styles — paragraph and character styles.

- To create styles (1) apply formats to a sample of text then create the style from those formats, (2) adapt an existing style, or (3) copy styles from other documents (or templates).

- Use keyboard shortcuts to help you apply styles.

- Make sure headings (1) stay with the following paragraph — to prevent a heading being left at the bottom of the page — and (2) have a following style — to make sure your body style, say, is automatically applied when you press [Enter] or [⏎]. Use styles to do this.

- Use templates to speed up how you create good-looking documents. Templates hold skeleton information about a document — styles, graphics, some text — you only need to fill in the meat on the bones.

- If you find yourself using the same type of document over and over again, setup a template comprising the fundamental aspects of your document. Then, when you go to create a document following that type, create it from your template.

7 Technical thingamajigs

Print preview 140

Printing 142

Print options 143

Starting Word at turn-on 144

Shortcut keys 146

Toolbars 148

Summary for Section 7 150

Print preview

Before you print a document, it's best to stand back and take a look at it. Print previewing does this job for you, giving you an overall view of the document before you go ahead and waste your paper while letting you edit the document if you need.

Print preview brings with it its own toolbar, with some new buttons.

Basic steps:

1 Choose **File→Print Preview**, or type [Alt]+[F] then [V], or simply (best) click the Print Preview button on the Standard toolbar. The display changes to print preview, fitting complete pages of your document into the print preview window

2 Use buttons on the Print Preview toolbar to adjust the display to suit

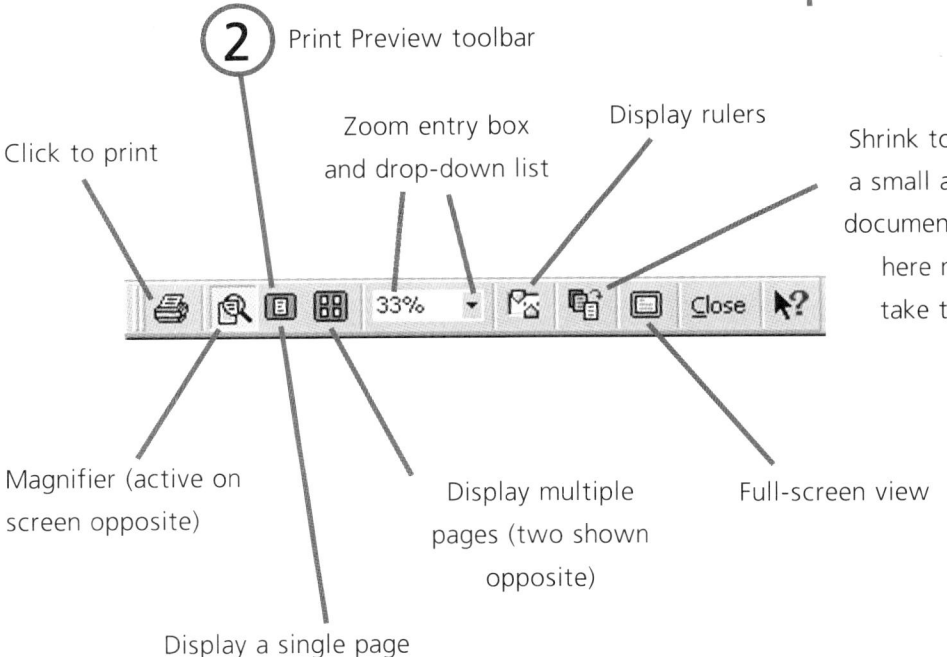

(2) Print Preview toolbar

Click to print

Zoom entry box and drop-down list

Display rulers

Shrink to Fit — if there's only a small amount of text on the document's last page, clicking here might (if you're lucky) take the text back to fit on one page less

Magnifier (active on screen opposite)

Display multiple pages (two shown opposite)

Full-screen view

Display a single page

140

① Print preview of document

Point to part of document with the zoom tool, click — and zoom in

Return to normal view by clicking here

Text, along with all character, paragraph and section formats and parameters, is displayed

Active page is highlighted

You can move to other pages with the vertical scroll bar (or you can type `Page Up` or `Page Down` to move to previous or next pages)

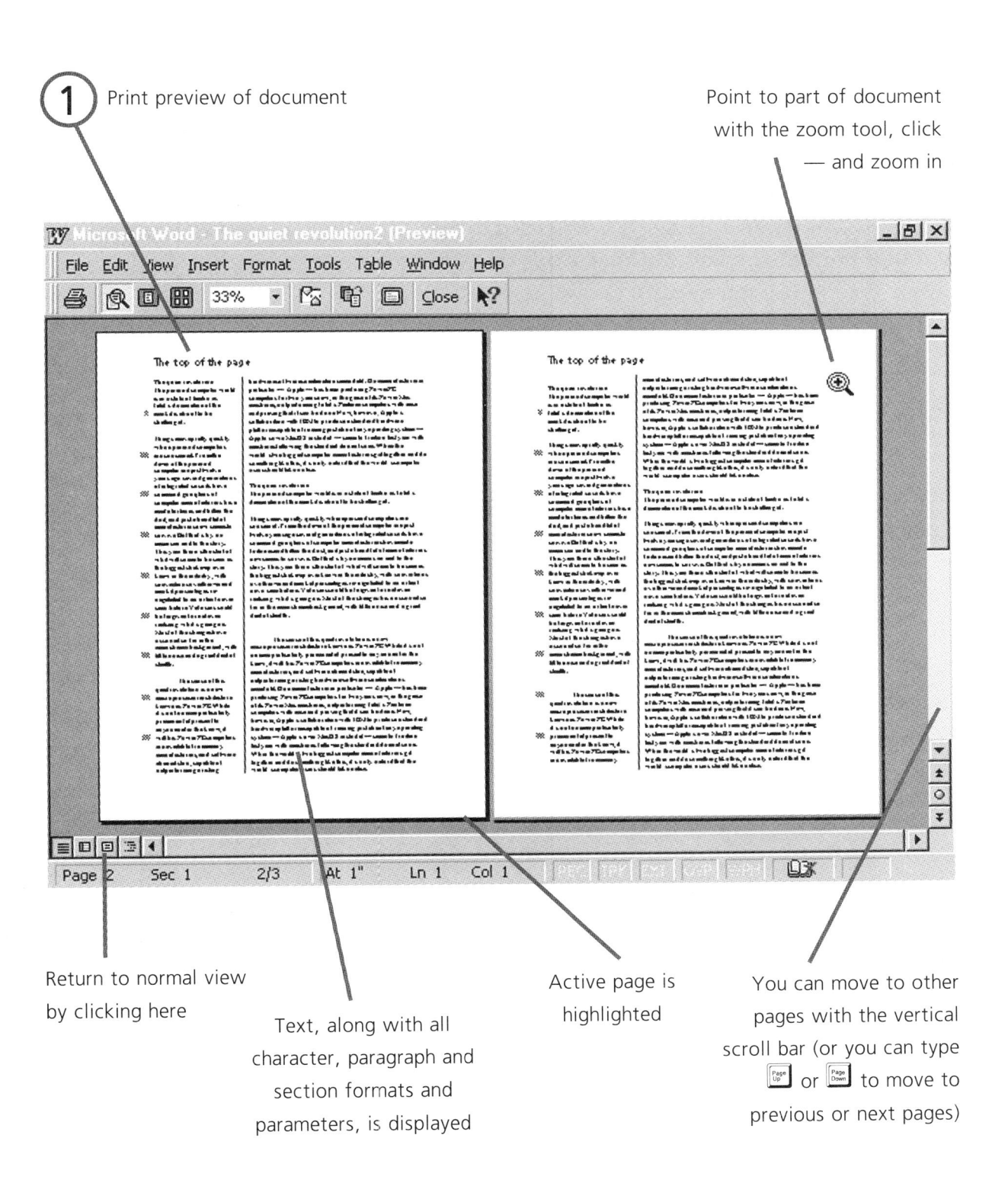

Printing

While printing from a PC can give many headaches, use of the Windows environment coupled with Word itself makes life a lot easier. We have, however, to assume that your computer is properly connected to a printer, and that both are on and working. After that, there are only a few things you need to know.

Basic steps:

1 Choose **File→Print**, or type `Alt`+`F` then `P`, or type `Ctrl`+`P`. This calls up the **Print** dialog box

2 As the default dialog box stands, if you click **OK**, one copy of the text in the active document will be printed to the printer shown — you can adjust controls and entries to change this

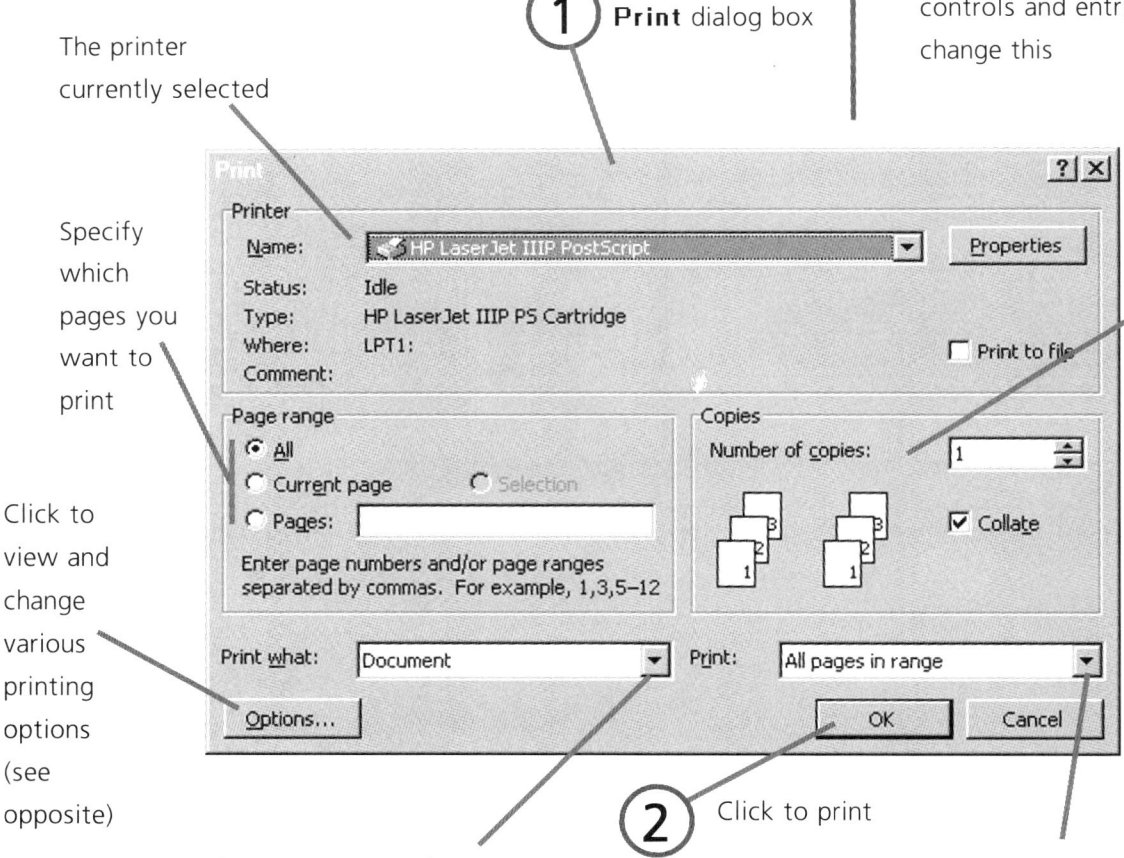

(1) **Print** dialog box

The printer currently selected

Specify which pages you want to print

Click to view and change various printing options (see opposite)

Drop-down list to specify which part of the document you want to print

(2) Click to print

How many copies do you want?

Drop-down list allows you to print both sides, or specified sides of double-sided documents

Print options

Apart from controlling print parameters such as number of copies, which pages and so on, you can specify other, more technical, things too. Important ones are shown below.

Basic steps:

1 From the **Print** dialog box, click **Options**. This calls up the **Print options** dialog box

Tip:

You can speed up the printing process by simply clicking the Print button 🖨 on the Standard toolbar. This bypasses the Print dialog box altogether and prints the document with default settings – for most printing purposes this is fine

① **Print options** dialog box

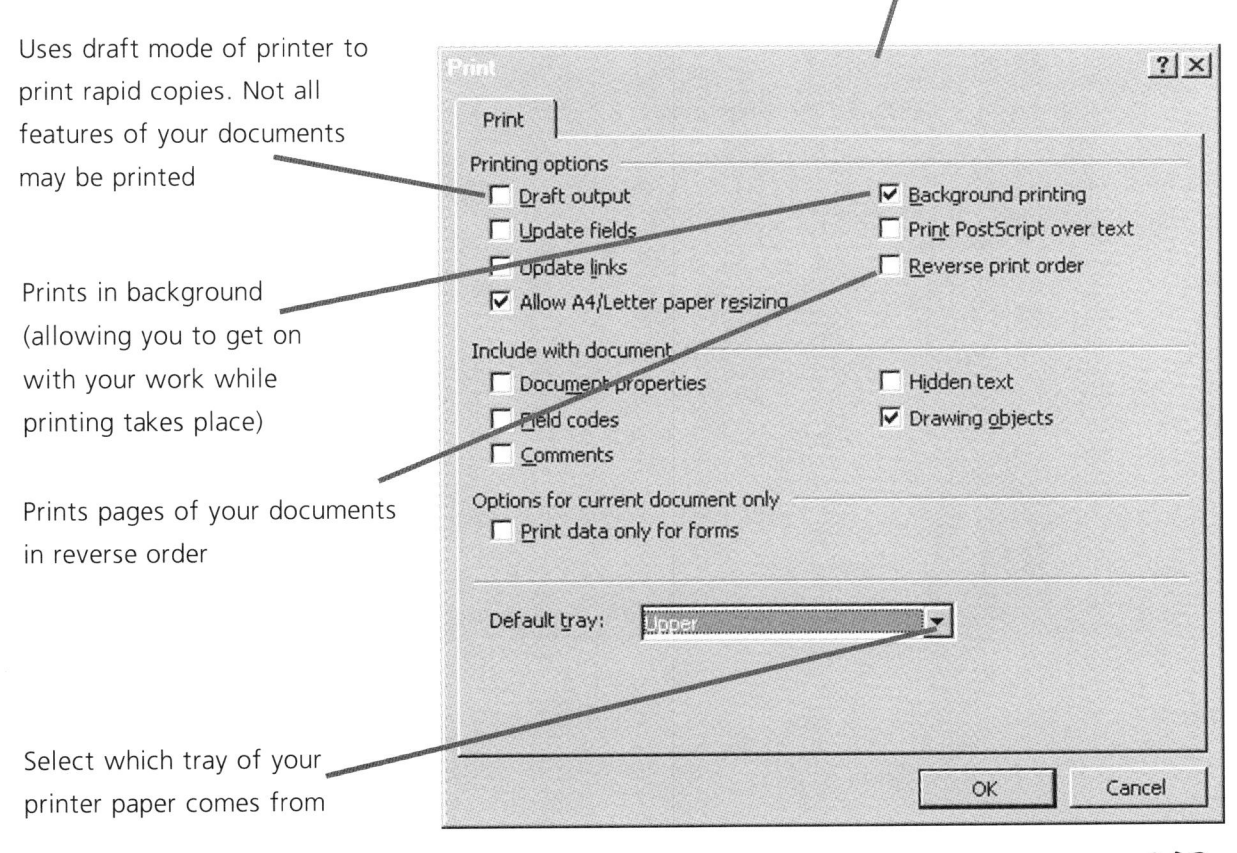

Uses draft mode of printer to print rapid copies. Not all features of your documents may be printed

Prints in background (allowing you to get on with your work while printing takes place)

Prints pages of your documents in reverse order

Select which tray of your printer paper comes from

Print

Printing options
- ☐ Draft output
- ☐ Update fields
- ☐ Update links
- ☑ Allow A4/Letter paper resizing
- ☑ Background printing
- ☐ Print PostScript over text
- ☐ Reverse print order

Include with document
- ☐ Document properties
- ☐ Field codes
- ☐ Comments
- ☐ Hidden text
- ☑ Drawing objects

Options for current document only
- ☐ Print data only for forms

Default tray: Upper

[OK] [Cancel]

Starting Word at turn-on

If you use Word just about every time you turn on your computer, you can set it up to start Word (or any other program for that matter) automatically.

Basic steps:

1. Choose **Start** → **Settings** → **Taskbar**, this calls up the **Taskbar Properties** dialog box
2. Click the **Start Menu Programs** tab
3. Click **Advanced**. This calls up an Explorer window, for the Start Menu

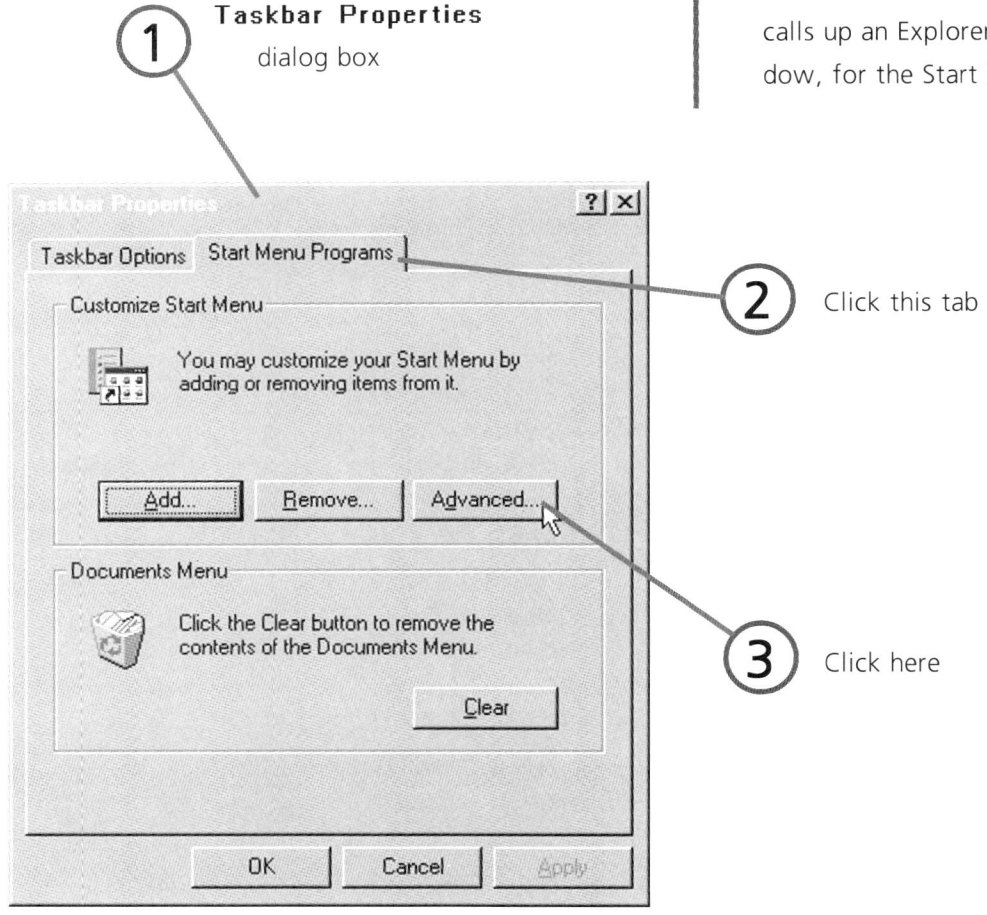

① **Taskbar Properties** dialog box

② Click this tab

③ Click here

4 Click the + box, to open the **Programs** folder in the left half of the window. If Microsoft Word is in this folder, go to step 5. If MSOffice is in the **Programs** folder, open the **MSOffice** folder in the same way

5 Hold down `Ctrl` and drag the Microsoft Word icon from the right half of the window to the **StartUp** folder in the left half

> **Tip:**
>
> Holding down `Ctrl` while dragging *copies* the Word icon to the StartUp folder. Dragging without holding `Ctrl` would merely move it! Now, whenever you restart your computer Word will automatically startup. If you ever want this *not* to happen, simply delete the icon

Open the **Programs** folder — you may need to open the **MSOffice** folder too, depending on how Word is installed on your computer

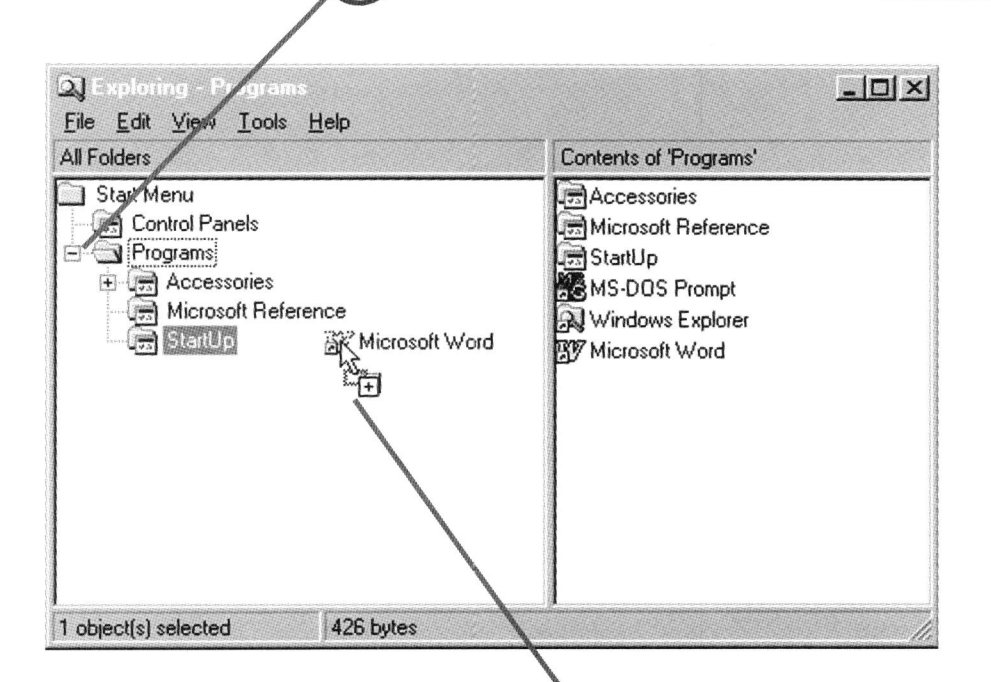

Hold down `Ctrl` and drag the Microsoft Word icon to the **StartUp** folder in the **Programs** folder — the + symbol indicates you are copying (the reason for holding down `Ctrl`) rather than moving it

145

Shortcut keys

A great many things you do in Word, you do a great many times. Some of these things can be called upon with the click of a button on a toolbar, or a shortcut key command. Although buttons are a boon over choosing a command through the ordinary menu method, undoubtedly shortcut keys are the quickest.

At first sight, you might think not all commands are available as shortcuts. However, you can assign your own shortcut key commands to *any* command available in Word.

Basic steps:

1 Choose **Tools→Customize**, or type `Alt`+`T` then `C`, to call up the **Customize** dialog box

2 Click the **Keyboard** button to display the **Customize Keyboard** dialog box

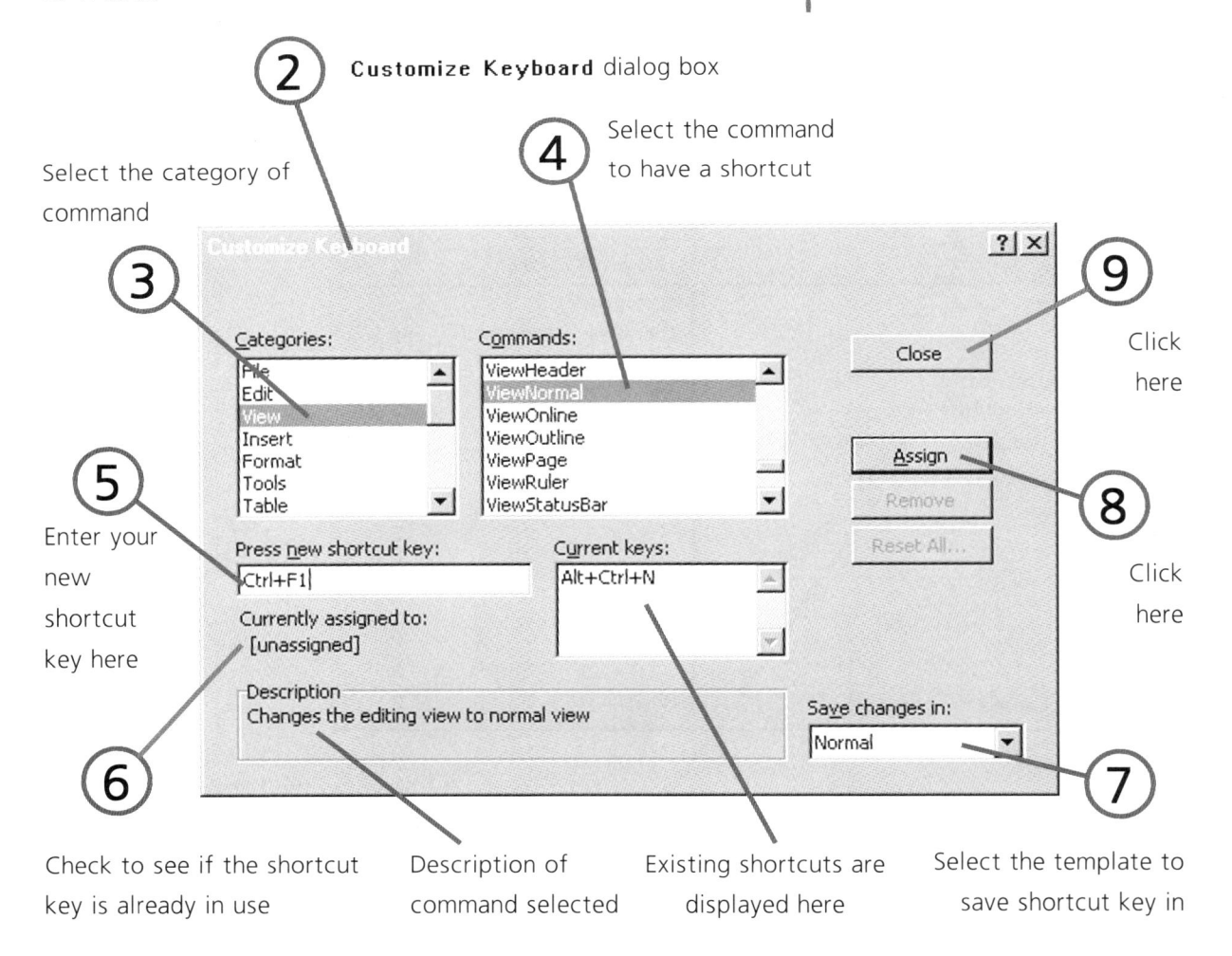

② **Customize Keyboard** dialog box

③ Select the category of command

④ Select the command to have a shortcut

⑤ Enter your new shortcut key here

⑥ Check to see if the shortcut key is already in use

— Description of command selected

— Existing shortcuts are displayed here

⑦ Select the template to save shortcut key in

⑧ Click here (Assign)

⑨ Click here (Close)

3 In the **Categories** scrollable list, select the category of the command you want to assign a keyboard shortcut to

4 In the **Commands** scrollable list, locate the command

5 In the **Press new shortcut key** field, enter your desired shortcut. Do this by literally pressing the keys you want as the shortcut

6 View the **Currently assigned to** field directly below the **Press new shortcut key** entry field — Word tells you whether the key is already in use or not. If the shortcut key you want is unassigned you can use it directly. If it's assigned already, you are about to override its previous use. Choose another shortcut key if you want, or go to step 7

7 Locate the template to save your shortcut

8 Click **Assign**

9 Click Close

Tip:

You can remove a shortcut key too, by locating the command in the Customize Keyboard dialog box, selecting the shortcut key in the Current keys field, then clicking the Remove button

Tip:

If you save a shortcut key in the default template (Normal.dot) it will be available in *all* new documents you create. If you save it in a *specific* template, on the other hand, it will be available only in new documents you create using that specific template

Tip:

You can revert back to Word's default shortcut key arrangement by clicking the Reset All button on the Customize Keyboard dialog box. Bear in mind though, that this reverts *all* shortcut key changes you have made

Toolbars

While Word has a large number of toolbars, they may not always be to a user's liking. Either they might have the wrong buttons on for your particular tasks, or they might not have the buttons you want at all.

You can customize toolbars (by adding, deleting, changing and moving around buttons), and you can create your own toolbars (designing buttons from scratch if you want). You can also choose from a wide range of built-in buttons to assign to commands in Word.

Basic steps:

ADAPTING A TOOLBAR

1. Choose **Tools** → **Customize**, or type `Alt`+`T` then `C`, to call up the **Customize** dialog box
2. Click the **Commands** tab if it's not already frontmost
3. Drag a button onto the toolbar of your choice to add it (or drag a button *off* a toolbar to delete it)

(2) Click **Commands** if not already frontmost

(1) **Customize** dialog box

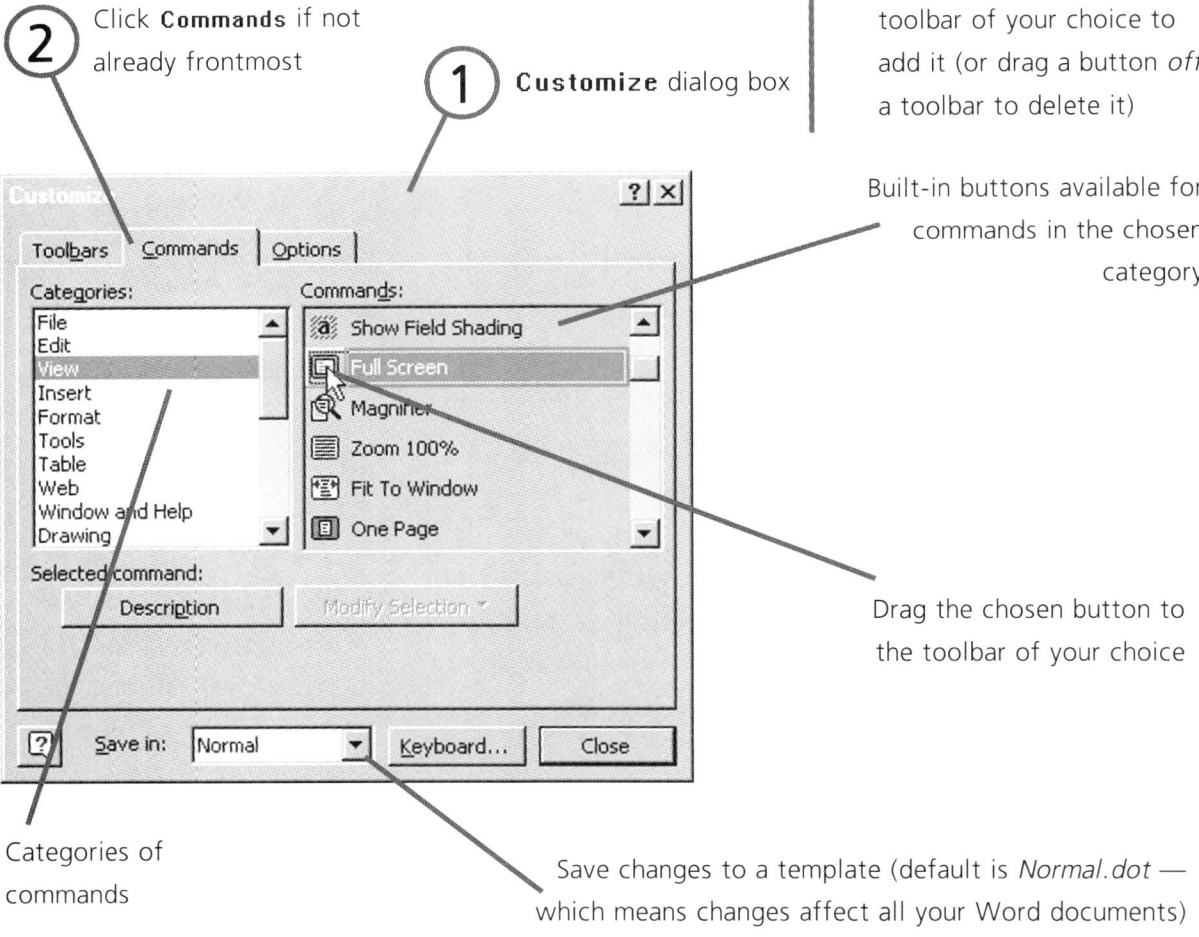

Built-in buttons available for commands in the chosen category

Drag the chosen button to the toolbar of your choice

Categories of commands

Save changes to a template (default is *Normal.dot* — which means changes affect all your Word documents)

CREATING A TOOLBAR

1 In the **Customize** dialog box, click the **Toolbars** tab

2 Click **New**, to call up the **New Toolbar** dialog box

3 Give the new toolbar a name

4 Click **OK** — the new toolbar is displayed as a floating toolbar on the screen and the **Customize** dialog box is called up with the **Toolbars** tab already frontmost (see below)

5 Drag buttons and adapt your new toolbar as before

> **Tip:**
>
> You can move (or delete) a toolbar button without the Customize dialog box. Just hold down [Alt] and drag the button to its new location (or drag it off the toolbar altogether to delete it). If you hold down [Alt] + [Ctrl] while you drag, the button is copied

Drag your toolbar wherever you want it to be

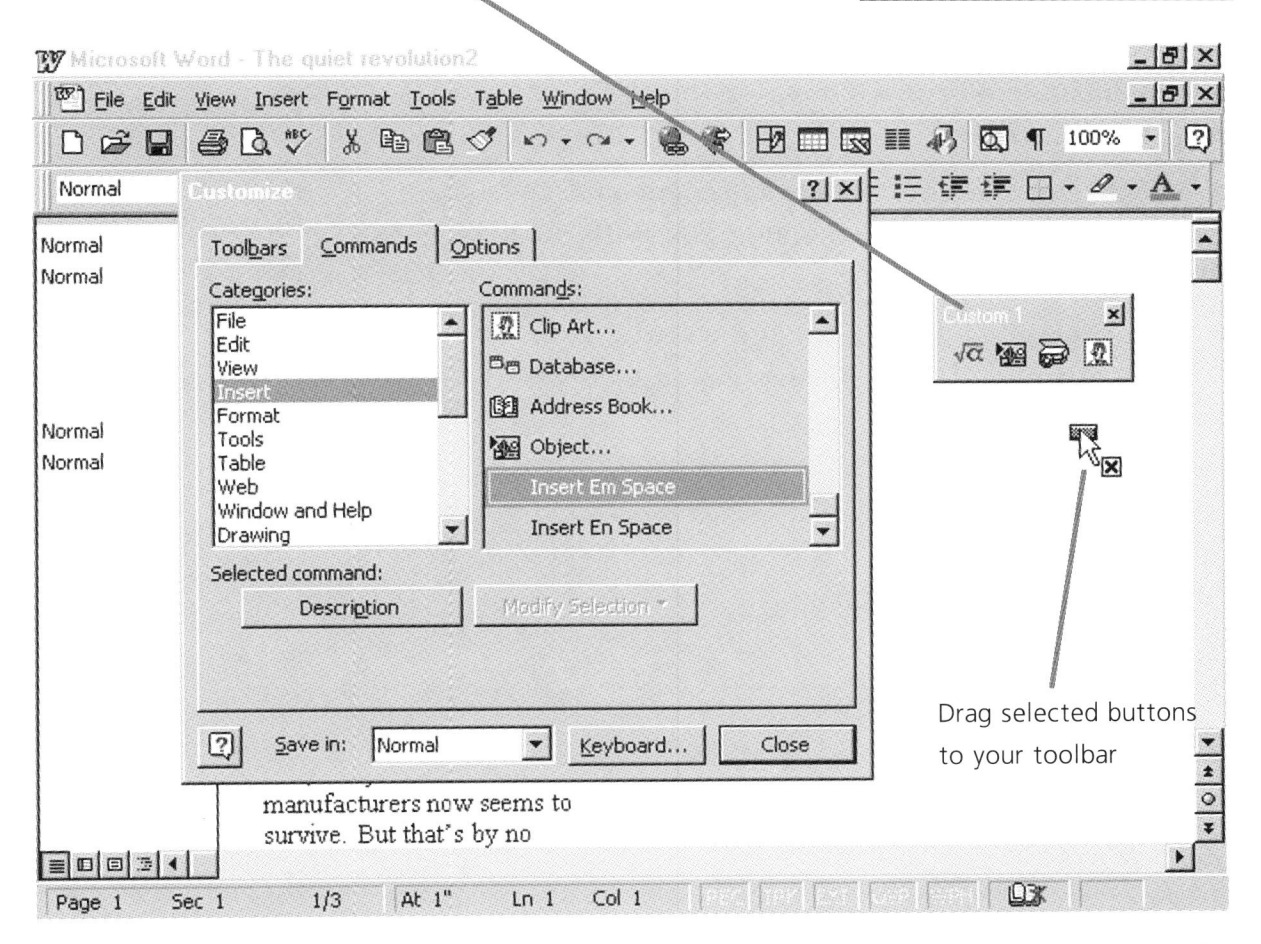

Drag selected buttons to your toolbar

Summary for Section 7

● Before printing, preview your work in Print Preview. This way you save some paper finding out where your overall problems are.

● Use the **Print** dialog box to adjust controls regarding the pages you print, the number of copies you want, and so on.

● Use the **Options** dialog box with the **Print** tab frontmost to adjust finer details of printing.

● Use the Print button 🖨 to print without any dialog boxes.

● Startup Word automatically each time you turn on your computer by copying Word's icon to the **StartUp** folder in the Explorer window for the [Start] menu's **Programs** folder.

● Assign your own shortcut keys to commands you use a lot through the **Customize** dialog box, with the **Keyboard** tab frontmost.

● Adapt existing toolbars, and create your own toolbars, through the **Customize** dialog box, with the **Toolbars** tab frontmost.

Index

A

AutoCorrect 100
AutoFormat 46
AutoText 102

B

Borders 47, 66
 toolbar 66
Borders and shading 66
Buttons 13, 149

C

Character
 formatting 48
Character styles 123
Clipboard 38
Columns 74, 86
Commands
 assigning shortcut keys 146
Counting
 words, lines, paragraphs 113
Creating a new document 22
Cut, copy and paste 38

D

Dingbats 42
Document 22
 based on template 130
 creating 130
 setting up 76
 window 3
Drag-and-drop editing 40

E

Edit menu 4
Editing
 drag-and-drop 40
 text 30
Entering
 symbols 42
Exiting 24

F

File menu 4
Finding
 formats 92
 text 92
Fonts
 formatting toolbar 49
 size 49
 TrueType 49
Format menu 5
Formats
 character 48
Formatting 46
 automatic 46
 character formatting 46
 creating styles 124
 painting 53
 paragraph 54
 paragraph formatting 46
 removing 52
 section 74
 styles 120
 tables 112
 toolbar 121
Formatting codes
 Word's lack of 56
Full screen view 18

G

Graphics 114
 editing 115, 117
 filters 115
 importing 114
 resizing 115
Gutter 78

H

Headers and footers 74, 80
 toolbar 80
Help
 for WordPerfect users 9, 29
 menu 5
 on-line Word system 6

I

Indenting
 keyboard shortcuts 59
 paragraph dialog box 57
 paragraph formats
  paragraph dialog box 57
 toolbar buttons 13, 56
Insert menu 5
Insertion point 3, 51, 55, 75

K

Keyboard shortcuts
 assigning your own 127

L

Leaders 65
Line count 113
Line numbering 74, 84

M

Margins 16, 74, 77
Mathematical symbols 42
Menu bar 3, 4
Menus 4
Minimize 25
Mistakes 36

N

Normal template 134
Normal view 14

O

On-line help 6
Opening 21
Orphan 58
Outline view 17, 104
Outlining 104
    procedure for 106
    symbols 105
    toolbar 105

P

Page count 113
Page layout view 16, 79
Painting a format 53
Paragraph
    formats 54
    formatting 46
    styles 46
Paragraph count 113
Paragraph dialog box
    indenting 57
Paragraph formats 54
    indenting 56
Paragraph formatting 46
Print preview 140
    toolbar 140
Printing 142, 143
    options 143

R

Replacing
    formats 94
    text 94
Ruler
    indent stops 56

S

Saving 20
Section 74
    end 74
    formatting 74
Selecting text 32
Setting up a document 76
Shading 66
Shortcut keys 146
    assigning commands 146
Spelling
    checking 96
    spelling button 96
    underline highlighting 96
        turning off 99
Starting up
    at turn-on 144
Status bar 3, 29
Styles 120
    character 123
    copying 128
    creating 124, 126
    deleting 131
    modifying 126
    paragraph 123
Symbols 42

T

Table menu 5
Tables 108
    AutoFormat 112
    converting into text 111
    converting text into 111
    creating from toolbar 109
    dragging boundaries 110
    dragging gridlines 110
    formatting 112
    moving around 109
    simple, using tabs 62
Tabs 60, 64
Templates 22, 130, 134
    creating 136
    modifying built-in 137
    normal 135
Text
    editing 30
    selecting 32
Text flow
    orphan 58
    widow 58
Toolbars 3, 10, 12
    creating, modifying 148
Tools menu 5
ToolTips 6
TrueType 49
Typographical symbols 42

U

Undo 37

V

View menu 4

W

Widow 58
Window menu 5
Word count 113
WordPerfect users help 9, 29

Z

Zooming 19